GREAT CAMPAIGNS

MacARTHUR'S NEW GUINEA CAMPAIGN

GREAT CAMPAIGN SERIES

GREAT CAMPAIGNS

MacARTHUR'S NEW GUINEA CAMPAIGN

Nathan Prefer

COMBINED BOOKS
Pennsylvania

PUBLISHER'S NOTE

Combined Books, Inc., is dedicated to publishing books of distinction in history and military history. We are proud of the quality of writing and the quantity of information found in our books. Our books are manufactured with style and durability and are printed on acid-free paper. We like to think of our books as soldiers: not infantry grunts, but well dressed and well equipped avant garde. Our logo reflects our commitment to the modern and yet historic art of bookmaking.

We call ourselves Combined Books because we view the publishing enterprise as a "combined" effort of authors, publishers and readers. And we promise to bridge the gap between us—a gap which is all too seldom closed in contemporary publishing.

We would like to hear from our readers and invite you to write to us at our offices in Pennsylvania with your reactions, queries, comments, even complaints. All of our correspondence will be answered directly by a member of the Editorial Board or by the author.

We encourage all of our readers to purchase our books from their local booksellers, and we hope that you let us know of booksellers in your area that might be interested in carrying our books. If you are unable to find a book in your area, please write us.

For information, address:
Combined Books, Inc.
151 East 10th Avenue
Conshohocken, PA 19428

Library of Congress Cataloging-in-Publication Data
Prefer, Nathan.
    MacArthur's New Guinea campaign / Nathan Prefer.
        p. cm.   — (Great Campaigns)
    Includes bibliographical references.
    ISBN 0-938289-51-9
    1. World War, 1939-1945—Campaigns—Papua New Guinea.
2. MacArthur, Douglas, 1880-1964.   I. Title.   II. Series.
D767.95.P74   1995
940.54'26—dc20   95-15824
                                                                          CIP

Printed in the United States of America.
Maps by Beth Queman.

Contents

Sidebars

Maps

Preface to the Series

*J*onathan Swift termed war "that mad game the world so loves to play." He had a point. Universally condemned, it has nevertheless been almost as universally practiced. For good or ill, war has played a significant role in the shaping of history. Indeed, there is hardly a human institution which has not in some fashion been influenced and molded by war, even as it helped shape and mold war in turn. Yet the study of war had been as remarkably neglected as its practice commonplace. With a few outstanding exceptions, the history of wars and of military operations has until quite recently been largely the province of the inspired patriot or the regimental polemist. Only in our times have serious, detailed and objective accounts come to be considered the norm in the treatment of military history and related matters.

Yet there still remains a gap in the literature, for there are two types of military history. One type is written from a very serious, highly technical, professional perspective and presupposes that the reader is deeply familiar with the background, technology and general situation. The other is perhaps less dry, but merely lightly reviews the events with the intention of informing and entertaining the layperson. The qualitative gap between the last two is vast. Moreover, there are professionals in both the military and academia whose credentials are limited to particular moments in the long, sad history of war, and there are interested readers who have more than a passing understanding of the field; and then there is the concerned citizen, interested in understanding the military phenomena in an age of unusual violence and unprecedented armaments. It is to bridge the gap between the two types of military history, and to reach the professional and the serious amateur and the concerned citizen alike, that this series, **GREAT CAMPAIGNS** is thus not merely an account of a particular military operation, but is a unique reference to the theory and practice of war in the period in question.

The **GREAT CAMPAIGNS** series is a distinctive contribution to the study of war and of military history, which will remain of value for many years to come.

Introduction

When the Japanese had entered the Second World War, their objectives had been limited to establishing what they referred to as the "Greater East Asia Co-Prosperity Sphere." After the destruction of the United States Pacific Fleet, the Japanese believed that they could seize Malaya, the Netherlands East Indies, the Philippine Islands, and an outer defensive perimeter extending from the Japanese Kurile Islands west to Wake Island, the Marianas and Rabaul in the Solomons. They believed that if they could hold the outer defensive perimeter and cause the Allies, particularly the Americans, sufficient losses to prevent an immediate response, a negotiated peace would be agreed upon by both sides. The Japanese expected to keep the essential parts of the Co-Prosperity Sphere.

They initially succeeded beyond their highest hopes. The attack on Pearl Harbor on December 7th, 1941 crippled the United States fleet in the Pacific. The gallant defense of Wake Island delayed its conquest but caused the Japanese only a little inconvenience. The British bastion of Singapore fell to the Japanese so quickly that the Japanese were as surprised as the Allies. Initial results in the Philippines were equally swift, although the later prolonged defense of Bataan and Corregidor sullied some Japanese had accomplished all of their goals except in Southern China. According to plan, the Allies should now approach them for negotiations.

Yet no such negotiations took place. Instead the Allies, in particular the Americans, gave every indication that they were still very much in the war, preparing counteroffensives against the newly established perimeter defending the Co-Prosperity Sphere. Having misjudged their enemy, the Japanese High Command turned to plans that had been prepared earlier but discarded in favor of the plan they had just completed. In the earlier plan the defensive perimeter was to encompass a much larger area and included a plan to seize Australia. In order to cut the lines of communication between the United States and Australia, the Japanese planned to seize New Caledonia, Samoa and the Fiji Islands. The flanks of this new perimeter were to be secured by the seizure of Southern New Guinea and the American Aleutian Islands.

Initial attempts by the Japanese to implement this enlarged plan of conquest led directly to the New Guinea campaign. The Japanese attempted to secure the flank objectives in New Guinea by sea. These attempts were thwarted by the naval battles of the Coral Sea and Midway, which did serious damage to the resources of the Japanese Navy as well as challenging its control of the Pacific Ocean.

Unable to move by sea, the Japanese tried the overland route. Landing on the northern coast of New Guinea, and in the Solomon Islands at Guadalcanal and Tulagi, the Japanese Army established bases from which they expected to support the next conquests. These, too, were stopped by the American counter landing in the Solomons and the Australian defense of Port Moresby. Late in the Port Moresby battles American infantry was committed in support of the Australians, beginning the United States' military commitment to the New Guinea campaign.

Having been stopped in their campaign to expand the defensive perimeter the Japanese now determined to hold what they had seized in the expectation that the Allies would still be willing to agree to a negotiated settlement once they learned how costly it could be to regain the territory now under Japanese control. In support of this plan the Imperial Headquarters in Tokyo now established several defensive sectors and allocated resources to each. At Rabaul in the Northern Solomons the headquarters of the *8th Area Army* was established to control events in the Solomons and New Guinea. Under its command, the *8th Area Army* had the *17th Army* which was located in the Solomons and directed to hold them against the already in progress American counteroffensive, and the *18th Army* which was directed to move to New Guinea from Rabaul.

The failure of the *8th Area Army* to hold both Guadalcanal and Southern New Guinea caused *Imperial General Headquarters* to again re-evaluate their situation. They estimated that the Allies would launch a two pronged attack towards recovery of the Pacific, one from the newly acquired Solomon Islands, and the other along the north coast of New Guinea. Accordingly they established a defensive perimeter which would be withdrawn strategically in order to gain time to prepare additional bases to the rear, while husbanding resources for an eventual counterattack. This new defensive line ran from Wewak in eastern New Guinea through Rabaul, New Georgia in the Solomons, the Gilbert and, Mariana Islands in the Central Pacific, to Wake Island and the Aleutians.

In New Guinea the *18th Army* moved its headquarters from Rabaul to Lae on the north coast of New Guinea in March of 1943. The *41st Infantry Division* was moved from China to New Guinea to join the *51st Infantry Division* already fighting there. Later, the *20th Infantry Division*, already in New Guinea, was added to the strength of the *18th Army*. Further attempts to reinforce the *18th Army* were halted when the *115th Infantry Regiment* was largely destroyed during the Battle of the Bismarck Sea when American air power destroyed the convoy carrying it to New Guinea. The Japanese were now in the position they had hoped to place the Allies in at the start of the war, communications cut, supply lines attacked regularly, and reinforcement of advanced positions difficult when not impossible. The result was to place the *18th Army*, with it's existing resources, in the position of defending eastern New Guinea with what it had available. These available resources consisted of the *20th* and *41st Infantry Divisions* and the decimated *51st Infantry Division*. Naval support was non-existent, and air support, still significant, was provided by the *6th Air Division* based at Hollandia. Although other Japanese forces were in New Guinea, particularly the *19th Army* in South Western New

Guinea, the burden of defending New Guinea would fall largely on the *18th Army*.

By early 1944 great sections of the Japanese defensive perimeter had been breached. The Aleutians had been recaptured, as had the Gilbert Islands. Clearly the Americans were moving faster than expected. *Imperial General Headquarters* now instituted another strategic withdrawal which left most of the front east of Hollandia as a secondary holding front to a new defensive line which began at Hollandia. Major supply bases were established on islands in Geelvink Bay and at Manokwari on the Vogelkop Peninsula at the tip of western New Guinea. Eastern New Guinea was, for all practical purposes, written off by *Imperial General Headquarters*.

Having written off eastern New Guinea, *Imperial General Headquarters* now had to find forces to defend Western New Guinea. There was no hope that the *18th Army* could move west intact, or in time, to defend that area. In any case, that army was engaging Allied forces, mostly Australian, which could otherwise be used against the Japanese elsewhere. So Tokyo established the *2nd Area Army* to control the defense of Western New Guinea. This force had under its command the *2nd Army* and the already in place *19th Army* which included two infantry Divisions defending south western New Guinea. Plans to send the *3rd, 36th* and *46th Infantry Divisions* to the *2nd Area Army* were altered when the *3rd Infantry Division* was retained in China, and the *46th Infantry Division* lost major elements to Allied submarines. Only the *36th Infantry Division* arrived intact. Later, in yet another change of plans, the *35th Infantry Division* would be added to the troop list of the *2nd Army*. As a result of all these changes and adjustments, the Japanese had by April of 1944 in New Guinea a command structure which consisted of the *2nd Area Army* commanding the *2nd, 18th* and *19th Armies*. The *2nd Army* had the *32nd, 35th* and *36th Infantry Divisions* under its control, totaling some 50,000 soldiers. The *18th Army* had its veteran divisions still under command, numbering now about 20,000 effective fighters. The *19th Army's 5th, 46th* and *48th Infantry Divisions* numbered around 50,000 troops, but they would see little of the coming battle.

The Americans had come a long way by April, 1944, as well.

The forces under General MacArthur's command had grown considerably from the two untrained National Guard divisions and supporting troops he had found upon his arrival in Australia in March of 1942.

The failure of his defense of the Philippine Islands rankled heavily with General MacArthur. He had repeatedly stated that he had been prepared to die with his troops on Bataan or Corregidor. The General blamed Washington for failing to come to the aid of his command. Prewar plans and subsequent promises had caused the General to believe that all he need do was delay the Japanese invasion forces, and an enormous convoy of troops, equipment and naval support would come swiftly to his aid. The failure of the reinforcements to arrive had stunned the General, whose concept of the war centered solely on his own theater of command. His troops had indeed delayed the enemy invasion plans, so much so that the enemy commander came close to being relieved in disgrace. Yet no help arrived. Left to his own resources, General MacArthur announced that he, at the head of his troops, would stand and die in the Philippines.

Then, suddenly, had come an order to General MacArthur from Washington to leave the Philippines and report to Australia. No less an authority than the President of the United States, Franklin Delano Roosevelt, had originated this order.

Two years later General MacArthur was still determined to keep the promise he made to the Philippines when he arrived in Australia and declared "I came through, and I shall return." Yet he was still not close to realizing his dream of liberating the islands he had left in disgrace on PT 41. Many obstacles had indeed been placed in his path. Upon arrival in Australia, expecting to find a large American force waiting for him to lead back to the Philippines, he was disappointed to find only two combat infantry divisions, the 32nd and 41st Infantry Divisions, available. Both of these divisions were untrained in jungle warfare and had been drawn from the National Guards of Michigan, Wisconsin, Washington, Oregon, Idaho and Montana. They had been strengthened with draftees and volunteers from across the United States. Neither was combat ready. The General found a similar situation in his air and naval forces. He was commanding an army that didn't yet exist.

It was the Japanese who forced General MacArthur, despite his misgivings about his resources, to begin the long road back to his beloved Philippines. The Japanese had not expected to achieve their initial goals so easily, and soon came to suffer from what they would later describe as a "victory disease." This was another way of expressing the fact that the Japanese High Command became extremely overconfident. As victory after victory fell into their hands at little or no cost to themselves, they began to broaden the scope of their planned conquests. For them, "Defeat was unthinkable in the early months." Hong Kong, the Philippines, Singapore, Batavia, Rangoon, Burma, Rabaul all fell to the Japanese onslaught. There was no reason not to push further than originally planned, to keep the Allies from retaliating against the homeland and the essential raw materials which had been captured.

The next steps were the capture of New Guinea and the Solomon Islands. This was intended to rupture communications between the United States and Australia, preventing a coordinated defense and delaying the inevitable offensive the Japanese knew would eventually come. The goal of the Imperial Japanese Navy, a decisive win-all battle, had been attempted and lost at Midway. Yet still the Japanese attempted to advance their defensive perimeter. In the Solomons the United States Navy and Marines invaded Guadalcanal and the six month struggle for supremacy there began. In New Guinea, the Japanese invasion force had been turned back by allied naval forces at the battle of the Coral Sea. Not deterred, the *Imperial Japanese Army* ordered its troops to march overland to the coast of New Guinea nearest Australia. Here they met and initially defeated Australian troops. The Australians quickly learned from the Japanese their tactics, and the fighting over some of the most difficult terrain in the world wasted Japanese resources. The Australians pushed back, and by the end of 1942 had pushed the enemy into the pockets known as Buna-Gona on the north coast of eastern New Guinea. The Australians, with most of their army fighting in North Africa against the German Afrika Korps, were near the end of their resources as were the Japanese. They needed help.

General MacArthur had reached an agreement with the commander of the U.S. Naval forces in the Pacific, Admiral Chester Nimitz, concerning the means and methods by which each would fight the Japanese. Admiral Nimitz with his Navy and Marine forces would begin an offensive in the Solomon Islands, beginning at Guadalcanal. General MacArthur and his Army forces would strike via New Guinea. Planning by General MacArthur's staff had selected the villages of Lae and Salamua, Japanese strongpoints, as the initial targets of their offensive. The enemy's strike at Port Moresby, although defeated by the Australians' stand, upset those plans. Air support needed to be established to support any attacks against Lae, and the Buna-Gona area had been selected as a likely place to establish those essential support bases. The enemy's withdrawal into defensive positions at those locations changed everything. At first, based upon his intelligence service's conclusions that the enemy would not settle at Buna-Gona, General MacArthur refused to move into the area ahead of the Japanese. As would repeatedly happen over the next three years, General MacArthur's intelligence service had evaluated incorrectly. MacArthur made himself unpopular with the Australians when he openly criticized the 7th Australian Division as not having had a hard fight. In fact, the Australians had performed miracles in holding, then defeating, the Japanese forces in the most difficult terrain in the world. To make matters worse, General MacArthur then complained to his superior in Washington, General George Catlett Marshall, that the Australians were no match for the Japanese, and that he was going to send in his American troops to clear matters up.

General MacArthur's assumption that his American soldiers would do better than the Australians quickly proved erroneous. Like their counterparts, the Americans found the jungle, the climate and the entire atmosphere of New Guinea oppressive. Combined with the dedicated opposition of the Japanese, who had orders to hold or die at their positions, the Americans also made unsatisfactory progress. The 32nd Infantry Division had been sent in first, and their lack of jungle training, combat experience and poor physical conditioning caused the division to wreck itself against the jungle and the Japanese. Yet the valiant attacks by the newly committed Americans availed them little at General MacArthur's headquarters. Commanders were relieved with depressing regularity. In desperation General MacArthur sent for the one American commander in his area he thought could do the job, General Robert L. Eichelberger. The degree of General MacArthur's frustration can be seen in the instructions given by him to General Eichelberger when he sent him to take command at Buna-Gona, "Bob, take Buna or don't come back alive." Fortunately, General Eichelberger was the man for the job, as he would prove time and again, and Buna fell early in 1943.

As would occur during the remainder of the New Guinea campaign, with one notable exception, neither General Mac-Arthur nor any of his staff visited the front lines. They never experienced the conditions under which they sent men to fight, and they never saw the Japanese at their determined best in defensive posture. Here, too, began General MacArthur's disturbing tendency to discount events which did not fit into his preordained timetable. During the Buna-Gona campaign an announcement from General MacArthur's headquarters declared the campaign over on January 9th, 1943. In fact, another three weeks and 3,500 casualties were needed to put truth into the communique. This tendency, first displayed in the Philippines and refined during the Papuan Campaign, continued throughout the war. This did little to enhance the General's popularity with either his own troops or his allies. Nor did his field commanders appreciate hearing that in the midst of a desperate struggle, their efforts had been declared "mopping up activities" by official communique. Indeed, because on occasion the truth blatantly contradicted the communique, some field commanders found themselves relieved of command because they did not keep up with a pronouncement issued hundreds of miles away and in complete ignorance of the facts.

All of these factors only made the job of the troops serving under General MacArthur's command that much more difficult. Yet MacArthur's soldiers, airmen and sailors turned in one of the most credible performances of the Second World War, one that is little recognized today due in large measure to the General's habit of issuing communiques which usually ignored the truth. Habitually claiming quick victories at minimal losses, the General cultivated an aura of invincibility and strategic brilliance that upon examination is belied by the facts. Yet despite their lack of recognition the troops under General MacArthur defeated in detail a major Japanese force, conquered an island bastion as difficult as Saipan and isolated some 135,000 enemy troops who would do no further damage to Allied interests for the duration of the war. Both of the divisions that General MacArthur had so callously tossed into the crucible of Buna would redeem themselves before the year was out. At the Driniumor River Battle, the reinforced 32nd Infantry Division would completely defeat the entire Japanese *18th Army*. At about the same time, the 41st Infantry Division would assault Biak Island and set an example for conquering a defended coral island that would last throughout the war. In both cases, and for many other American units at other battles in Western New Guinea, the odds were with the enemy, as both numbers and terrain favored the Japanese. Yet time after time, the American infantryman, supported closely by artillery, engineers, armor, medical, air and naval counterparts, defeated whatever the enemy put in front of him. It is long past time when the accomplishments of these valiant men be recognized as their own, not those of an ungrateful and often ungracious leader.

Although Washington still considered Europe the main theater of operations, General George C. Marshall did manage to siphon off units and supplies to the Southwest Pacific. The threat of the Japanese seizing Australia had concerned both Washington and London, and initial forces were sent to prevent this from happening. With that foot in the door, additional troops had been sent to General MacArthur so that by April of 1944 he could send into combat a complete United States field army. Under General Walter Krueger, the Sixth United States Army had two Corps, the I Corps under General Eichelberger and the XI Corps under General Hall. Ground forces under Sixth Army's control included the 1st Cavalry Division, the 6th, 24th, 31st, 32nd, 33rd, 38th, 40th, 41st, 43rd Infantry Divisions, the

11th Airborne Division, and the independent regimental combat teams of the 112th Cavalry, 158th Infantry and 503rd Parachute Infantry. Support troops consisted of the 2nd, 3rd and 4th Engineer Special Brigades and numerous aviation engineer battalions, as well as medical, quartermaster and transport units. The only noticeable difference between the Sixth United States Army and American armies stationed in England was the lack of any large armor contingent. Not all of these units were immediately available for commitment in New Guinea, as some such as the 1st Cavalry Division were busy occupying the recently seized Admiralty Islands. Yet the resources were greater than expected by the enemy.

CHAPTER I

Moving West—Hollandia

The Papuan Campaign had taken six months to complete. In addition to the 32nd and 41st Infantry Divisions, the Australian 14th, 16th, 18th, 21st, 25th and 30th Infantry Brigades had taken part in the campaign. Casualties from all causes had decimated most of these units, and further campaigns waited upon the rehabilitation of these units, while building up supplies and reserves from newly arriving units.

The victory at Buna-Gona had set the stage for future operations. General MacArthur was as anxious as ever to return to the Philippines, and the situation at the end of February, 1943, was in accord with his earlier concept of advancing towards his goal by moving his land based air support from base to base, each progressively closer to the Philippines. Because the Navy was still building itself into the overwhelming force it would be by war's end, they had little to spare to assist General MacArthur's Southwest Pacific Theater of Operations. Throughout 1943 they would have barely enough resources to conduct their own campaign against Japan, in the Central Pacific. Those operations, under Admiral Chester Nimitz's Pacific Ocean Areas Theater, would progress parallel to General MacArthur, each initially directed towards the Philippines. The situation tied General MacArthur to his land based air support, which in turn needed landing strips and harbors to move forward.

As a result, General MacArthur planned a progressive movement along the north coast of New Guinea, moving against the Japanese by capturing their bases, establishing his own air and

162nd Infantry storm ashore during realistic training exercise.

naval support at those bases, then repeating the process until the entire 1,400 mile coast of northern New Guinea was in Allied hands. Meanwhile, Admiral Nimitz's Central Pacific drive would protect General MacArthur's flank while driving eastward through the Gilbert, Marshall and Palau Island chains of the Central Pacific. The bloody conquest of Buna stirred unrest in some quarters, and General MacArthur determined to attack only those areas absolutely needed to support his campaign, while bypassing others.

The balance of 1943 was spent in clearing operations. In the South Pacific the allied forces moved eastward. Operations involving Army and Marine forces, supported by the U.S. Navy, seized New Georgia, Munda, and Bougainville. In New Guinea Australian forces, supported by segments of the 41st U.S. Infantry Division, moved eastward against moderate opposition. It was a slow and sometimes costly process. The Australians would later describe it as "a ghastly nightmare" to fight for months on end in the "primeval swamps, the dank and silent bush." Worse, in terms of a swift return to the Philippines, it was much too slow.

One base that originally was scheduled to be attacked was Rabaul. This Japanese strongpoint on the offshore island of New Britain was discovered to have become weaker as its resources were drained off to fight the combined MacArthur-Nimitz drives, and a landing under General MacArthur's command had been scheduled for the Admiralty Islands as the prelimi-

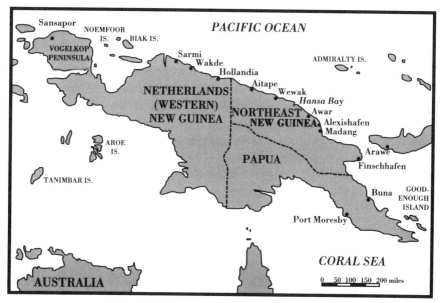

nary step in moving against Rabaul. Air crews bombarding the islands in preparation for the attack began to report little or no Japanese opposition during their attacks. General MacArthur, anxious to speed up the advance, ordered an immediate reconnaissance in force to land and determine whether the Japanese had evacuated the islands, as was suspected. Elements of the 1st U.S. Cavalry Division, an infantry unit despite its designation, landed and found that the Japanese had not evacuated, but had simply withdrawn from the target areas to await the assault they knew would come. General MacArthur followed the initial waves ashore and made the decision on the spot to bring in the entire 1st Cavalry Division and force the issue to conclusion. The General's presence on the field had been critical to a successful conquest of the islands, but unfortunately it would be his only visit to the front lines during the New Guinea Campaign.

The speedy capture of the Admiralties, and the isolation of Rabaul by a landing of the 1st U.S. Marine Division on New Britain under General MacArthur's command, had presented new opportunities to speed the advance. In consultation with Admiral Nimitz, Admiral William H. Halsey, and the Joint

41st Division DUKW on the beach near Aitape.

Chiefs of Staff in Washington, it was decided to cancel several invasions planned, and to proceed further up the coast of New Guinea. Admiral Halsey, who had commanded General Mac-Arthur's Naval support, had argued that the Allies had no need of many of the scheduled bases, and that the weakened condition of those bases posed no threat to the Allied advance. Convinced by these arguments, both General MacArthur and Admiral Nimitz revised their planning to bypass Japanese positions wherever possible. For General MacArthur, with Rabaul neutralized and his flank covered by Admiral Nimitz, the next step would be the major Japanese base at Hollandia, a series of airfields from which the Japanese had launched air strikes against the Allies. The choice was based upon two main factors. The bases at Hollandia could be quickly adapted for allied use, and Hollandia was within the extreme range of the allied aircraft from existing bases. Three landings were planned, one at each end of the Hollandia area, to create a pincer attack against what was expected to be a strong defense, and a third to establish a buffer against the large Japanese forces known to be fighting the Australians west of the landing area.

During March 1944, several meetings and communications were conducted between the Joint Chiefs of Staff in Washington, General MacArthur, and Admiral Nimitz. Progress against the enemy and future projections were weighed and decisions were made as to how to proceed against the remaining enemy

Interesting shot of 105mm howitzers test-firing on an LST before the Hollandia landings.

defenses. During these meetings General MacArthur, who declined to travel outside his own area of responsibility, was represented by his unpopular Chief of Staff, General Richard K. Sutherland. General Sutherland made a noticeable argument for the appointment of an over-all Pacific Commander, and of course he had in mind his own commander, General MacArthur. When it was pointed out to him that if such a plan was formally proposed, the commander appointed might well be Admiral Nimitz, General Sutherland replied that if Admiral Nimitz was appointed over General MacArthur, the General "would retire one day, resign on the next, return to the United States as a civilian and undertake an active newspaper and radio program to educate the public." While General MacArthur's rather remarkable position for a wartime Theater commander to the threat of subordination to another officer was ignored, no further discussion of an overall commander for the Pacific was raised for the duration of the war. The result of all these conversations was a directive by the Joint Chiefs of Staff to General MacArthur and Admiral Nimitz, setting out the schedule of future operations. Hollandia was set for April 15th, the Southern Marianas for June 15th by Admiral Nimitiz's forces, the Palau Islands by September 15th by Admiral Nimitz's forces, Mindanao by November 15th by General MacArthur's command, and finally Formosa by February 15th by Admiral

41st Signal Company boards landing craft for Hollandia operation.

Nimitz's forces. The directive left several questions open, such as what was to be done about the Japanese naval base at Truk, and the Philippines. Although the Joint Chiefs directive did not specifically direct General MacArthur into the Philippines, there was no doubt in the General's mind about his destination.

First, however, there was the rest of New Guinea to conquer. The staff of Southwest Pacific Headquarters had originally considered a number of closer localities as the next step in advancing up the coast of New Guinea, but now with the directive from the Joint Chiefs, the problem was Hollandia. It was, indeed, a problem. The Japanese base had three airfields, Hollandia, Cyclops, and Sentani. These were located in an area lying between Humboldt and Tanahmerah Bays, with the immediate region being dominated by the 6,000 foot peaks of the Cyclops Mountains which ran parallel the coast in steep cliffs which drop to the coast forming a saddlelike basin around Lake Sentani. Although known to be a major Japanese base, little in detail was known of either the area or the enemy defenses. From radio intercepts the Allies knew that the principal defenders of Hollandia were the *Fourth Air Army*, commanded by Lieutenant General Kunachi Teramoto, an experienced air officer who had fought in Manchuria. Although the *Fourth Air Army* officially consisted of the *6th* and *7th Air Divisions*, the latter had been so depleted in combat that it had been withdrawn for replacements and retraining. Only Lieutenant General Giichi Itabana's *6th Air Division*'s two brigades, the *14th* and *30th Air Brigades*, remained in New Guinea, with most of their strength stationed at Hollandia.

The Japanese had not expected anything to happen at Hollandia. Although when he had first arrived in New Guinea, in April of 1942, General Adachi had declared that Hollandia would be the final bastion of defense should the attack on Port Moresby fail, the concept of failure was so foreign to the Japanese military that no garrison had been provided. They knew that the Allies were bogged down in the jungles of eastern New Guinea, and would not be near Hollandia for months. This lack of foresight caused them to leave Hollandia without a garrison. While occupied by the *6th Air Division*, there was no ground force garrison other than local security forces. Fooled by the Allied deception measures indicating an attack at Wewak, the enemy continued to leave Hollandia undefended. And to the Allies benefit, the base was not only without a strong garrison, but was in the midst of a command upheaval. The commander of the *6th Air Division* had been relieved in disgrace, and his replacement had only just arrived when the Allies struck. In addition to Major General Masazumi Inada's recent assumption of command of the *6th Air Division*, the ground force commander had also only just arrived from the *18th Army*. Major General Toyozo Kitazono had arrived from the forward units of the enemy forces and assumed command at Hollandia only ten days before the first Allied landings. Although there was little he could have done in those ten days, he had undoubtedly arrived convinced that the main Allied attentions were directed at Hansa Bay and Wewak, not Hollandia. As it turned out, General Kitazono was missing in action during the battle, but survived the war. General Inada assumed direct command of the defenses at Hollandia.

Landing craft assemble off-shore for Hollandia landings.

The condition of the *6th Air Division* was only little better than that of the withdrawn *7th Air Division*. Lack of spare parts, poor maintenance, and loss of heavy equipment in earlier battles had made life very difficult for General Itabana's flyers. Allied estimates put some 319 planes in or around Hollandia, of which at most 239 planes were believed serviceable. Against these, the Fifth U.S. Army Air Force could throw over 800 fighters, 780 bombers, and 173 reconnaissance planes. Hundreds of transport planes were also available for re-supply emergencies. In addition, about 500 Royal Australian Air Force planes were in the area and available. But the Allies, too, had maintenance problems, and estimated that only some fifty per cent of their planes were combat ready for the coming battles. Even with half of their available planes out of service, the Allies outnumbered the enemy five to one in combat planes.

The Air Forces had other problems, however, which made their supremacy of numbers less than decisive. Their nearest base was at the valley of Nadzab, in the lower Markham River Valley, which had been seized by the Australians in January. Although the Allies now had nine airstrips there, Nadzab was 448 nautical miles from Hollandia, outside the range of most of the Allied planes. While the Fifth Air Force's heavy B-17 Flying Fortress and medium B-24 Liberator bombers could reach Hollandia, the mainstay of the Fifth Air Force's fighter force, the P-38 Lightning could not accompany them for more than 350 miles, making the bombers sitting ducks for the enemy fighter opposition around Hollandia. In order to reduce enemy air opposition at Hollandia for the coming attack the bombers and

Troops of the Hollandia Assault Force rush ashore from their beached landing craft at Tanahmerah Bay. (National Archives)

the fighters had to bomb the airfields into disarray and also to reduce enemy fighter opposition at Hollandia. The only possible solutions were to extend the range of the P-38's or to use naval air support for the landings.

Admiral Nimitz was approached for the loan of his naval air power. The Admiral agreed readily, and loaned his powerful Fifth Fleet's aircraft carriers to General MacArthur for the Hollandia operation. Control and coordination were worked out by the staffs. Not to be outdone, Lieutenant General George C. Kenney, commanding both General MacArthur's overall Air Forces, and also the Fifth U.S. Army Air Force, increased efforts already in progress to extend the range of the P-38 fighter plane. By modifying the planes existing wing fuel tanks, the aircraft's range could be extended from the former maximum of 350 miles to 650 miles. By April 1, two P-38 Groups had been converted into long range fighters, and were available to escort the bombers to Hollandia. During March these resources were directed against the forward enemy base at Wewak, and by the end of the month all enemy air opposition had ceased. So effective were the Allied attacks that General Teramoto was forced to move his *Fourth Air Army's* headquarters back to Hollandia. As the Allies controlled the sea, the withdrawal was by land. As would happen again in this campaign, the jungle claimed hundreds of Japanese ground crew specialists so urgently needed elsewhere.

The first daylight mission against Hollandia was launched on March 30th. Seven B-24's, seventy-five B-25's escorted by newly converted long range P-38's dropped tons of bombs on Hollandia. The intent was to destroy enemy air power, and so the runways were not a prime target. If possible, they were to be saved for Allied use. Enemy opposition was moderate, and about twenty five enemy fighters attacked the 65th Bombardment Groups while another thirty five were engaged by the 80th Fighter Squadron. Results of the bombing were evaluated as quite good. Again on March 31 an identical mission was sent over Hollandia. Against the same type of opposition as the day before, the Fifth Air Force again destroyed enemy planes and installations on the ground and in the air. After a break caused by bad weather, a third strike was launched on April 3rd. Reinforced by more heavy bombers and this time with A-20 Attack Bombers in the strike force, another devastating attack put 355 tons of bombs and 175,000 rounds of strafing ammunition into Hollandia. A diary written by a Japanese airman found later by Allied forces expressed the opinion that this last strike marked "the annihilation of our Army Air Force in New Guinea." Although additional strikes continued to the day of the amphibious assault, the way had been smoothed for the ground forces.

At dawn, on April 22, 1944, the three great operations took place. The eastern attack group moved towards Aitape, the central attack group for Humboldt Bay, and the western attack group to Tanahmerah Bay. Captain A. G. Noble, U.S.N., commanding Task Group 77.3 was the first to break off from the main convoy. Covered by the escort carriers and with minesweepers preceding him, his task group arrived safely off the

U.S. infantry prepare to move off the beaches at Tanahmerah Bay after leaving a landing craft. The narrow beaches were a problem to supply forces. (National Archives)

designated landing beaches at 0500. Every ship, including the transports, was used to provide a pre-invasion bombardment. In addition to the shore, the four offshore islands were also subjected to shelling. Most of the Japanese in the area were service troops who ran at the first explosions. Aircraft from the carriers and from Fifth Air Force planes were on call to provide air support during the morning.

All this preliminary bombardment, carried out without opposition from the Japanese, had caused considerable smoke and dust clouds over the target area. As a result the actual landing missed the planned beaches by some 1,200 yards to the east. However, in the absence of enemy opposition this proved to be a minor error. As it turned out the beaches on which the troops landed, at the village of Wapil, proved to be at least as good for the assault force as the planned beaches would have been. The

Mortar team pushes inland during Hollandia operation.

2nd and 3rd Battalions, 163rd Infantry, landed and found Japanese equipment and hot food abandoned. These units immediately moved off the beaches and established a beach-head perimeter defense line some 500 yards inland. Opposed only by the occasional rifle shot, the battalions had captured 3 Japanese and freed more than 50 Javanese slave laborers by the end of the day.

The 1st Battalion, 163rd Infantry, came ashore and moved past its sister units towards Tadji Bomber Strip. At the same time, the 2nd Battalion moved on Tadji Fighter Strip, leaving the 3rd Battalion to defend the beachhead. Both battalions reached their objectives before lunch. No Japanese were seen. Defense perimeters were quickly established and patrols sent out to locate the enemy. The cost of capturing two enemy air strips had been two soldiers killed and 13 wounded. By mid-day Number 62 Works Wing of the Royal Australian Air Force was at the strips preparing to rehabilitate them for Allied use. Within the next few weeks the Australians and the 872nd and 875th U.S. Army Aviation Engineer Battalions rebuilt both strips for the

Sherman tanks support the advance at Hollandia. These early-pattern cast-hulled versions were long obsolete in other theaters.

larger and heavier Allied planes. Within 48 hours of the landing aircraft of Number 78 Wing, Royal Australian Air Force, were operating out of the Hollandia base.

The follow-up ground force, the 127th Infantry Regiment of the 32nd Infantry Division, landed without incident on April 23rd. So meager was Japanese opposition that half of the covering aircraft carriers were released for replenishment during the afternoon of April 23rd. Indeed, the only effective Japanese opposition came on April 27th, when three enemy planes managed one torpedo hit on the cargo ship *Etamin*. Damaged but not sunk, the *Etamin* was towed to the allied base at Finschafen for repairs. No other naval casualties occurred at Aitape.

Lieutenant General Walter Krueger, in overall command of the operations, was satisfied. A unique individual in the U.S. Army, General Krueger had begun his military career as an enlisted man during the Spanish-American War, rising to the rank of sergeant after service in Cuba and the Philippines. Commissioned directly from the ranks, he never attended the U.S. Military Academy at West Point. Despite that neglect, he successfully completed the course of study at the Infantry and Cavalry School at Fort Leavenworth, Kansas, and later graduated the Staff College. He served in both the Mexican Punitive Expedition and the First World War as a staff officer. He capped his military education by graduating in subsequent years from the Infantry School at Fort Benning, Georgia, the Army War College and finally the Naval War College. Between the wars he held various command and staff appointments, culminating in his appointment to command the Third U.S. Army in May of 1941. During his career, he had come to the attention of General MacArthur, who asked for his assignment to the Southwest Pacific Theater when the newly created Sixth U.S. Army was formed in that Theater. General Krueger took command of the Sixth Army in January of 1943. Although it was known as "Alamo Force" during much of its service in New Guinea due to General MacArthur's desire to keep Australian commanders from high profile operations, it nevertheless operated in effect as a U.S. field army.

At Aitape, the balance of the month was spent in expanding the perimeter and in trying to locate the elusive enemy. Artillery came ashore but fired not one hostile round. There were simply no targets. Both the 127th and 163rd Infantry Regiments expanded their perimeters behind a screen of patrols. Still no contact was made with the Japanese. In view of the complete lack of opposition, the commander of the infantry force, Brigadier General Jens A. Doe, felt that progress could have been faster. General Doe, who was the assistant division commander of the 41st Infantry Division, repeatedly urged Colonel Francis W. Mason, commanding the 163rd Infantry Regiment, to move faster. Colonel Mason continued to halt expansion while sending out patrols to ensure the safety of his troops. This, General Doe felt, had become overcaution, and General Doe requested that Colonel Mason be relieved of his command. General Krueger approved the request, but Colonel Mason retained command until May 9th, when another commander could arrive. April at Aitape ended with the first skirmish of note when troops of the 3rd Battalion, 163rd Infantry, found themselves surrounded at the village of Kemti. Some 200 Japanese troops harassed this force on April 27th and 28th, after which the Americans withdrew to let the artillery fire of Battery A, 126th Field Artillery Battalion have room to fire. Returning to

Kamti the next day, Company L found the village deserted. Shortly after this skirmish the 163rd Infantry was relieved by additional elements of the 32nd Infantry Division.

While General Doe's Persecution Task Force was securing the air strips at Aitape without difficulty, Reckless Task Force was operating as well. This operation had difficulty from the start. Information about this area was scanty. The pre-war Dutch colonizers had failed to develop the area, and information on any development the Japanese may have made was non-existent. In order to remedy this situation, Alamo Force ordered a scouting party into the area a month before the landings, to discover exactly what the infantry would be facing when they landed. An earlier attempt to scout the area using a Dutch group had ended in disaster when the party was killed before leaving Eastern New Guinea. This time the party would be Australian, part of the Coastwatcher network that the Allied forces had come to rely on so much. Codenamed "Ferdinand" after the docile bull, it had since the early days of Guadalcanal and Port Moresby provided all Allied combat forces with advance intelligence of Japanese strengths and movements. Composed of Australian military personnel, most of whom were recalled reservists who had lived in the South Pacific before the war, these men lived precariously behind enemy lines, hiding and observing enemy movements. Reporting by radio, their lives in constant danger, they had saved many a life in the Allied camp.

Commander Eric A. Feldt, Royal Australian Navy, commanded the Coastwatcher organization. He selected the group to land at Hollandia as requested by Sixth Army. The party was to be commanded by Lieutenant G. C. "Blue" Harris. Lieutenant Harris picked another Australian Lieutenant, R. B. Webber, an Australian army sergeant and three privates, an Australian sailor, three native policemen, and an Indonesian interpreter. Lieutenant Harris and his party boarded the U.S. submarine *Dace* and departed for the beaches off Hollandia. Plans called for the scouts to spend two weeks in the area, after which *Dace* would return and take them home.

On March 22nd *Dace* surfaced of the selected beaches in darkness. As the party prepared to land, a searchlight was sighted on the beach. Harris and *Dace* withdrew, and the

163rd Infantry makes a river crossing at Aitape.

following night the party landed at a small beach further along the coast. Harris arranged with *Dace*'s commander, Commander D. B. Claggett, a system of signals in case anything went wrong. Divided into two groups, Harris led the first ashore. Heavy breakers at the beach overturned the rubber boat, making their radio useless. Natives spotted them as they came ashore. Harris ordered the signal to *Dace* which would prevent the second group from coming ashore. However, aboard *Dace* Commander Claggett received the signal to land the second group, which he did. The signal mixup has never been explained, but may have been caused by signals which the natives were observed sending. Like the first group, the second overturned on the beach and lost much of its equipment. The local natives seemed friendly, but Harris relied on the sixth sense he had developed in more than a year in the jungles of New Guinea and didn't trust them. As it turned out, he was correct.

The natives had reported the presence of the scouts to the Japanese immediately. After camping for the night in the jungle, the party was attacked the next morning by Japanese troops. Harris and two of the Australians stood off the attackers for some four hours while the rest of the party escaped into the jungle. After his two comrades were killed and he was

Aerial view of U.S. airstrike on the Japanese defenses near Hollandia, 29-30 April, 1944. (National Archives)

wounded, Harris was captured and tortured about Allied intentions in the area. Already fatally wounded, Harris said nothing and was executed by the Japanese. The other five members of his group miraculously survived, some by hiding in the jungle and others by hiking under terrible conditions to Allied positions. Unfortunately this gallant episode availed the Reckless Task Force little in the way of information.

With no word from Harris' party, selection of landing beaches was made from aerial photographs. The nature of the terrain hidden under the jungle canopy could not be determined, and planners had hoped that the terrain would support allied operations. They also relied on a rumor that a Japanese road existed just behind the beaches selected. Plans were made on these assumptions. So the Western Attack Group moved into Tanahmerah Bay, not really knowing what they were facing.

The opening operations went well. As at Aitape, bombardment started on time and was unopposed. Admiral R. A. C. Crutchley's cruisers and destroyers, after completing their bombardment, moved west to Demta Bay where they found and destroyed Japanese supply dumps and transport barges. Pre-invasion air strikes by planes of Task Force 58 were canceled when no opposition appeared.

The 24th Infantry Division's 2nd Battalion, 21st Infantry and 3rd Battalion of the 19th Infantry were carried ashore by landing craft of the 542nd Engineer Boat and Shore Regiment. The landings were unopposed. While the main body of the battalions took up perimeter defense positions around the beachhead, Company I of the 21st Infantry was sent to locate the expected Japanese trail behind the beachhead. It turned out, as Company I investigated, that there were numerous trails behind the beachhead. There were so many, in fact, the proper trail could not be identified. During this search occasional Japanese stragglers were seen, but no serious opposition developed. This proved fortunate given the almost complete lack of knowledge of the area by the Americans.

The depth of the American's lack of knowledge quickly became evident when the follow-up forces and supplies began to come ashore. The area immediately behind the assault beaches was primal swamp. There was simply no room for the mass of men and supplies coming shore. Small areas on the beach and a few dry areas inland could be used, but the inland areas could only be reached by cutting a dry road through the swamp, a task the engineers found impossible. The trail believed to be behind the landing area which would connect both landing areas did not exist. Nor were the engineers able to build one. Only two artillery pieces could be emplaced to provide covering fire, should it be needed. Company A, 1st Marine Tank Battalion, came ashore in support and found themselves stranded on the beach. There was no path usable even by tracked vehicles. General Frederick A. Irving, commanding the 24th Infantry Division, ordered the establishment of a shuttle system to divert supplies from Red Beach 2 to Red Beach 1, where conditions were slightly better.

Fortunately for Sixth Army, the landings at Humboldt Bay went much smoother. Led by the 2nd Battalion, 162nd Infantry

Brig. Gen. Jens A. Doe, assistant division commander, 41st Infantry Division, observes the 163rd Regimental Combat Team's landing at Aitape. (National Archiver)

of the 41st Infantry Division, the landings were likewise unopposed and quickly completed. Here, as at Tanahmerah Bay, only occasional enemy rifle fire disrupted the advance. All first day objectives were taken before dark, at a cost of 6 killed and 16 wounded. The combat elements of the 41st Infantry Division, the 162nd and 186th Infantry Regiments, 116th Combat Engineer Battalion and part of the 603rd Tank Company were prepared for the next day's advance on Hollandia.

The fortune of the Sixth Army during the early stages of these operations was unique in Pacific War operations. In each case the Japanese, including combat experienced units, ran from the assaulting forces rather than confront them. This type of demoralization was rarely encountered in Japanese combat units. In one instance, at Pancake Hill just inland from the 41st Infantry Division's beaches, the 3rd Battalion, 162nd Infantry, found a Japanese anti-aircraft gun sited to give direct fire on the beaches the battalion had just crossed. The gun was in perfect working order with ammunition stacked nearby. Its weather proof cover was still in place. Yet it never fired and was undefended when

BAR team probes remaining Japanese holdouts in Hollandia area.

seized by the Americans. The lack of morale in these Japanese units has never been adequately explained.

The Americans did not question their good fortune. The advance continued and by the morning of the 23rd, Hollandia Town had been seized by the 162nd Infantry without opposition, while the 186th Infantry reached the shores of Lake Sentani. By this time, many American commanders were beginning to worry about the lack of opposition. Their intelligence reports, provided by the Sixth Army, indicated large enemy forces in the area. Hollandia was also supposed to be a major enemy base. Where was the enemy? There were occasional pinprick attacks, such as the one against the 186th Infantry at Lake Sentani on April 23rd, but there was no organized Japanese defense. There were no large enemy forces identified. More and more the combat commanders sent out patrols and found nothing. The Japanese continued their attacks on a small scale, delaying the advance on occasion but no determined opposition developed. Colonel Oliver P. Newman, who had replaced Colonel Mason as commander of the 186th Infantry, continued his advance towards Cyclops Drome, the major enemy air strip in the area. Using landing craft of the 2nd Engineer Special Brigade, the regiment moved by land and water. They approached the airfield on the 25th, but artillery fire from friendly forces, probably the 24th Infantry Division, and some Japanese artillery were falling on the field. Colonel Newman directed that the field would be seized the following day despite reports from patrols that there were strong enemy defensive positions around the field. Colonel Newman had assumed, correctly as it turned out, that the Japanese had abandoned the airfield. The almost complete lack of opposition in the advance to the field, and the Japanese artillery fire on their own field had led him to believe that the enemy was not going to fight for Cyclops Drome. By noon the next day the 186th Infantry had secured the airfield against light enemy fire. Before dark, patrols of the 1st Battalion met patrols of the 21st Infantry Regiment, 24th Infantry Division. All objectives had now been secured.

The advance of the 24th Infantry Division to the air fields was very much like the advance of the 41st Division. Led by the 1st Battalion, 21st Infantry, the Americans had advanced along native trails. These were narrow and winding. "At any one of the numerous hair-pin turns and defiles over the first two or three miles of the track, a squad of Japanese riflemen could have delayed an entire Infantry Division." There were no Japanese left in the area. Defensive installations were found undefended. Only conditions of terrain and supply difficulties hindered the advance of Lieutenant Colonel Thomas E. Clifford, Jr.'s battalion. Events followed exactly as they were developing for the 186th Infantry. Snipers harassed the advance. Patrols became the only source of reliable intelligence. A small Japanese force attacked the perimeter on the night of April 22nd, doing little damage. The advance on the 23rd was a repetition of the preceding day. The 3rd Battalion, under Lieutenant Colonel

41st Division equipment is moved up from Humboldt Bay to Pancake Hill.

Chester A. Dahlan, came up in support during the day. The rest of the regiment, commanded by Colonel Charles B. Lyman, would follow the next day.

The next day, April 24th, brought the first serious opposition to the advance of the 21st Infantry. While attempting to cross a stream, the leading elements of Company B came under rifle and machine gun fire. Repeated attempts to force a crossing or to outflank the enemy position were unsuccessful. Supporting fires were called for and planes from Task Force 58, still waiting offshore, bombarded the enemy in concert with artillery fire from the 52nd Field Artillery Battalion reinforced by the mortars and machine guns of Colonel Clifford's battalion. The enemy would not be dislodged, however, and the battalion pulled back from the stream and established a defensive perimeter for the night. Colonel Clifford and his men had encountered one of the few aggressive groups of Japanese present at Hollandia. The Japanese continued to fire on the American's positions throughout the night, using in addition to mortar, grenade and small arms fire, artillery bursts from a dual purpose 90mm antiaircraft gun.

Dawn brought new problems for the 21st Infantry. The entire regiment was strung out over 12 miles of jungle trail. Supplies were fast disappearing. The 1st Battalion did not have enough food for breakfast on the 25th. Ammunition, especially in the 1st Battalion which was engaging the enemy, was in short supply. There was now an aggressive enemy force facing the regiment, which further aggravated the supply problem. During the planning stages of the operation, the division supply officer had determined that one infantry regiment could be supplied over a native track by hand carried supplies. Provided that the track remained dry, this method was to be used in the event the Japanese motor road did not exist. By April 24th, all these calculations were inoperative. The motor road did not exist, and now rain began to fall, making the track impassable to a heavily laden soldier.

General Irwin decided to see conditions for himself. He went up the trail on April 23rd, and quickly concluded that supply under these conditions was impractical. He ordered the forward positions consolidated while the following units continued as best they could in the re-supply effort. He also assigned the 1st Battalion, 19th Infantry Regiment, to become fully involved in carrying supplies forward. General Irwin also considered the possibility of flying in supplies and parachuting them to the 1st Battalion, 21st Infantry. One look at the weather and the general conditions under which the drop would have to be made canceled that idea. For the time being, the only action to be taken was to re-supply the leading troops. Both the 1st and 2nd Battalions of the 19th Infantry were committed to getting supplies inland from the beaches, where the antitank and cannon companies of both the 19th and 21st Infantry Regiments moved them forward. The men of Colonel Clifford's battalion patrolled during the day, finding that the enemy force defending the stream had departed.

General Irwin hoped that the next day would be better. He requested an air drop on the line of march and also ordered Colonel Clifford to move forward. As ordered, the 1st Battalion moved forward at dawn. There was no opposition, although terrain and jungle conditions slowed the advance. Towards noon, two Japanese armored vehicles were discovered abandoned along the trail. The battalion continued its advance after destroying these vehicles and reached the Dajaoe River. Here they encountered a small Japanese force which offered resistance. Outflanking this force the battalion next encountered automatic weapons fire. The American's own mortars and machine guns soon drove off these Japanese. Continued harassment by small groups of Japanese slowed the advance for the balance of the day, and the battalion progressed only about 500 yards past the Dajaoe River before stopping for the night.

Behind the advance things had not gone well. Despite General Irwin's optimism the rain continued all day, precluding an air drop. There was no improvement in the supply situation. General Irwin ordered greater efforts in bringing supplies forward. By dawn of April 26th, two infantry battalions, two antitank companies, two cannon companies, two service companies and several engineer, artillery and medical units were engaged in bringing supplies to the 1st Battalion, 21st Infantry, the only unit in contact with the enemy.

The 24th Infantry Division had a high morale. When it became apparent that the 1st and 3rd Battalions of the 21st Infantry were beyond supporting artillery fire, Company A, 641st Tank Destroyer Battalion, sent one gun, all that could be manhandled, and two crews over the trail to assist the infantry. An entire platoon carried the ammunition for the gun. Similarly, Battery A of the 52nd Field Artillery Battalion manhandled a 105mm howitzer forward. Battery C, 11th Field Artillery Battalion, volunteered every man to hand carry supplies forward. All these gallant efforts proved unavailing. When the 1st Battalion attacked again on the 26th, none of these weapons or supplies had reached effective range.

General Irwin had lost none of his optimism, and the response of his men had strengthened his resolve to continue the attack. Continuing to believe that the weather would improve, he ordered the two leading battalions into the attack. Relying on instinct and intelligence that the Japanese would not defend the airfield, he ordered that the leading battalions go on half rations and make the best of their ammunition situation. The General was fully aware of the risk he was taking, for if the Japanese resisted or the weather failed to improve, disaster was a foregone conclusion. As often happens, fortune favors the bold. The 1st and 3rd Battalions attacked into the same kind of resistance that they had encountered earlier. Here and there a few determined enemy defended an unsupported position. These few were quickly overcome without heavy ammunition expenditure. By midday, the 3rd Battalion had reached the airfield, and Colonel Lyman could report by midafternoon that

New Guinea natives at times aided both sides during the campaign.

the entire airfield was secure. Hollandia Drome was in American hands.

The day continued to be good to the 24th Infantry Division. The weather finally cleared enough for B-24 Bombers of the 17th Reconnaissance Squadron, 5th Air Force, to drop ammunition and rations along the trails. Once the rain stopped, the 2nd Battalion, 21st infantry, moved swiftly up the trail to join its sister battalions, bringing with it additional supplies. Engineers working on the trails had made them partially passable for jeeps, which eased the resupply burden. Hollandia Drome, the objective of the campaign, was secured. And finally, contact had been made with the 41st Infantry Division, connecting the two beachheads.

Both Divisions engaged in mopping up operations for the remainder of their stay in Hollandia. Small groups of Japanese were encountered and eliminated, the largest group of about

400 being destroyed by the 186th Infantry on Hill 1000. Shortly after this engagement, the 24th Infantry Division assumed responsibility for the zone of the 41st Infantry Division, which moved to its next assignment. Patrols and intelligence reports indicated that the survivors of the *Hollandia Garrison* had assembled at the village of Genjem, some 15 miles west of Lake Sentani. From here they were moving in groups west to Wakde-Sarmi. This involved a march of 125 miles in the most primitive jungle in the world. There were no reliable maps and few supplies. Some 7,000 Japanese were reported to be in this force. Reportedly, the first attempt to make the march began May 9th and consisted of the *Headquarters, 6th Air Division*, which included stranded pilots and ground crews. These extremely valuable specialists set out as ordered with little in the way of medical supplies, avoiding Allied combat bases set up in the jungle along their expected route. These bases, manned by companies I and K of the 19th Infantry, sent out regular patrols to catch these travelers. The patrols killed and captured nearly 500 Japanese, but the jungle accounted for far more. The Japanese estimate of only seven per cent surviving this trek is considered quite accurate. For the Japanese, the Hollandia operation opened with a major disaster. Not only were several important airfields given to the enemy, but many irreplaceable specialists desperately needed for future air operations were lost. Worse was yet to come.

New Guinea and its Inhabitants

New Guinea was probably first inhabited by migrants from the Asian mainland who moved south and east by way of Indonesia. Because of the extremely rugged terrain, the early communities had little or no contact with each other and became intensely independent and self sufficient. Several differing languages and customs developed as a result.

The island was first sighted by Spanish and Portuguese explorers in the early 16th century and was known at first as the Isla de Oro, or island of gold. Largely neglected for another century, traders began to appear in the mid-19th century. British, Dutch and German colonizers also soon appeared and a mutual division of the territory of New Guinea was agreed upon, without reference to the inhabitants. Later, Australia tried an annexation attempt which was stymied by British and Dutch authorities. Britain then established a protectorate over the eastern half of the island.

The British protectorate passed to Australia in 1902. Renamed the Territory of Papua, the island now had Dutch, German and Australian masters. With the outbreak of the First World War, Australia seized the German territories and administered them until the Japanese seized them in early 1942. While World War One had passed New Guinea and its environs without much notice, World War Two would bring New Guinea rudely into the twentieth century. Its legacy is felt there still, as when on April 27th, 1992 a World War Two bomb was responsible for killing two natives of Valur, Papua New Guinea when they tried to open it to remove its explosives.

Concept of an Air Division

The Japanese military structure as it existed during World War II contained an air force which was modeled on Army lines. Much like the United States at the time, the Air Force was a part of the Army, with an identical rank structure and an organizational structure as similar to ground forces as possible. The defenders of Hollandia were the troops of the *6th Air Division*. It had arrived in New Guinea as a part of the *Fourth Air Army* in September of 1943. The *Fourth Air Army* consisted of the *6th* and *7th Air Divisions,*

much like the ground forces *18th Army* consisted of the *20th, 41st* and *51st Infantry Divisions*. Because of commitments elsewhere, the *7th Air Division* left New Guinea in November of 1943, leaving the *6th Air Division* and some elements attached directly to *Fourth Air Army* as the main air support for the Japanese forces in New Guinea.

The *6th Air Division* consisted of two *Air Brigades*, the *14th* and the *30th*. Each brigade in turn consisted of an assortment of fighter and bomber regiments. For example, at

45

one point the *8th Air Brigade*, attached to *Fourth Air Army*, had three fighter and two bomber regiments under its control. As the campaign for Western New Guinea began, *Fourth Air Army* had under its command a total of twelve flying regiments, two separate flying squadrons and an air transport unit. These units were based all along the coast of New Guinea and the islands offshore.

CHAPTER II

Taking the Outposts

The securing of the airfields at Hollandia, and the destruction so easily of the Japanese *6th Air Division* freed Sixth Army planners to move on the next in the list of objectives. The objective was still the Philippines, and the step by step forward advance of the essential air power of the 5th United States Army Air Force, soon to be joined by the 13th U.S. Army Air Force. Advancing further up the coast of New Guinea required moving to the edge of Geelvink Bay. Airfields there would cover the entire remainder of the New Guinea area scheduled for conquest, and allow the Allies to move anywhere they pleased secure in the knowledge that air cover would be available.

Planning at General MacArthur's headquarters centered on the area known as Wakde-Sarmi. Sarmi was the former center of the local Netherlands East Indies Government, now in exile. Located on a peninsula of land jutting into Geelvink Bay, it also had a reputation as a local center of commerce before the war. In 1943, with the Allies' intentions clearly focused on re-conquering New Guinea, the Japanese had begun base development there, including the construction of air bases. About twenty miles east of Sarmi lie the Wakde Islands. These two islands, Insoemoar and Insoemanai Islands, were about two miles offshore, and Insoemoar Island had been developed into a major airdrome. Seizing these bases would greatly advance the Allied drive up the north coast of New Guinea, while at the same time reduce the potential Japanese air threat to allied bases to the east.

There was yet one more reason to seize bases in this area. By March of 1944 coordination between the Central Pacific Forces under Admiral Nimitz and the Southwest Pacific area under General MacArthur required that Geelvink Bay be secured to prevent any flank attack on either force. The March 12th, 1944 directive from the Joint Chiefs of Staff confirmed that the Southwest Pacific Forces would be required to seize Geelvink Bay, to secure the coming Central Pacific attack into the Mariana Islands in the Pacific.

The planners had already determined that a full infantry division would be required to seize all the objectives within Geelvink Bay. It was believed that one regimental combat team would be sufficient to seize the Wakde-Sarmi area, a second to secure the coast opposite the Wakde Islands, and a third for a reserve force in the event unexpected opposition occurred. Intelligence reports indicated the presence of approximately 6,500 enemy troops in the general area. These were believed to be from the *224th* and *223rd Infantry Regiments* of the *36th Infantry Division*. The rest of the *36th Infantry Division* was believed to be spread out over the various posts ashore and the offshore islands, including Biak Island, a future objective in the center of Geelvink Bay. The exact dispositions of the enemy forces was not known.

General Krueger had originally allocated either of the two newly arrived infantry divisions to the task of seizing Wakde-Sarmi. These new arrivals, however, had no training in jungle warfare and needed at the very least to acclimatize themselves to the strange conditions under which they would be fighting. Generals MacArthur and Krueger decided that given the crucial nature of these operations an experienced combat unit would be preferable to an untried new arrival. First to be selected for the task was the 32nd Infantry Division, the oldest and most experienced unit in the entire Southwest Pacific Theater. However, the rapid conquest of Hollandia made it more practical to use the 41st Infantry Division, the next most experienced formation in the theater. Planners set May 12th as the date for the attack.

Planning in wartime is always subject to change. No sooner had the plans for the Wakde-Sarmi operation been drawn than

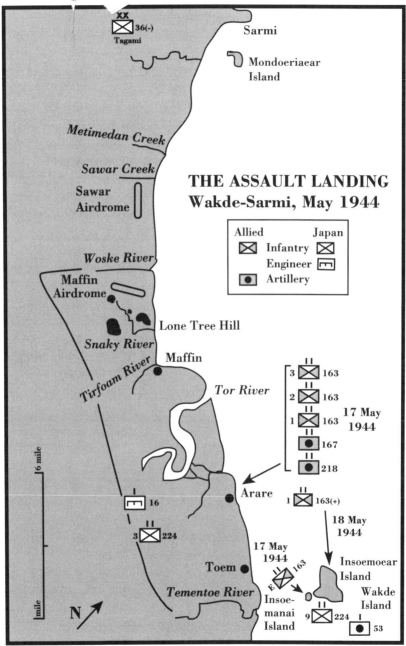

THE ASSAULT LANDING
Wakde-Sarmi, May 1944

Sarmi

Mondoeriaear
Island

Metimedan Creek

Sawar Creek

Sawar
Airdrome

Allied		Japan
Infantry	⊠	⊠
Engineer		⊡
Artillery	⦿	

Woske River

Maffin
Airdrome

Lone Tree Hill

Snaky River

Maffin

Tirfoam River

Tor River

3 ⊠ 163

2 ⊠ 163

1 ⊠ 163   **17 May
1944**

⦿ 167

⦿ 218

XX 36(-)
Tagami

6 mile

⊡ 16

3 ⊠ 224

Toem

17 May
1944

Tementoe River

Insoe-
manai
Island

Arare

1 ⊠ 163(+)

**18 May
1944**

Insoemoear
Island

Wakde
Island

E ⊠ 163

9 ⊠ 224

⦿ 53

N

Rear Admiral L niel E. Barbey (right), Br. Gen. Clarence Martin (center) and Brigadier R.N.L. Hopkin (left) observe an Allied landing. (National Archives.)

changes began to appear. One of the first changes was the date of the attack. Vice Admiral Daniel E. Barbey, who commanded the Seventh Fleet Amphibious Force, noted that the tides in the area would be more favorable later in the month than on the planned date. Recalling the serious losses incurred by the Navy-Marine assault on Tarawa the previous year, when the tides had failed to carry the Marines ashore as planned, the date was changed in accordance with Admiral Barbey's suggestion. The Admiral also gave as an additional reason for postponement the need to familiarize his officers and men with the needs of the assault units in order to ensure proper combat loading of the vessels needed to carry the troops to battle. Here, too, earlier experience, this time at Guadalcanal, had shown that the Navy had to load their ships in accordance with the needs of the assault forces, and not necessarily in the most economical or convenient way. This would result in less casualties in the assault forces by allowing the Navy to respond to their needs promptly.

Vice Admiral Daniel Edward Barbey graduated the United States Naval Academy at Annapolis in the class of 1912. He served in various posts during his career, including battleship, destroyer and tanker duty. He was instrumental in establishing the Amphibious Warfare section in the Navy Department in 1941. His many contributions to amphibious warfare tactics included his development of the DUKW, the soon to be famous amphibious truck known to the soldiers and sailors as the "Duck." Appointed Rear Admiral in December of 1942, he received command of the newly formed VII Amphibious Force of the Seventh Fleet. He served with distinction throughout the war in this capacity, earning the trust and confidence of General MacArthur and his army subordinates.

The objections raised by Admiral Barbey were the subject of a conference called by General Krueger on May 6th. All Allied forces sent representatives, and the general consensus was that the Navy's objections were well founded, and should be heeded. General Krueger notified General MacArthur's headquarters of the changes in the plan.

The news from General Krueger postponing the Wakde-Sarmi operation prompted General MacArthur to review once again the planning for the operation. New information had become available in the interim since approval had been given to the plans, and with that data now available, General Mac-Arthur decided that the ground around the Sarmi area was unsuitable for the type of airfields which the Allies planned to construct there. Heavy bomber fields could not be accommodated in the Sarmi area. Concluding that there was now no need for that part of the operation, General MacArthur decided that the Sarmi portion of the assault be canceled, while the seizure of Wakde and the coastal area around Arare proceeded as originally planned. This latest change prompted a new conference at General Krueger's headquarters on May 9th.

This second conference determined that the proposed Wakde-Sarmi Operation be changed to a Wakde-Biak Operation. Sarmi would be eliminated from the plan, and an assault on Biak Island would be substituted. It had always been planned that Biak would be seized as a part of the ongoing march to the Philippines. The rapid progress thus far, and the decision by General MacArthur to eliminate the need for Sarmi, had provided the planners with both time and resources previously dedicated to Sarmi. These would now be directed at Biak. The conference also determined the resources which would be used

_.n phase of the operation. One regimental combat team of
_.e 41st Infantry Division would seize the Wakde-Arare area,
while the remainder of the division would seize Biak. Ten days
between operations was considered sufficient to make logistical
and transportation adjustments. Landings were now scheduled
for Wakde on May 17th and for Biak on May 27th.

Brigadier General Jens A. Doe, assistant division commander
of the 41st Infantry Division, would command the attack on
Wakde. His force, codenamed Tornado Task Force, would seize
that portion of the New Guinea coast nearest Wakde, around
Arare, and then seize the Wakde Islands. The forces assigned to
Tornado Task Force were the 163rd Regimental Combat Team,
which included the 167th and 218th Field Artillery Battalions in
addition to the 163rd Infantry Regiment and supporting units.
Mainland landings would take place on the 17th, while the
islands were to be seized on consecutive days. Arare, a small
native village four and a half miles from Wakde, was selected as
the site of the mainland assault and as a future headquarters
and staging area. The purpose of the landings at Arare was in
fact limited to providing a nearby base for the 191st Field
Artillery Group to support the Wakde assault. Grouped under
the command of the Task Force artillery commander, Colonel
George M. Williamson, Jr., the 167th and 218th Field Artillery
Battalions would be joined by the cannon company of the 163rd
Infantry Regiment. They were to begin firing on Wakde as soon
as they were established ashore.

The 163rd Infantry Regiment would assault in column of
battalions, with the 3rd Battalion leading. The 1st Battalion was
assigned the Wakde Islands assault. Topographical information
was "meager" although experience thur far in the campaign
promised the usual jungle conditions. This would be the Sixth
Army's first real experience with island warfare, however. The
Wakde and Schouten Islands, of which Biak was the largest,
were coral outcroppings covered with thick jungle growth and
with all the natural defenses previously associated with the
Central Pacific island assaults of the Navy and Marine Corps.
All these islands had dozens of caves, ridges and swamps which
could only strengthen the defense. Water on these islands was
scarce. Naval access to them was limited by breaks in the coral

163rd Infantry, 41st Division, during the invasion of Wakde. Flag identifies friendly troops to artillery and air support.

reefs surrounding each island, openings which were known to the enemy and which allowed him to place his defenses opposite these openings. Size was also a factor. Insoemoar was described as "a generally flat island about 9,000 feet long by 3,000 feet wide, containing approximately 540 acres." Insoemanai was a much smaller island with little to distinguish it from its bigger neighbor. Both Army and Air Force reports took to referring to Insoemoar as Wakde, ignoring Insoemanai, and the names became interchangeable.

The 5th and 13th Air Forces were aware that the Japanese had received reinforcements in men and planes in recent weeks. Experience with prior reactions by Japanese airpower to assaults had convinced air planners that the Japanese would limit their attacks to night raids and general harassing missions. It was reconnaissance missions by the 5th Air Force's 17th Reconnaissance Squadron which convinced Generals MacArthur and Krueger that conditions at Sarmi were unsuitable for their purposes. Protection of the assault force from Japanese air attack was made the responsibility of the 5th Air Force. The 5th Air Force assigned the 310th Bombardment Wing to both defend Hollandia and support the assaults on Arare-Wakde-Biak. Consisting of the 3rd and 475th Fighter Groups, the 3rd and 345th Bombardment Groups, the 310th was responsible for the protection of Allied bases, Allied naval forces and the pre-invasion bombardment in the coming attacks. Pre-invasion strikes would be made against Toem, Manokwari, Moemi, Ransiki and Noemfoor. The purpose of these far ranging strikes was to deplete enemy air power and to deceive him as to the location of the next landing. Support of ground operations would follow the pre-invasion bombardment.

Tornado Task Force's problems began with the preparation for the landing. Loading was constantly delayed. The constant changing plans required new orders, new loadings. Sarmi was dropped from the plan and Arare substituted. The assault vessels used to carry the troops and equipment were eight hours late arriving for the loading. Once loaded, the Landing Ships, Tank (LSTs) were further delayed in departing by adverse wind and surf conditions. An additional twelve hours were lost. Finally, the 533rd Engineer Boat and Shore Regiment also arrived at Aitape, the staging area, late. Unloading their equipment would only further delay matters. General Doe asked General Krueger for a postponement of the attack for two days so that all these delays could be rectified. After consulting with the naval force commander, Captain Noble, General Krueger allowed only an additional six hours for the departure of Tornado Task Force. Departure was now scheduled for midnight on May 14th.

General Doe was a native of Chicago, Illinois. A graduate of West Point with the class of 1914, he was commissioned in the infantry in June of that year. While assigned to infantry duties in Texas, he enrolled and became a machine gun officer, and in that capacity he commanded the 15th Machine Gun Battalion in France during the First World War. He participated in the St. Mihiel and Meuse-Argonne Offensives and later became an instructor at the Army Machine Gun school in France. After the war he served in the usual assignments, and combined service in China with attendance at the Command and General Staff School and the Army War College. Continuing to serve with infantry units, he was a regimental commander at the outbreak of the Second World War. Assigned as a regimental commander of the 163rd Infantry Regiment, he rose to assistant division commander by February, 1943. General Doe was, therefore, no

Soldiers of the 163rd Regimental Combat Team crawl off the beaches of Wakde under enemy fire. (National Archives)

stranger either to combat or its difficulties. He substituted the Shore Battalion of the 593rd Engineer Boat and Shore Regiment for the unit originally assigned to Tornado Task Force, since the 593rd had already been combat loaded. The soldiers of Tornado Task Force worked around the clock to load their ships. Finally the Task Force departed Aitape at 0100 Hours on May 15th, one hour late. By dawn of May 17th the assault and naval covering forces combined and moved into their attack positions off Arare.

As usual, the Navy's Seventh Amphibious Force was providing transportation and supporting fires. Two Naval covering forces were organized to support the landing at Arare and on the Wakde Islands. Under Rear Admiral V. A. C. Crutchley, Royal Navy, the Australian cruisers *Australia* and *Shropshire*, supported by H.M.A.S *Warramunga* and *Arunta* with the U.S.S. *Mullany* and *Ammen*, shelled the mainland targets at Sawar and Sarmi. The second force, under the command of Rear Admiral

Russell S. Berkey, U.S.N., consisted of the cruisers *Phoenix*, *Boise* and *Nashville*. Their targets were the Wakde Islands. In addition to these cruiser groups ten American destroyers under the command of Captain Richard F. Stout bombarded various targets between Toem and Maffin Bay.

Plans called for the cruiser groups to depart the area once the 191st Field Artillery Group had established itself ashore, to avoid naval losses from Japanese air or naval forces.Those destroyers not needed to protect the cruiser groups would remain in the area for supporting fires as needed. Lack of air or naval opposition on May 17th made this plan unnecessary.

The day dawned cloudy and rainy. Troops were roused at 0530 and loaded into assault craft. By the time the troops were aboard the landing craft the day had cleared and the sun rose. The 3rd Battalion, 163rd Infantry, moved towards the selected beaches. Company I, 163rd Infantry landed unopposed by 0715 near Arare. Quickly followed by the rest of the 3rd Battalion, the troops fanned out along both sides of the landing area and secured the beachhead. The bulk of the 3rd Battalion, using a coastal trail they discovered, formed a beachhead perimeter. Next ashore were the combat engineers of Company A of the 116th Combat Engineer Battalion and the entire 27th Combat Engineer Battalion. The 1st and 2nd Battalions of the 163rd Infantry quickly followed and all assault troops were ashore by 0930.

The 1st Battalion, 163rd Infantry, moved east along the coastal track to the village of Toem, where they prepared for the next day's attack on the Wakde Islands. Company L of the 3rd Battalion moved west, where the first Japanese opposition occurred in the form of sniper fire. Supported by the bulk of its parent battalion, Company L pushed on to the Tor River, its objective for the day. Company I remained at the beachhead to unload supplies. The heavy weapons companies of all three battalions were also kept near the beach in preparation for the next day's assault on Insoemanai.

Reconnaissance of Insoemanai Island by landing craft had determined that it was undefended. A platoon of Company E, 2nd Battalion, was transported to Insoemanai and found it deserted. Transporting the heavy weapons companies from

Arare to Insoemanai began at once and by midday these mortars and machine guns were firing on Insoemoar. Confidence increased with the continuing lack of Japanese opposition. The 191st Field Artillery Group came ashore at Arare, moved to Toem, and prepared to fire in support of the next day's attack. Still, no Japanese opposition was encountered. Destroyers moved in to close quarters with Insoemoar Island without reply from the enemy. Aircraft strafed at low level without opposition. American troops moved about freely on Insoemanai Island, in plain sight of any enemy on Insoemoar, without drawing fire. The earlier confidence soon turned to cockiness. "The commander of the Insoemanai Island detachment sent word that if his orderly didn't have sore feet, the two of them could wade over and take Wakde." This cocky soldier would be very grateful the next day that his offer was rejected.

General Doe insisted on sticking to the plan and the timetable. This called for a full scale pre-invasion bombardment by air, naval and artillery forces before the assault troops landed on Insoemoar. May 17th ended with the bombardment proceeding according to plan. The beachhead at Arare had been secured by the 163rd Infantry as scheduled. The assault force was poised and ready to board the attack craft for the trip to Insoemoar. This unit, the 1st Battalion of the 163rd Infantry reinforced by Company F of the regiment, was joined at the departure point by four Sherman tanks of the 603rd Tank Company, an attached 41st Infantry Division unit. As the light began to fade on May 17th the Japanese on Insoemoar began to finally react to all the attention which had been directed at them during the day, and mortar and machine gun fire began to strike Insoemanai Island. While these caused no casualties, it was now clear that tomorrow would not be the easy day many had expected it would.

Meanwhile, on the mainland there was no organized Japanese opposition. The Americans found 21 dead Japanese in the area and suffered losses of 2 killed and 11 wounded, some by misdirected "friendly fire." Most now knew that tomorrow would be more difficult.

While the Americans had been making their preparations, the Japanese on Insoemoar had not been as idle as they seemed at first to the 163rd Infantry. They had constructed nearly one

Infantrymen of the 163rd. Regimental Combat Team move off the beach at Wakde. (National Archives)

hundred bunkers for defense while awaiting the almost predictable American assault. There were numerous slit trenches and foxholes, with the American bombardment providing additional craters quickly adapted for defense. There were also two concrete air raid shelters for protection from the Americans' fire, and the Japanese as always used the available caves for both shelter and defense. As usual with the Japanese, camouflage was excellent throughout, leading to the early overconfidence by some inexperienced Americans. While some of the island's defenses had been damaged in the pre-invasion bombardment, most were still intact. Indeed, the only major contribution of the pre-invasion bombardment was the destruction of the major portion of the enemy's artillery.

May 18th opened with a heavy preparatory fire directed at Insoemoar Island. More than two thousand rounds of naval gunfire were directed at the island. Known defenses were particularly targeted. The attacks of the Fifth Air Force and the artillery of the 191st Field Artillery Group added additional thousands of pounds of explosives designed to destroy the Japanese capacity to resist the coming invasion. Confidence was still high among the assault troops and their commanders, despite the evidence late the previous day of the enemy's continued intent to resist.

The assault on Insoemoar would come in six waves, each consisting of four Landing Craft, Vehicle, Personnel (LCVPs). Losses in equipment began even before the assault waves left Arare. During the loading of the reinforced 1st Battalion, 163rd Infantry, one of its supporting tanks was disabled by the heavy surf's shorting out its electrical system. With loading completed, the landing craft began movement towards Insoemoar Island. At 300 yards offshore, the Japanese began to fire on the approaching boats with rifles and machine guns. Despite this fire, the assault continued into the beach and all four companies landed shortly after 0900 hours. The closer to the beach they came, the more intense the enemy fire became. Casualties were taken even before landing. "Several coxswains and boat operators were killed and, although no boats had to turn back, several got out of control and disrupted the wave and boat organization." Things might have been worse except that the Japanese had misjudged the direction of the American attack and had not fully defended the landing beaches. The temporary dislocation of their defenses and the continuing heavy supporting fires reduced the effectiveness of the Japanese defenses, but even so the Americans were not going to have an easy time on Insoemoar.

During the landing many of the small supporting Navy craft made valiant efforts to distract enemy fire from the more vulnerable assault craft. Two landing craft in particular, Landing Craft Infantry 34 and LCI-73, deliberately drew enemy fire and suffered casualties as a result. Company A of the 542nd Engineer Boat and Shore Regiment, manning the small landing boats, succeeded in putting the troops ashore in generally good order, despite the casualties and boat damage. One naval officer who accompanied the assault waves ashore recorded his first few moments on the beach. Landing in the third wave he moved

Browning .30 caliber machine gun team of 163rd Infantry covers an incoming patrol on Wakde. (National Archives)

out onto the beach and "From then on it was a matter of shifting from one log to another. We were pinned on the beachhead for 30 minutes." Upon finally moving off the beach conditions changed little. "I do not suppose we got more than a hundred yards when a machine gun from our rear opened on us. Everyone dove for cover. I dove for a tree but no matter where I went someone continued to pop at me." This officer, a public relations photographer, survived the landing, but several of his companions did not.

Company A moved off to the southeast after landing. The objective was a small peninsula which was reported to harbor an enemy strongpoint. Within minutes the leading elements came under machine gun fire from a bunker which was quickly eliminated by rifle fire and grenades. Using this method, the company continued to work its way to the end of the peninsula and secure the area.

The early success of Company A was due in large part to the

surprise of the Japanese at the American selection of a landing beach. This prevented them from deploying their heavier weapons to best oppose the actual landing. Despite this failure the combat troops among the garrison did make good use of their personal weapons. The early loss of three of the four American company commanders is ample evidence of the fighting efficiency of the garrison of Wakde. The loss of so many key leaders threatened to reduce the American attack to a leaderless confusion. Major Leonard A. Wing, the battalion commander, acted quickly to prevent such confusion. Company executive officers were quickly moved up and into position to replace the fallen leaders. Two tanks were attached to Companies B and F which had started to expand the beachhead westward. Despite these steps "Resistance being encountered was the toughest that had thus far been put up by any enemy garrison along the New Guinea Shore." Many of the troops found themselves pinned down on open beaches by machine guns and rifle fire. In addition to the prepared Japanese defense positions the widespread wreckage added numerous defensive locations for enemy snipers and automatic weapons. These poured effective fire into the American positions.

Slowly, using every possible concealment, the veteran American infantry moved to better positions from which they could effectively return the enemy's fire. Losses on the beach, besides the three company commanders, now included the third supporting tank which while unloading fell into seven feet of water, making it useless for the duration of this operation. The remaining tanks, however, aided the riflemen by drawing fire away from them. It seemed that every Japanese defender fired at the two remaining tanks. The Americans used this diversion to move inland. The tanks also gave the Americans local fire superiority when using their cannons and heavy machine guns. Supported by this fire the infantry continued to push inland, leaving 150 enemy dead behind. Companies B and F, with the tanks in support, found that once off the beach resistance to the west collapsed. The central Japanese defenses lay to the east, allowing those Americans moving west relatively rapid progress. Still, the Japanese could not accept that the Americans had brought tanks with them. "Stories were told of Japs shaking angry fists at the steel monsters and charging them with sabers and bayonets. A few Japs managed to get atop the tanks but were killed before they could do any damage." It was just as well that the tanks suffered no crippling damage. There were no more immediately available, and without them the advance would have been far more costly.

Moving inland from the center of the beachhead, Company C encountered several pillboxes about two hundred yards inland. A standard infantry assault using small arms and grenades eliminated these positions after an hour of intensive combat. Yet, only one hundred yards further inland a second set of pillboxes was discovered. Company C called for tank support, and as the opposition in the area of Companies B and F had diminished, the two tanks were redirected to Company C. Using the tanks cannon and machine guns, Company C cleared this second set of pillboxes. By midday Companies B, C and F had reached the airstrip. Company A, assigned to what had been believed to be a Japanese strongpoint, had found only snipers. With opposition continuing to be heavy against the rest of the battalion, Company A was recalled to join the attack across the airstrip.

As things were clearing at the front, confusion reigned in the rear. Supply unloading had begun and naval and merchant marine personnel were ashore. Japanese stragglers, bypassed by the infantry, opened fire on the beachhead and wounded two naval personnel. Telephone lines just installed were destroyed by bulldozers working on the beach. An underwater cable link established from Arare to Wakde refused to function. The heavy combat at the front increased the amount of messages to command posts in the rear, overloading those circuits still working. Beaches were overcrowded. Landing craft were everywhere. The last unit of the 1st Battalion, Company D (Heavy Weapons), was ordered to Insoemoar and briefly added to the confusion on their way to the front. Nevertheless, supplies critical to the fighting continued to flow and the infantry, busy with its own fight, was largely unaffected.

Company A now took the lead and quickly faced the same type of opposition which its sister companies had experienced. A group of bunkers delayed the advance until the tanks came up and opened fire. Japanese infantry, hidden in foxholes behind the bunkers attacked the tanks and supporting infantry. Automatic riflemen of Company A quickly eliminated these attackers and the Americans moved forward. No further serious opposition faced Company A and they reached the north coast of Insoemoar by 1330 hours.

The rest of the American force was not so fortunate. Companies B, C and F were moving in line abreast eastward against considerable opposition. Rifle, machine gun and mortar fire from prepared positions at the eastern end of the airstrip delayed the advance. Company D's heavy weapons were now available but did little to suppress the enemy fire. Major Wing decided to envelop the enemy position with all his infantry and clear out the few remaining pockets of enemy resistance elsewhere on the island. Much of the afternoon was spent in trying to reorganize for the final attack, but the loss of so many key leaders, including the three company commanders early in the battle, delayed moving the companies into position. Many key noncommissioned officers had also become casualties and the replacements available had inadequate experience to reorganize under fire. While Company C was moving into new positions it was split in half by enemy fire which prevented the two halves from moving together. Artillery fire from the 167th and 218th Field Artillery Battalions finally suppressed the enemy fire long enough for the company to consolidate. However it was now late in the day and the attack to clear the last of the enemy force from Insoemoar Island was put off until the following day. Although some effort was made to begin the attack by Companies B and F, with tank support, little progress was made. Daylight was needed to complete the attack successfully.

The night of May 18th-19th was used by the Americans to consolidate forces and resupply the combat troops. Meanwhile the Japanese were equally active. The battalion command post near the front was attacked at 0230 by a small group of Japanese. Fighting lasted for some thirty minutes until the defense force, part of Company D, repulsed the enemy who left behind twelve dead. This skirmish did little to hinder preparations for the coming attack.

That attack began with an artillery bombardment lasting one hour. At the cessation of the artillery and mortar preparation, Company C and the two remaining tanks moved against the last Japanese positions. These included bombproof bunkers and pillboxes. "Some of these had walls of coconut logs, ten to fourteen inches in diameter, with six to eight inches of coral rock and soil between them. In some cases gas drums filled with sand, truck bodies and frames, and steel landing boats were incorporated in the construction. Roofs were usually of three to five feet of coral." Company C and its attached tanks used a standard method long used in Pacific campaigns to reduce these defenses. Covered by close infantry support, the tanks advanced upon a bunker and blasted away with their 75mm cannon and machine guns. Enemy efforts to destroy the tanks were thwarted by the riflemen, who shot down any Japanese who appeared in the open. Slow and costly, it was the only method that worked. Opposed by so many bunkers, caves and pillboxes Company C advanced slowly. The other assaulting unit, Company B, had similar experiences and Company F was moved from reserve into the line alongside Company B. Two additional tanks from the 603rd Tank Company had arrived from the mainland and these were now added to the assault forces. Each tank, covered by a platoon of riflemen, attacked an assigned sector. Begun at 0915 in the morning, the attack did not clear its objectives until 1400 that afternoon.

Company A had been assigned a holding mission, in the event the Japanese tried to attack on the American flank or to escape into other parts of the island. By midday it was apparent that the Japanese had no such intentions, and Company A was also called forward. All four of the assault units were working together when the last organized resistance was crushed at about 1640 hours. The Japanese still occupied a small area of about 500 yards at the northeast corner of the island. Major Wing, however, decided that his men had done enough for one day. He withdrew most of the troops to the middle of the island for hot food and rest. An outpost line was left to contain the remaining enemy force.

Some of the Japanese were not content to await the next American attack. A number of them slipped past the Company

Australian infantry move along a dust choked road after retreating Japanese forces who have turned to face the American landing behind them. (National Archives)

C outposts and reached the beachhead. They quickly attacked the engineer units they found there, but the combat engineers quickly reacted and destroyed the enemy force, killing 36 and taking one prisoner. Companies A, C and F scoured the northeast end of the island on May 20th, killing those few enemy troops they found. As usual in these vicious encounters the Japanese refused to surrender and many were sealed in their caves, while others committed suicide. By afternoon Major Wing felt the Japanese had been eliminated and withdrew his battalion to the mainland.

However, the Japanese were not quite finished on Insoemoar. Continual harassment by snipers against the aviation engineers working on the airstrip prompted Brigadier General Doe to send Company L, 163rd Infantry, to clear the island once again. They spent four days on Insoemoar and killed eight enemy snipers.

The islands were quickly put to the use for which they had been seized. Even before the island had been declared secure, the 836th Engineer Aviation Battalion had begun work on the airstrip and facilities. Working continually, the aviation engineers had the strip operational by midday on May 21st. The first aircraft landed on the island that afternoon. By the time Biak was invaded the airstrip was available for aircraft to use in support of that operation. The final accounting for the seizure of the Wakde Islands included some 759 Japanese dead and another 4 captured. Fifty more Japanese had been killed in or around Arare. The Americans had lost 40 men killed in action and 107 wounded. An additional three men had been killed and 32 wounded on surrounding islets seized during the operation. The outposts leading into Geelvink Bay had been seized. Now it was necessary to secure the mainland base to prevent any Japanese interference with those outposts.

The Infantry Division

During the Second World War the United States Army fielded a total of ninety divisions. Sixteen of these were armored divisions, all of which served in the European or Mediterranean Theaters. Five were airborne divisions, one of which, the 11th Airborne Division, served under MacArthur's command during the liberation of the Philippines. Two were known as cavalry divisions, but were in fact infantry. One, the 1st Cavalry, served under General MacArthur while the other, the 2nd, a unit composed primarily of African-Americans, was disbanded before it saw combat in North Africa. The remaining 67 divisions were infantry, which saw combat in every theater of war except the China-Burma-India Theater.

The total included 18 infantry divisions made up of National Guards from all the states. Seven of those served in the Southwest Pacific Theater. The evolution of one of these highlights the development of the infantry division from its World War One organization to the final product, changing constantly, used throughout World War Two. The first of MacArthur's divisions to arrive in Australia was the 32nd Infantry Division. The division was drawn from the National Guards of Michigan and Wisconsin. Inducted into federal service on October 15, 1940, it was still in its World War One configuration. It consisted of two infantry brigades, the 63rd and 64th. Each brigade had two infantry regiments assigned to it. The 125th Infantry and 126th Infantry Regiments made up the 63rd Brigade, while the 127th and 128th Infantry Regiments were in the 64th Brigade. The other major component of the division was the 57th Field Artillery

66

Brigade which contained three field artillery regiments, the 120th, 121st, and 126th. The division was also supported by the 107th Combat Engineer Regiment and the 107th Medical Regiment.

Events in Europe had caused American military planners to decide to streamline the American infantry division to conform to the successful examples of the German Army. In this streamlining each division was reduced to three infantry regiments, four field artillery battalions, one engineer combat battalion and one medical battalion. The infantry brigade disappeared from the organizational charts. The sole exception to this new organization was the 1st Cavalry Division, which for some reason retained the two brigade, four regiment organization throughout the war.

In this re-organization, the 32nd Infantry lost its 125th Infantry Regiment, had its combat engineer regiment reduced to battalion strength, as well as its medical allotment. The result of such reassignments provided material to form new divisions, while also leaving several regiments as "orphans." Some of these saw combat as regimental combat teams, like the Arizona National Guard's 158th Infantry Regimental Combat Team which served in New Guinea. Others, like the 32nd Infantry Division's 125th Infantry Regiment, drawn from Michigan, served continually within the United States as training and demonstration units. The regiment served in that capacity until the war's end, when like its old division, it was disbanded and returned to State control.

The "new" 32nd Infantry Division modeled the typical infantry division which saw combat throughout the world. It now consisted of three infantry regiments, the 126th, 127th, and 128th. Its artillery was now four battalions, without a regimental organization. They were the 120th, 121st, 126th and 129th Field Artillery Battalions. All were using 105mm Field Artillery pieces except the 121st, which fired 155mm guns. The engineer battalion was numbered the 114th, while the medical battalion retained the old 107th numerical designation. Other organic units included the 32nd Reconnaissance Troop, 32nd Signal Company, 32nd Quartermaster Company and 32nd Counter Intelligence Corps detachment. All were standard to the U.S. World War II infantry division.

One thing that was missing from the 32nd Infantry Division was an attachment of tanks. In the early months of the war in the Pacific, none of the Army infantry divisions had organic tank battalions. This was because it was believed that they would be useless in the jungle conditions prevalent in the Pacific. However, the Australians used light tanks with considerable success in reducing Japanese defenses during the struggle for Buna-Gona, and slowly tank units began to appear in the Pacific. In the European and Mediterranean Theaters all the infantry divisions had at some point a tank battalion more or less permanently assigned to it. Some of these shifted from division to division as needed, but most could rely on one or more tank battalions as regular members of their company.

The 32nd Infantry Division was therefore typical of the structure of all United States infantry divisions in World War Two. Only an attached tank unit was missing, and these were never considered a permanent part of the division, anyway. The "triangular division" proved highly successful in all of the combat conditions met in the Second World War. It could detach a regimental combat team for a small mission, receive attachments of a regimental combat team or two, as did the 41st Infantry Division when it added the 34th Infantry Regiment at Biak, or all other types of detachment and attachments. Versatile, flexible, and durable, it was one of the major military innovations of the Second World War.

The Australians

Few American histories of the Second World War detail the contribution made by the Australian Army. Yet, for the first eighteen months of the New Guinea campaign, they formed by far the bulk of General MacArthur's forces. One of the reasons why their contribution is so little understood today in the United States is the relationship between General MacArthur and the senior Australian Army commander during World War II, General Sir Thomas Albert Blamey.

General Blamey was a native Australian who had begun a career as a schoolteacher but who decided in 1906 to join the newly forming Australian Army. Blamey received a commission in this new force, consisting mainly of militia units built around a small core of regular soldiers. In 1912, as one of the few regulars in the Australian Army, he attended the Staff College at Quetta, India. He graduated the following year, just in time to take part in Australia's contribution to the First World War. Assigned first as a staff officer to the 1st Australian Division, he rose to chief operations officer. Between brief periods

commanding a battalion and a brigade at the front, he rose in grade until he became a brigadier general and chief of staff to the senior Australian Army commander on the Western Front, Lieutenant General Sir John Monash. He served with the Australian Corps throughout the war, and was still its Chief of Staff at war's end.

After the war Blamey continued to serve with the Australian Army until 1925, when he retired to accept an appointment as the Chief Commissioner of the Victoria Police. Ten years later, after several difficulties in that position, he resigned under fire and also resigned his commission in the militia. This eclipse lasted but two years. As a new war loomed over the horizon, Blamey was recalled to active duty largely due to the fact that he was the most experienced senior officer available to the Australian Government. He was appointed Chairman of the Manpower Committee and his main responsibility was to prepare Australian forces for war. Upon the outbreak of the Second World War in September, 1939, General Blamey was appointed commander of the newly raised 6th Australian Division. Later, when a second division was raised, Blamey was given the Corps command over the two new divisions. He spent eighteen months commanding the Australian Corps in North Africa and Greece, where despite his opposition to the plan, his troops were put into an impossible situation trying to support an already defeated army. Successfully withdrawing his surviving forces, he was appointed Deputy Commander in Chief of the British Middle East Theater and left his Corps command behind. In September of 1941 he was promoted full general and became the only active service Australian general to hold that rank for the next twenty-five years.

Shortly after his promotion, General Blamey was called home to defend a now threatened Australia. Arriving just five days after General MacArthur's arrival from the Philippines, he found himself facing a myriad of problems. He had to establish a coalition relationship with the Americans, defend Australia with insufficient forces, and had to create an army for Australia where none existed. General Blamey soon found himself performing a dual role. In one he was the senior Land Forces commander under General MacArthur's command, a subordinate to General MacArthur. In the other he was the Senior Military Commander, Australian Forces, or equal to General MacArthur and with the power not only to disagree with General MacArthur but to refuse his cooperation. It was a situation uncomfortable for all concerned.

Most uncomfortable of all was General MacArthur. He wanted no part of another commander of equal rank and with the prestige of being a national leader in his theater of operations. This conflict would continue for the duration of the war. General Blamey, although often bypassed by General MacArthur and relegated to lesser roles, together with his Australian troops, nevertheless remained a loyal subordinate to General MacArthur to the end of the war.

In the beginning there was little choice for General MacArthur but to depend on the Australians. His own troops, the 32nd and 41st Infantry Divisions were still arriving and needed additional training. So when the enemy made a push to seize the southeastern tip of New Guinea, in and around Papua, it was General Blamey's forces, mostly militia backed by the few regulars who had returned from the Middle East, who stopped them. These same troops pushed the Japanese back, in incredibly difficult terrain, to the strongholds at Buna-Gona. By this time General MacArthur felt that he could commit American troops, but he did not want them under Australian control. In order to prevent this, General MacArthur moved his own headquarters forward to Port Moresby to take a more direct role in the coming battle. He had been critical of Australian performance during the Port Moresby battles, claiming that they were not good in the field or the jungle, that they were all recruited from the slums of Australia, and that they lacked fighting spirit. General MacArthur also criticized the Australian commanders, with the exception of General Blamey. He expected his Americans to show the Australians how to fight.

Unfortunately for General MacArthur, his Americans reacted exactly as had the Australians when first confronted with the horrors of combat. American commanders were overconfident, troops lax about security and camouflage, and when confronted by a stubborn Japanese defense, they too failed utterly. It was shortly after this that General MacArthur sent urgently for General Eichelberger.

General Eichelberger saved the situation, and incidentally rated General Blamey as a better tactician than any of his fellow American commanders. Nevertheless, General MacArthur wanted his own national troops kept from Australian command. He called for General Krueger to come from the United States to command the Sixth Army, an army which did not yet exist and for which there were insufficient troops available to justify such a command. And he began his subterfuge of creating task forces for missions that reported directly to him, bypassing the Australians.

Nevertheless the Australians, commanded by a constantly suffering General Blamey, continued to make a decisive contribution to the Southwest Pacific Theater's campaigns. The 6th, 7th and 9th Australian Divisions fought for more than two years to clear New Guinea of the enemy bypassed by the Americans. Twelve Australian militia brigades maintained bridgeheads on islands left by the advancing Americans. General MacArthur, ungracious as always, later claimed that

this was all unnecessary and led to a waste of Australian lives but neglected to mention that it had all been done at his direction. So reliable had he privately begun to consider the Australians that his original plan for seizing the Philippines called for an Australian corps of two divisions to make the first landings. When General Blamey refused to give up control of the Corps, the plans were changed, eliminating all Australian participation.

During the Philippines campaign, General MacArthur used his Australian troops to secure his flanks, having them seize islands around the Philippines to prevent any enemy interference with his own Philippine operations. In most cases these operations were unnecessary. In one case General MacArthur ordered General Blamey to use two Australian divisions, under an Australian corps, to seize Java. At his new headquarters on Morotai General Blamey reviewed General MacArthur's plans for Java, then refused to let Australian forces participate. Post war research convinced at least one historian that to have gone through with the Java operation would have resulted in one of the bloodiest invasions of the Pacific war.

General Blamey's career ended with his appearing as the Australian delegate at the signing of the surrender instrument aboard the U.S.S. *Missouri* in September of 1945. Shortly afterwards, he was retired from the Australian Army he had served so faithfully during the most severe crisis of its existence.

CHAPTER III

Securing the Outposts

While the 1st Battalion, 163rd Infantry was engaged on the Wakde Islands, the rest of the 163rd Infantry Regiment established a perimeter on the mainland. The 2nd Battalion moved east, without Company F engaged on Wakde, and established a line of defense and patrolled along Tementoe Creek. This unit found no Japanese. On the west, the 3rd Battalion moved to the Tor River and awaited further orders. It was in this direction, towards Sarmi, that General Doe expected to find the Japanese.

Satisfied with progress on Wakde, General Doe gave permission for the 3rd Battalion to cross the Tor River late on the 18th. Patrols crossed late in the afternoon and again the following morning. Reports from these patrols indicated that the Japanese were present in strength and had developed some defensive positions. Additional reports from Sixth Army Headquarters cited intelligence reports of Japanese plans to counterattack the Arare landings. Verification of these reports came quickly, when on the 19th and 20th, Japanese patrols probed heavily against the Company K units holding the bridgehead across the Tor River. Although no major assault took place, the Japanese continued to patrol and harass the Americans with heavy mortar and artillery fire.

Reinforcements arrived for the Americans on May 21st. The 158th Regimental Combat Team landed at Toem. Designated as task force reserve, its arrival gave General Doe some depth to his defense.

General Doe's peace of mind did not last long, for almost

coincident with the arrival of the new troops, General Krueger ordered the mission of the Tornado Task Force expanded. In effect he was going back to the original concept of Wakde-Sarmi in that he ordered the task force to expand in a westerly direction the amount of mainland under its control. He ordered a push towards Sarmi, some sixteen miles westward.

Tornado Task Force would now be facing the Japanese *36th Infantry Division*. Under the command of Lieutenant General Hachiro Tagami, this unit had only been in New Guinea some five months, arriving from North China in late December, 1943. One of its regiments, the *222nd Infantry*, was on Biak Island. The remaining two, the *223rd* and *224th Infantry Regiments*, were in the Sarmi area. Some detachments had been scattered about, but the bulk of the division lay around the Sarmi area. One reinforced company of the *224th Infantry Regiment* had just been destroyed on the Wakde Islands. The 36th Infantry Division was reinforced with the usual service and supply units together with some Naval Guard Forces.

While the Japanese were gathering their forces, the Americans were making their own adjustments to conform to the new orders from Sixth Army. The major change in American dispositions occurred when the 41st Infantry Division recalled General Doe and the 163rd Infantry Regiment for the assault on Biak Island. General Doe's place was taken by Brigadier General Edwin D. Patrick, while the 158th Infantry Regiment replaced the 163rd Infantry. The exchange was completed by May 23rd, when Company L of the 158th Infantry advanced across the Tor River.

Brigadier General Edwin Davies Patrick was a native of Indiana. He entered the U.S. Army by joining the Indiana National Guard as a second lieutenant of infantry on February 11, 1915. When the National Guard was federalized for border service, he served with sufficient distinction to later obtain a commission in the regular army. After service with infantry units in the United States, he was assigned as a machine gun officer and shipped to France to take part in the closing battles of the First World War. After the end of the war, Captain Patrick served in various infantry posts, attending the Infantry School at Fort Benning, and the Signal School at Camp Vail, New Jersey.

Supplies are landed on the beach at Wakde, against a backdrop of scenery typical of the campaign.

More infantry duty followed, including China service, before Major Patrick was ordered to attend the Command and General Staff School at Fort Leavenworth, Kansas. After attending both the Army and Naval War Colleges, he was appointed commander of the 357th Infantry Regiment, and later assigned as Chief of Staff of the Sixth Army. After serving for a year in that post, he assumed command of the recently created 158th Infantry Regimental Combat Team in May, 1944.

General Patrick had committed the entire 158th Infantry to the capture of Sarmi. Led by its 3rd Battalion, the regiment was to advance by stages until Sarmi had been secured. In the first stage, the 3rd Battalion was to seize a village known as "Maffin Number One," about 3,000 yards west of the Tor River. The second stage involved seizing a second village, "Maffin Number 2," after which the entire regiment would descend on Sarmi. Both enemy dispositions and terrain conditions were sketchy or unknown. There were, however, two enemy airfields which were the prizes of a successful seizure of the Sarmi area. On the morning of May 23rd Company L advanced toward "Maffin Number One."

Among the information not available to General Patrick or his troops was the nature of the opposition. General Tagami had quickly organized his division and its attachments into three large defense forces. Although the names and compositions of these forces varied as events developed, the 158th Infantry Regiment was facing at this stage the *"Right Sector Force"* under the command of Lieutenant Colonel Kato, an engineer officer. Colonel Kato had some 1,200 troops to defend the Tor River line. In addition to a battalion of the *224th Infantry Regiment*, he had the *16th Field Airdrome Construction Unit* and a battery of artillery using 75mm mountain artillery guns. Not under Colonel Kato's command but nearby was another battalion of the *224th Infantry Regiment*.

Captain Clarence Fennell, commanding Company L, led his men against increasing opposition for some 1,800 yards towards "Maffin Number One." Japanese resistance pinned down the infantry with rifle and mortar fire. The balance of the 3rd Battalion moved up to support Company L, and by mid-afternoon some 400 yards had been gained. This failed to satisfy the regimental commander, Colonel J. Prugh Herndon, a former bursar at the University of Arizona and long time commander of the National Guard regiment, and so he ordered up the regiment's 1st Battalion in support. As the newly ordered infantry could not get up to the front before nightfall, the advance was halted for the day.

Early the next day, the battalion moved against the Japanese, after a preliminary bombardment of artillery and mortar fire had been laid down. Japanese opposition was still strong, but the 158th Infantry now had tank and engineer support. Tanks from the 603rd Tank Company and engineers from the 27th Combat Engineer Battalion armed with flamethrowers, dispersed the Japanese and the infantry was able to advance to "Maffin Number One." There was no opposition in the village, so once again Company L led the advance to the next river line, at the Tirfoam River. Here efforts to secure a crossing met determined opposition. Tanks were brought up to suppress the enemy fire. Suddenly, before the tanks could open fire, Japanese infantry charged out of the bush. Led personally by Colonel Kato, men of the *224th* and *223rd Infantry* charged at Company L and its tank support. During the attack the Japanese brought an anti-tank gun into position and damaged severely three of the four supporting American tanks. Company L recovered quickly and repulsed the attack, killing Colonel Kato and destroying the gun crew. Company L consolidated its positions and sent patrols across the river late in the afternoon. Captain Fennell's 200-man company, which remained in the forefront of the battle, would shrink to less than 90 men in the coming week of combat. The continual Japanese pressure on the 3rd Battalion prompted Colonel Herndon to call forward his 1st Battalion, which he ordered into the jungle to outflank the Japanese defenses.

The 1st Battalion attempted to follow its orders, but Companies A and C were quickly stopped cold by machine gun and rifle fire from the jungle. Both the 1st and 3rd Battalions settled into positions for the night. Attention was given to the 28 men killed and 75 wounded during the day's bitter fighting. Additional casualties from heat exhaustion were also evacuated. Japanese casualties had been much higher, especially in the mid-day counterattack. Colonel Kato's place was taken by Major Yasake Matsuoka, a battalion commander in the *223rd Infantry*. His orders were unchanged from those given earlier to Colonel Kato, defend the approaches to the Sarmi airstrips. Major Matsuoka also learned that help was on the way. Another of General Tagami's defense groups was moving into the area. Colonel Kato's sacrifice had enabled this force, known as the *"Eukie Group"* to arrive in time to face the next American attack. Although it had suffered losses from the pre-invasion bombardment, this force was still capable of a strong defense.

May 25th started well for the Americans. Lieutenant Colonel Paul Shoemaker, a pharmacist from Tucson, Arizona, and his acting executive officer, Captain Herbert Erb, of the 1st Battalion carefully planned the advance. After withdrawing from the river front, the 158th Infantry called in heavy artillery and mortar fire to clear the enemy defense along the Tirfoam River. The 1st Battalion relieved the exhausted 3rd, and reinforced by Company E of the 2nd Battalion, moved across the river. Little opposition was found, but evidence that the Japanese defense had been hurt by the artillery preparation abounded. Opposed by rifle fire alone, the battalion secured the next village by

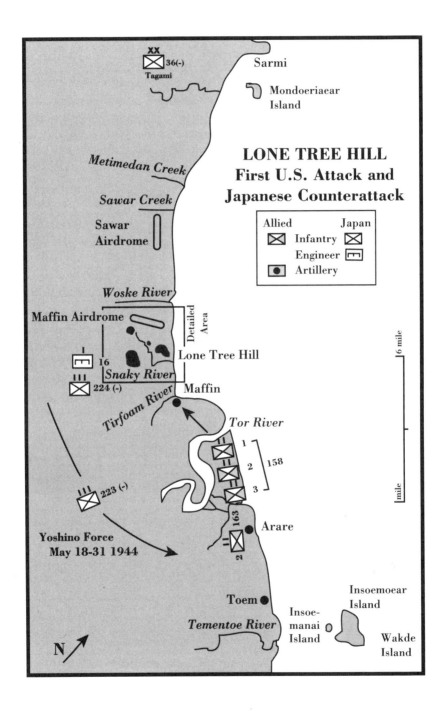

LONE TREE HILL
First U.S. Attack and
Japanese Counterattack

mid-morning. Again using a heavy preparatory fire, this time of machine guns and mortars, the 1st Battalion moved forward to its next assigned objective, some 600 yards west to a pier. Again, only scattered rifle fire opposed the movement. The objective was secured before lunch, and the 2nd Battalion, commanded by Lieutenant Colonel Frederick R. Stofft, moved up to join the 1st Battalion.

Colonel Herndon, using an inaccurate map supplied by Sixth Army, designated the next objective as "Lone Tree Hill." On his map this terrain feature rose from the coast some 2,000 yards west of the jetty just seized, and was depicted by a lone tree on the crest. In actual fact, this was a coral hill mass covered with thick jungle growth. It was also the main Japanese defensive position on the route to Sarmi. Lone Tree Hill was also a part of an integral group of terrain features, including hills, rivers, and defiles which would give the Japanese many advantages and make the American's task much more difficult than it first appeared.

Both the "Right Sector Force" and the "Eukie Group" were on or near Lone Tree Hill. In mid-afternoon the 1st Battalion approached a native village at the foot of Lone Tree Hill. Rifle and machine gun fire halted the advance. Artillery fire began to come down on the Americans, who mistakenly thought this was friendly fire. Upon verifying that this was Japanese artillery fire, General Patrick ordered the advance halted for the night. The infantry was ordered to withdraw far enough from Lone Tree Hill to allow American artillery fire to concentrate on the newly discovered Japanese positions. Another 22 dead and 26 wounded had to be evacuated. Still unaware that they had confronted the crucial Japanese defense position, the Tornado Task Force prepared to renew the attack in the morning.

Plans called for a thirty minute naval bombardment and a fifteen minute artillery concentration before the infantry again advanced on Lone Tree Hill. Events, however, did not conform to plans. The naval bombardment by two destroyers lasted but twenty minutes, the artillery concentration, supposed to follow directly on the heels of the naval bombardment, was about an hour late, letting the Japanese repair any damage done by the U.S. Navy. Finally, the infantry, having been withdrawn the night before, had to march some 1,000 yards before coming near the enemy positions, again permitting the Japanese time to repair any damage done by the American artillery fire. Company B, leading the attack, did not get any farther than it had the day before. Japanese machine gun and rifle fire stopped the attack as it began. Heavy machine gun and artillery concentrations were used throughout the morning to gain small advances. During this day Company A twice fought at a creek, dubbed the "Snaky River," and was twice forced back. Company B, assaulting the village at the foot of Lone Tree Hill, spent the day gaining very little yardage. Supported by Company E, Company B made repeated attempts to outflank the enemy without success. Finally, having made no real progress, the Americans settled in for the night.

Colonel Herndon reviewed both the infantry's progress and the many patrol reports he had received during the day. He now felt this was a serious obstacle and that more time and some detailed planning were needed to overcome it. His views were not shared at Task Force headquarters, however. Again, the 1st Battalion was ordered to push on and secure Lone Tree Hill. The 2nd Battalion was assigned a supporting and flanking role. Artillery support was moved closer to the front. Tank support remained unavailable because the tanks could not cross the Tirfoam River.

One again the infantry advanced, on May 27th, the day Biak was assaulted. Supported by naval guns, artillery and mortar fire, the infantry moved out to the attack. It had by now become clear to the infantrymen that they were attacking not one hill, but at least three. In addition to Lone Tree Hill itself supporting fire for the enemy came from two other terrain features, known as Hill 225 and Mount Saskin. Each was defended by a Japanese force which in turn supported the other positions. The hills were coral and covered with caves, ravines, steep cliffs and thick jungle. The thick jungle growth gave the defender additional concealment. Artillery fire was only partially effective, since it could not reach into the many caves or the deeper ravines which shielded the Japanese. As the 41st Infantry Division was about to learn on Biak, there was only one way to destroy such

B Company, 163rd Infantry near Wakde airstrip.

defenses, using infantry and engineers combining to destroy each enemy position in turn.

May 27th was a repetition of the days before. Small advances were made at heavy cost. Nearly 300 men of the 158th Infantry had to be evacuated at the end of the day, for a gain of a foothold on Lone Tree Hill and Mount Saskin. Colonel Herndon now demanded tank support, which he suggested come by landing craft to the west side of the Tirfoam River. New plans were drawn up for the battle to come on the 28th.

The next day dawned brightly for the Americans. After an effective artillery bombardment, Companies A and C secured the crest of Lone Tree Hill. However, when Company A tried to move off the hill to the south, Japanese fire stopped the attack. Unable to fire on the enemy from the crest, Company A was forced to withdraw. The 3rd platoon became separated from the rest of the company and was pinned down in an unknown location. Captain Herbert Erb, who had been with Company A before his advancement to battalion headquarters, volunteered to find and bring in the lost platoon. This he managed to do, bringing in the platoon safely and eliminating an estimated 37 enemy soldiers while doing it. Captain Erb also led stretcher bearers through enemy fire to bring in nine seriously wounded men. During this second volunteer trip, Captain Erb lost a man killed and had eight men wounded. Lieutenant Colonel Shoemaker put the captain in for the Silver Star for his work this day.

Meanwhile Company C, moving west from the top of Lone Tree Hill, was attacked by the Japanese garrison. The attack was repulsed and Company C found itself pinned down by enemy mortar and machine gun fire. Rifle and mortar ammunition began to run low in both companies, and they were ordered off Lone Tree Hill. Down on the beach, Companies B and E were once again unable to get past the native village. Later that afternoon, an engineer platoon, covered by heavy mortar fire from Company B, completed clearing a beach area to permit landing craft to land the tanks demanded by Colonel Herndon. The Colonel, confronted everywhere by a strong and aggressive Japanese defense, advised General Patrick by radio that he was withdrawing his forces to more tenable positions. He intended to use the "Snaky River" as a line of defense for the night and to reorganize for a renewed effort in the morning. General Patrick approved Colonel Herndon's request. The first battle for Lone Tree Hill had gone to the Japanese.

General Patrick had other worries besides the failure of the attack at Lone Tree Hill. Japanese had become active on the eastern flank of the Arare perimeter and the 163rd Infantry had been ordered to Biak without delay by General Krueger. Sixth Army did propose sending a regimental combat team from the 6th U.S. Infantry Division to replace the departing 163rd Infantry, but they couldn't arrive immediately. General Patrick was also advised that they might come without their artillery support. He needed combat troops within his perimeter in the event the Japanese counterattacked anywhere other than at Lone Tree Hill, which occupied his only available combat infantry. General Patrick had to consider all his responsibilities, and so on the morning of May 29th he ordered Colonel Herndon to send his 1st Battalion back to the beachhead for security, and to relieve the departing 163rd Infantry.

Like General Patrick, Colonel Herndon now had to reconsider his position. With only two depleted battalions, he could not hope to continue the attack with any possibility of success. He ordered his remaining units into defensive positions along the "Snaky River" and in some outposts on the west bank. He would await the arrival of reinforcements.

While the 158th Infantry waited for reinforcements reorganization and rest were the orders of the day. There were serious matters needing attention. Private Joseph Palma, a former steel worker from Pennsylvania and now a member of the regiment's Ammunition and Pioneer Platoon, was ordered to take a jeep to the area of Lone Tree Hill to bring in a wounded man, in the darkness of May 27th. Palma at first protested, knowing that the unit he was directed to, Company F, was made up entirely of Native Americans and was commanded by Captain Jacob F. Duran, himself a Pueblo Indian. The Indians had a reputation for stoicism and it was unusual for them to call for help. Not until his officer explained that the wounded man was from Long Island, New York, did Private Palma agree to go. Joined by a medical aide man named Murphy, they journeyed in the noisiest jeep in the unit through the darkness to Company F. Loading the wounded man into the jeep, they began the return journey. Palma had taken with him his M-1 carbine and some grenades in the not unlikely event they were ambushed. Halfway back, the jeep became mired in mud and rocks. Quickly unloading the wounded man, Palma and Murphy hid themselves in the jungle. Within minutes a Japanese patrol came upon the jeep. Palma knew that if the patrol found the grenades he had left in the jeep they would search the area and find the Americans. Armed with only two carbines, his and Murphy's, they couldn't hold out long. But the enemy patrol looked over the jeep and departed without searching the area. Getting the jeep going again, the threesome returned safely to American lines, where Murphy confessed that the grenades had scared him so much that he had tossed them out at the start of the trip.

During the wait for reinforcements, the Americans continued to patrol and harass the enemy. During one such patrol, led by

Lieutenant Hal Braun of Company B, the Japanese let the Americans proceed several hundred yards into the ravine which separated Lone Tree Hill, or Mount Irier as the Japanese knew it, from Mount Saskin. Lieutenant Braun could feel the enemy eyes upon him the entire time, but not a shot was fired, nor was there any firm sign of the enemy. Briefly, Lieutenant Braun played with the idea of proceeding the last few hundred yards to the airdrome, which was the regimental objective, but realized that he was in effect considering suicide for himself and for his men. Knowing that he was in enemy rifle sights the entire way, he and his patrol returned safely to American lines.

Encouraged by the American's defensive attitude, the Japanese went over to the attack. On May 29th, as the 1st Battalion was relieving the 163rd Infantry at the beachhead, Company F of the 2nd Battalion, holding an outpost position on Mount Saskin reluctantly visited by Private Palma recently, was attacked and forced to withdraw to the position of Company G along the beach. The Japanese continued to be active in patrols and skirmishes all along the "Snaky River." Colonel Herndon became concerned about a Japanese counterattack. His original withdrawal had been approved by General Patrick with the specific stipulation that the line of the "Snaky River" be held. Under the continuing enemy pressure, Colonel Herndon called his senior officers together for a council. Present were Lieutenant Colonel Paul Shoemaker of the 1st Battalion, Lieutenant Colonel Frederick Stofft, commanding the 2nd Battalion, and Lieutenant Colonel George Colvin, 3rd Battalion commander. Asked if they thought the regiment could hold their positions against a full scale enemy counterattack, the three battalion commanders felt that they could not. Colonel Herndon agreed with his battalion commanders and telephoned General Patrick that he intended to withdraw his two remaining battalions to the line of the Tirfoam River, from where the attack had started days ago. General Patrick at first refused permission for the withdrawal, but upon the continued insistence of Colonel Herndon ordered the 2nd and 3rd Battalions, 158th Infantry, to withdraw some 2,000 yards to the east bank of the Tirfoam River. The movement began immediately.

Upon arriving at his new command post east of the Tirfoam

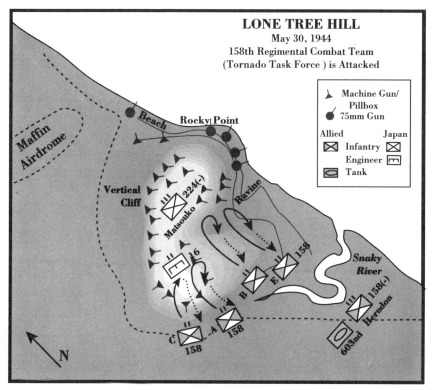

LONE TREE HILL
May 30, 1944
158th Regimental Combat Team
(Tornado Task Force) is Attacked

River, Colonel Herndon found General Patrick waiting. After discussing the recent events, General Patrick relieved Colonel Herndon of command, replacing him with his own chief of staff, Colonel Earle O. Sandlin. General Krueger at Sixth Army Headquarters was informed of General Patrick's decision. Meanwhile, the 158th Infantry established itself in defensive positions along the east bank of the Tirfoam River. The soldiers of the regiment were not told why Colonel Herndon had been relieved and rumors arose that he had been taken ill, promoted, or called home for a family emergency. Some of the ranking officers in the regiment later learned some of the details of the relief. Lieutenant Colonel Stofft, who had been at the war council with Herndon, later spoke with General Krueger before taking command of the 127th Infantry Regiment, 32nd Infantry Division. During the conversation General Krueger reportedly showed Colonel Stofft a pair of brigadier general's stars and remarked that they had been intended for Colonel Herndon but that "he lost them at Lone Tree Hill." Other officers, including the regimental adjutant, Major Boise Day, heard that the relief had been planned earlier and that this was the reason for Colonel Sandlin's presence in the forward area. Whatever the truth, Colonel Herndon's two decades with his regiment were over.

Ironically, within hours of Colonel Herndon's relief, his fears were realized. Japanese attacks from the south showed that they had indeed outflanked the 158th Infantry and were on their lines of communications. Probing attacks were beaten off by infantry and combat engineers. It was now the Americans who were defending while the Japanese attacked.

The 2nd and 3rd Battalions, 158th Infantry, had withdrawn in good order to the east bank of the Tirfoam River. There were no personnel or equipment losses under Colonel Herndon's careful direction. With the infantry, backed by the 147th Field Artillery Battalion, holding a position along the east bank and with a flank guard in a line running east from the river, Colonel Sandlin took command. In addition to the regimental combat team, he found within his defenses the regimental cannon company, Company C of the 27th Combat Engineer Battalion, and some medical units. By nightfall, all these had been enclosed with a defensive perimeter and were dug in awaiting the Japanese.

The enemy came that night. Flanking the perimeter, they struck the engineers, who fought back successfully, repulsing the attack with light loss. Nevertheless, sporadic rifle and artillery fire harassed the Americans all the next day and more attacks were expected. With the Japanese on the offensive, the Tornado Task Force was dangerously exposed. The Task Force was spread out along twelve miles of coast, scattered units often beyond supporting distance of one another. The Japanese were now moving in the jungle south of the coast, unopposed. They could attack at their own time and place. Moreover, the infantry contingent of the Task Force continued to shrink. The 163rd Infantry had gone to Biak and the 158th Infantry couldn't possibly defend twelve miles of jungle even with attached engineers and artillery. No reinforcements were immediately available. As on the previous night, the initiative remained with the Japanese.

General Tagami, commanding the Japanese forces, had not been idle. While ordering the defense of Lone Tree Hill, he had also set in motion other of his forces to get on the American's flank. These forces, known as the *"Yoshino Force"* and the *"Matsuyama Force"* had by the evening of May 26th, succeeded in placing themselves in the jungle south of the American positions. With the Americans holding within their perimeters, the two forces moved to the attack, while the *"Right Sector Force"* held the bulk of the 158th Infantry at the Tirfoam. Preliminary attacks, made against the departing 163rd Infantry, had identified many of the American positions to the Japanese. These attacks were beaten off, but they were not designed to overrun the Americans, only to identify their positions and heavy weapons locations. General Patrick, misinterpreting the nature of these attacks, felt that they had been made by stragglers who posed no real threat to his forces. Actually, there were over 8,000 Japanese troops in his immediate area, in organized units, commanded by experienced officers and with nearly half of the troops having prior combat experience in China. General Patrick's estimate to General Krueger that there were only some 3,000 troops opposing his Task Force wasn't even half right.

The Americans faced the night of May 30th spread out in some 21 separate perimeters. The only combat troops within the beachhead area, the 158th Infantry, was defending the Tirfoam River line, with one battalion defending the main headquarters and supply area around Arare. Randomly divided amongst the other perimeters were supply, anti-aircraft, engineer, artillery and medical units. It was upon these that the Japanese attack fell.

The attack began at dusk, and the first unit to suffer was Battery B of the 202nd Antiaircraft Artillery Battalion, which had a number of isolated positions along the beach designed to protect the beachhead from enemy air attack. The number 6 gun position was overrun, and other gun positions, including those of Battery A, were attacked throughout the night. Using weapons and ammunition captured from Battery B, the Japanese also moved after the Americans' supply dumps. Here they came against the only infantry force in the area, the 1st Battalion, 158th Infantry, which fought them off for four furious hours.

Company B, the unit which bore the brunt of this fight, engaged in hand-to-hand combat before driving the Japanese back into the jungle.

Captain Hal Braun, who had made that strange patrol a few days earlier, now commanded Company B. His command had less than one hundred men left to it when the Japanese struck the headquarters area. With three heavy machine guns from Company D under Sergeant Dixie Walker, he had to hold a beachhead of about 150 yards. The Japanese, after overrunning number 6 gun position, turned American weapons, particularly the heavy machine guns, against Company B. For several hours the Japanese, estimated to number several hundred, roamed through the American defensive positions. The soldiers of Companies B and D remained in their two-man holes and fired at enemy shapes in the dark. Fighting quickly became hand-to-hand. Men literally couldn't see their hands in front of their faces, so dark was the night. Only by flare light and smell, or the sudden attack of an enemy, could either side tell who was who in the darkness. Desperate, Captain Braun called in a mortar strike on his own positions, knowing that his men were in the ground while the enemy was above ground and exposed. This desperate act saved part of his defensive perimeter, but one of Sergeant Walker's gun positions was overrun, the crew dead or wounded. Japanese troops took over the position, while the wounded Americans played dead. One wounded American was taken prisoner, tied to a tree and bayoneted to death. A few yards away was another American, also tied to a tree and wounded. This man managed to get a hidden knife from his clothing and release himself. After killing his sleeping guard, he reached American lines safely. With dawn the Japanese withdrew, leaving Company B to repair what damage it could. Considering the ferocity of the fight, American losses of 12 dead and 10 wounded were remarkably light. At least 50 Japanese were killed in this night engagement.

With dawn of the 31st, General Patrick moved swiftly to consolidate his units. Now convinced that his estimate was incorrect, he ordered all defenses consolidated and strengthened. Isolated units were moved together to form a stronger defense. Elements of the 158th Infantry on outpost duty to the east were withdrawn into the perimeter. Finally, General Patrick ordered all offensive activity stopped pending the arrival of reinforcements. Colonel Sandlin, now commanding the 158th Infantry Regiment, was also made responsible for the entire Task Force defenses. He quickly ordered parts of his regiment to reinforce areas which had been attacked during the night. Company K, for example, was ordered to reinforce the 1st Battalion defending the supply and headquarters positions of the Task Force. By the time night came again, the Americans had consolidated into eight perimeters, still along the beach, with more infantry included in the defense. General Patrick, despite orders to the contrary, kept the 2nd Battalion, 163rd Infantry, ashore as a reserve. They were ordered to wait on the beach until morning, when they would be permitted to complete their movement to rejoin the rest of their regiment on Biak.

To the immense relief of the Americans, no attack developed that night. The Japanese, despite a reputation to the contrary, had difficulties in jungle combat as did the Americans. Their liaison between units was often poor, as was their knowledge of local terrain. Their troops feared the jungle just as did the Americans, and avoided reconnaissance in deep jungle unless necessary for immediate operations. Most serious for the Japanese was their supply problem. At this stage of the war, with the Americans controlling the sea and air around New Guinea, the Japanese were forced to hand carry supplies over difficult, often trackless, jungle. It often proved impossible, even for the hardy Japanese soldier. For all of these reasons, the Japanese who surrounded Tornado Task Force could not move in to finish the job of destroying that force. General Tagami lost contact with both attacking units, who in turn lost contact with each other. Supplies disappeared rapidly, so much so that many of the Japanese were using captured ammunition and weapons. Distances had been underestimated, tracks had to be cut through the jungle, and the efforts had exhausted the troops. While attacks continued against the 2nd and 3rd Battalions, 158th Infantry, no further attacks materialized against the other perimeters of the task force. After ten days of fruitless attempts to right all the wrongs within their forces, both the "*Yoshino Force*" and the "*Matsuyama Force*" withdrew to the west.

While the Tornado Task Force rested from its close call with destruction, the Japanese withdrew to reorganize and prepare improved defenses. Sixth Army intelligence officers, reviewing reports from prisoners, captured papers, scouting patrols, and intercepted enemy radio transmissions, revised their previous estimates of enemy strength. Earlier, they had believed that only parts of the *36th Japanese Infantry Division* were stationed at Sarmi. Now, confronted with hard evidence identifying every major unit of that division, they revised their estimate to state that the entire *36th Infantry Division*, reinforced, was present. They doubled their estimates of enemy forces from 6,500 to 10,776, at least half of whom were classified as experienced combat troops. For Tornado Task Force this was good news, because Sixth Army Headquarters, heeding their intelligence officers, ordered the entire 6th U.S. Infantry Division to Arare, rather than the one regimental combat team proposed earlier.

The 6th U.S. Infantry Division traced its history back to the First World War, when it had been a part of General John J. Pershing's American Expeditionary Force on the Western Front. Inactive between wars, it had been reactivated on October 10, 1939 at Fort Lewis, Washington. In its brief career before arriving in New Guinea, it had been designated a "motorized" division, and later had trained in desert warfare. Ironically, it was now about to engage in its first combat in some of the most primitive jungle in the world, something it had not trained for in the United States.

The first units of the 6th Infantry Division to arrive in Arare were the 1st Infantry Regiment and the 6th Engineer Battalion (Combat) which came ashore on June 5th. However, these units came with a string attached, for the division commander, Major General Franklin C. Sibert, requested that they not be committed to combat until at least one more regimental combat team was ashore. The 1st Infantry Regiment did relieve those units of the 158th Infantry holding the perimeter positions along the beachhead. This allowed those units to move to the Tor River, where the 1st Battalion relieved the tired 3rd Battalion on the lines.

General Patrick decided not to wait for the 6th infantry Division to arrive. His confidence increased by Japanese inactiv-

Sherman of 603rd Tank Company, supported by infantry of the 163rd Regimental Combat Team, moves inland on Wakde. (National Archives)

ity for the past few days, he ordered the 158th Infantry to renew its aborted advance of May. The 158th Infantry moved to the assault on June 7th, covering the same ground it had struggled over two weeks earlier. It encountered the same Japanese defensive positions, stronger and reinforced. Supported closely by tanks of the 603rd Tank Company and artillery from the 167th Field Artillery Battalion, the advance was methodical. As before, the first position to be attacked was a group of bunkers and pillboxes at the small lakes east of the Tirfoam River. Infantry and armor reduced these positions in time to settle in for the night. Both the Japanese and the Americans passed a quiet night, and the assault was resumed in the morning where it faced the usual rifle, machine gun and mortar fire. The successful infantry and armor combination reduced the opposition, while long range fire from the heavy artillery of the 218th Field Artillery Battalion eliminated enemy artillery fire. By mid-afternoon the 158th Infantry had reached and secured its old positions along the Tirfoam River, and was preparing to continue the advance when new orders arrived from Sixth Army Headquarters.

General Patrick's intention in sending the 158th Infantry against Lone Tree Hill once again was in the form of a diversion. He had planned to send two battalions of infantry, provided by the 6th Infantry Division, in an amphibious end run to the Sarmi Peninsula, where scouts reported no defenses. These plans ran afoul of General Krueger's plans, which involved a campaign spanning hundreds of miles of jungle, ocean and islands. General Krueger was having trouble at a number of places, of which Arare was but one. With the 6th Infantry Division committed to the attack at Arare, he easily found need for the now experienced 158th Regimental Combat Team elsewhere in his Theater. Accordingly, orders were issued to the 158th Regimental Combat Team to consolidate their positions and await relief by the 6th Infantry Division. General Krueger needed the Arizonans elsewhere, specifically an island none of them had ever heard of, known as Noemfoor.

The 158th Infantry spent June 11th and 12th clearing its area, digging defensive positions, and patrolling. Some Japanese outposts which threatened the defensive positions of the Americans along the Tirfoam River were attacked and reduced. On June 14th the 20th Infantry Regiment of the 6th Division relieved the 158th Infantry at the Tirfoam River line, and by June 22nd the exhausted survivors of the 158th were preparing for their next assignment. Behind them the regiment left seventy dead, two hundred fifty seven wounded, and four missing. They had captured eleven prisoners.

The arrival of the entire 6th Infantry Division on June 14th coincided with the division commander, General Sibert, assuming command of Tornado Task Force. The objective of the Task Force remained the same, the seizure of Sarmi and the destruction of the Japanese forces defending it.

Major General Franklin Cummings Sibert was a native of

Bowling Green, Kentucky who graduated from the United State Military Academy at West Point with the Class of 1912. Appointed a second lieutenant of infantry, he served in a number of assignments until sent to France during World War I. After serving as an aide to General John J. Pershing, Commanding General of the American Expeditionary Force, he organized and commanded the 1st Machine Gun Battalion. Returning to the United States, he again organized and trained another Machine Gun Battalion, the 10th, and went back to France in command of this unit. He served with the 4th Infantry Division until the war's end. Between the wars he had the usual assignments, and attended the Infantry School Advanced Course, the Command and General Staff School, and the Army War College.

The son of Major General William L. Sibert, an engineer officer, and brother of Brigadier General E. L. Sibert who served on the staff of General Omar Bradley in the European Theater, General Sibert was assigned to the staff of Major General Joseph Stilwell, and made the historic "Burma Retreat" with General Stilwell. After returning to the United States, General Sibert was given command of the 6th Motorized Division. Subsequently, he would rise to command the X Corps in the invasion of the Philippines.

General Sibert was a thorough commander. While forced to relieve the 158th Infantry with his 20th Infantry Regiment, he did not rush into combat until all his troops and supplies were ashore. He also had his 1st Infantry Regiment secure his rear areas, the jungle from which the *Yoshino* and *Matsuyama* attacks had come from before the arrival of the 6th Infantry Division. General Krueger, faced with numerous deadlines and pending invasions which required that the Sarmi area be secured as a staging base, would not let General Sibert delay as long as he would have liked. He ordered an offensive towards Sarmi by June 18th. Accordingly, General Sibert ordered the 20th Infantry to attack, which he managed to delay until the 20th of June.

General Sibert ordered the 1st Infantry to replace the 20th Infantry in the defensive positions at the Tirfoam River so that the 20th Infantry could move into the attack unhindered with defensive responsibilities. The objective, as it had been since mid-May, was the enemy forces on and around Lone Tree Hill.

The attacking force was yet another regimental combat team. Yet this time there was a difference, for unlike the 163rd and 158th Infantry Regiments which preceded them, the 20th Infantry was backed up by an entire combat infantry division, with all the artillery, engineer, medical and supply support that comes with such a combat force. Its rear areas were secured by a sister infantry regiment and while there was still pressure from above for speed, few of the other difficulties faced by its predecessors were still present. There were still, however, the Japanese, and the 20th Infantry moved forward against Lone Tree Hill on June 20th.

Meanwhile the Japanese, knowing that the Americans could not leave such a sizable force as theirs waiting in the jungle, had worked diligently to improve their defenses. Caves were improved for defense. Bunkers were built both on Lone Tree Hill and along the approaches to it. At least seven 75mm field pieces of artillery were emplaced in the general area of Lone Tree Hill. Log and earth dugouts had been built low to the ground, restricting the Japanese fields of fire, but making them all but impossible to detect until they opened fire. Positions were even constructed in trees and expertly camouflaged. The Americans might have more troops available this time, but they would be facing even tougher defenses. There were some 850 soldiers from the *224th Infantry* and *36th Division Artillery* on Lone Tree Hill. In the immediate area, still grouped into the *"Right Sector Force"* were the survivors of the rest of the *224th Infantry*, the *16th Airdrome Construction Unit,* additional artillery, antiaircraft and service troops. In the Lone Tree Hill-Mount Saskin-Hill 225 area at least 1,800 Japanese troops waited, well dug in and prepared for the coming attack.

The 1st Battalion, 20th Infantry, followed by the 3rd Battalion, led the attack. Initially there was no Japanese opposition. When Company B, leading the advance, reached Lone Tree Hill heavy automatic weapons fire pinned them down, exactly as had occurred three weeks before to Company B, 158th Infantry. Even with tank support the Japanese positions could not be reached or neutralized. The tanks could not leave the road along the coast, and so their use was limited. Company A, sent to assist Company B, succeeded in reaching its sister unit after which

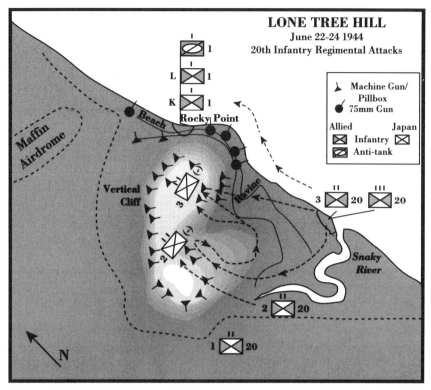

LONE TREE HILL
June 22-24 1944
20th Infantry Regimental Attacks

both were cut off from the rest of the battalion. The two companies spent the night in a tight defensive perimeter some 400 yards from the main force of Americans. The next day, rather than an all-out attack, the Americans patrolled extensively. A clearer picture of the terrain and the Japanese defenses began to appear. Companies A and B regained contact with their battalion, and they also scouted the enemy positions. No real ground was gained this day, but much valuable intelligence of both terrain and enemy dispositions had been gathered. For the first time, the American forces attacking Lone Tree Hill had a fairly clear idea of their opposition.

A result of the patrolling was to organize an attack by nearly all of the 20th Infantry Regiment. Previously individual Companies and occasionally a battalion had attacked. This time all three battalions of the 20th Infantry would be engaged in reducing the Japanese defenses of Lone Tree Hill. While the 1st Battalion held the Japanese attention by probing attacks along the beach access, the 2nd and 3rd Battalions would attack Lone

Tree Hill from a new direction, out of the jungle to the south. The initial 3rd Battalion attack ran into unexpected terrain difficulties, and even with support from Company B, 6th Combat Engineer Battalion, could not make progress. Once again, the Americans withdrew across the Snaky River for the night.

Early the next morning, June 22nd, a heavy artillery and mortar concentration was placed on the Japanese. Following this, P-47 fighter aircraft flying from the now secure Wakde airfields strafed and napalmed Lone Tree Hill. Immediately after the planes left, artillery opened fire again until the infantry was in a position to move into the attack. Companies E and I led the 3rd Battalion attack, and at first progress was met only by scattered rifle fire. The heavy and accurate bombardment had affected the defenders, and crippled their defense at least temporarily. As the morning progressed, machine gun and light mortar fire increased. Working together, the Americans reached the top of Lone Tree Hill shortly after noon, the first Americans there since Companies B and C of the 158th Infantry over three weeks before. They were soon joined by Companies F and L who had been unable to find their own way up the hill and had turned and followed Companies K and I to the top. Reinforced by heavy weapons from Company M, the four companies immediately formed a defensive perimeter around the top of their objective. More than a month after the first Americans had approached it, they held a strong position atop Lone Tree Hill.

The 2nd Battalion was immediately ordered up to support the 3rd Battalion and its own Company F. Moving out in the early afternoon, the troops struggled through heavy jungle and enemy opposition to a point some 400 yards short of the 3rd Battalion's perimeter. Approaching darkness forced them to dig in for the night. There were several soldiers in the 20th Infantry who felt that the day had gone too easily. Shortly after dark, Colonel Matsuyama and his *224th Infantry* proved the skeptics correct.

Launching a furious suicidal attack against the 3rd Battalion, two companies of the *224th Infantry* engaged the Americans in hand-to-hand combat. When the 2nd Battalion tried to send help, it found that although it was not under direct attack, it too was surrounded. All communication between battalions and the rear was cut off. After some six hours of confused heavy fighting the Japanese withdrew to their caves and bunkers, leaving some 30 dead and 100 wounded Americans in the 3rd and 2nd Battalions. Japanese losses were heavy as well, and Colonel Matsuyama was wounded in this attack. Despite his injuries, however, Colonel Matsuyama wasn't finished. He ordered a new attack at dawn against the 2nd Battalion. The Japanese, some wearing American uniforms and using American weapons, were allowed to get close to the American lines before they were identified. Again Japanese and American engaged in hand-to-hand combat before the Japanese were driven off. American heavy weapons positions were prime targets of Japanese rifle and artillery fire. Machine gunners fell at their guns, to be replaced by the assistant gunners. Riflemen fired at shadows, sheltered in mud and awaited the next burst of fire from the shadows. The Japanese, as was their custom, yelled and screamed insults at the Americans. Any American who revealed his position by replying was the next target of a Japanese assault. Only sunrise brought relief.

With the Japanese again under cover, the 2nd Battalion was ordered to make contact with the 3rd Battalion. However, the opposition in the 400 yards separating the two units was so strong that the battalion decided that it would be better to climb down the hill and find another way to join the 3rd Battalion. This it proceeded to do, although it would take all day and two attempts before a way could be found through the Japanese defenses. Meanwhile the 3rd Battalion retained its positions on the crest of Lone Tree Hill. No supplies could get through to them, and the heavy fighting of the past twenty four hours had completely drained the water supply. Fortunately, a rainfall in the afternoon temporarily replenished the water supply, but nothing could be done for other critical supply needs, such as food, ammunition and medical supplies. Wounded could not be evacuated, except at great personal risk.

One soldier who assisted the evacuation of the wounded was Private Robert W. Scrannage. Moving to an exposed position where several of his fellow infantrymen lay wounded, he moved each to a place of safety, then climbed upon a tank and directed its fire into an enemy pillbox which was preventing further evacuation of wounded. Knocked unconscious from the tank by an enemy grenade, he quickly regained consciousness and moved again to an exposed position between his wounded friends and the enemy. Keeping himself between the enemy and the American wounded for two hours, until he himself had to be evacuated, Private Scrannage saved many lives. He was later awarded a Silver Star.

Company L of the 1st Infantry was ordered to bring food, water and ammunition up to the 3rd Batalion, 20th Infantry. Heavily loaded with supplies Company L was ambushed and pinned down on the slopes of Lone Tree Hill. It, too, began to run out of ammunition, for it had not been prepared for a fight. Only the arrival of the 2nd Battalion, 20th Infantry, in its odyssey around Lone Tree Hill saved Company L. Even with the additional manpower supplies remained a problem, and it took all day to remove the 300 casualties, using volunteer carrying parties.

The night brought little relief to the men of the 2nd and 3rd Battalions, for the Japanese again attacked throughout the night. Clearly, Lone Tree Hill was not going to be easy to eliminate. At this point General Sibert considered bypassing the enemy entrenched on Lone Tree Hill but discovered he could not. Lone Tree Hill, even if bypassed, could place machine gun and artillery fire along the shores of Maffin Bay. This would prevent it from being used for staging subsequent operations. The 6th Infantry Division had to secure the entire shore of Maffin Bay, including Lone Tree Hill.

Like the 158th Infantrymen before them, the regular army soldiers of the 6th Infantry Division learned combat quickly. Patrols continued to be sent out, for information, for combat and to save wounded. Patrols were always dangerous. Some, like the patrol of Lieutenant Braun some weeks earlier, advanced without contact. Others were ambushed. One company strength patrol was hit by rifle, machine gun and artillery fire. Upon withdrawing, it was discovered that an officer had been left behind, probably dead. Technician Third Grade Arthur M. Renna, a medical corpsman, returned under intense machine gun fire and brought out the officer's body. He received a Silver Star for his efforts.

Unable to bypass Lone Tree Hill, General Sibert considered his other options. It was now apparent, with two infantry battalions cut off on top of the hill, that a frontal assault was not the answer. If soldiers as brave as Private Scrannage and Technician Renna couldn't make progress, there had to be a better way. So the General looked for ways to outflank the enemy. He decided on an amphibious landing beyond the main Japanese defenses. Orders went to the 1st Infantry Regiment and the 6th Reconnaissance Troop to make this landing.

The 3rd Battalion, 1st Infantry, chose Companies I and K, supported by the 6th Reconnaissance Troop, to make the amphibious assault. Boated in tracked landing vehicles, Company K landed on the beach and moved inland to an area known as Rocky Point. Here they were pinned down by Japanese machine gun and artillery fire from Lone Tree Hill. Company I landed about two hours later, a delay caused by the need to use the same landing vehicles for both units. The two companies joined forces on the exposed beachhead. Behind Company I four tanks of Company C, 44th Tank Battalion, landed. Even with this armored support, the infantry was only able to maintain its positions, but could not advance. Boats carrying supplies in and wounded out were fired upon by the Japanese 75mm artillery pieces on Lone Tree Hill. One boat loaded with wounded was sunk by this fire, but another boat managed to rescue the wounded passengers without loss. Unable to make any progress against the defenses of the *223rd Infantry* defending this sector, the American dug in for the night.

On the top of Lone Tree Hill, the 2nd and 3rd Battalions, 20th Infantry, began to systematically clear the hill of the enemy. With every available weapon, the 3rd Battalion cleared the hilltop of the Japanese positions in caves and dugouts, while the 2nd Battalion, reinforced with Company L of the 1st Infantry, secured the route up the hill, enabling supplies to flow and wounded to be evacuated. For the first night since the attack had started, there was no organized Japanese counterattack.

Even without an enemy counterattack, the infantrymen had to fight hard for every inch of ground. Second Lieutenant Theodore Frankel became known to his men as a human dynamo for repeatedly attacking Japanese positions with flame throwers and rocket launchers. Even after he was severely burned, Lieutenant Frankel led his squads up to each enemy position in turn and directed its destruction. When three of his men were wounded, he evacuated each of them to safety despite his own wounds and heavy enemy fire directed at him. He somehow managed to live to receive his Distinguished Service Cross. Many other soldiers made their contributions, as well. Technical Sergeant Harry Moskovitz took command of his platoon when its officer was wounded. Repeatedly he attacked Japanese positions, and then led his men in repulsing a counterattack despite the fact that he had been mortally wounded. Sergeant Moskovitz's Silver Star was awarded posthumously. There were also men like Private First Class Harry L. Williams, who although dying himself, further exposed himself to aid a wounded friend. He, too, received a posthumous Silver Star. Captain Jimmie C. Smith of the 51st Field Artillery Battalion finished his assigned duties of observing artillery support for the infantry, and then moved between American and Japanese lines to aid wounded. He further exposed himself to bring up supply vehicles to evacuate the casualties. He, too, was a Silver Star winner at Lone Tree Hill. The battle for Lone Tree Hill was clearly as severe as any fought in the Pacific.

The following day, June 25th, the two battalions with Companies L and M, 1st Infantry attached, continued clearing operations. Both battalions had suffered severely, with just over three hundred men left in each battalion which had numbered well over eight hundred men at the start of the battle. But despite these losses, the mopping up continued successfully. The Japanese had lost the fight for Lone Tree Hill, and now struggled only to satisfy their own need for survival or death. On the beach Companies I and K, 1st Infantry, continued to use mortar and machine gun fire to harass the enemy. By mid-afternoon, with the 20th Infantry making better progress, Companies I and K began to move inland. It became apparent to the Americans that the battle for Lone Tree Hill was nearly over.

Success had been costly. About 1,000 Americans had fallen during the 6th Infantry Division's attacks thus far, including 140 killed in action. The Japanese later estimated that they had lost 500 killed and 300 wounded in this phase of the battle. The *224th*

THE DOUBLE BAY "BUNKER"

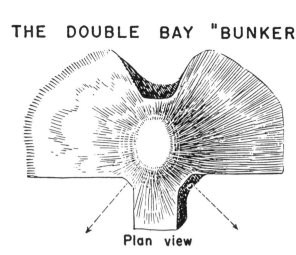

Plan view

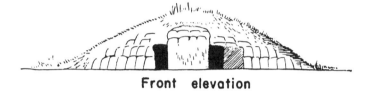

Front elevation

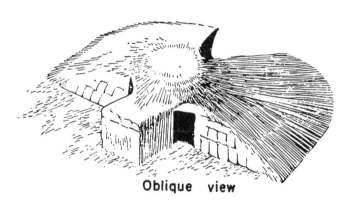

Oblique view

THE SINGLE BAY "BUNKER"

Front elevation

Plan view

Oblique view

Typical Japanese bunkers.

Infantry Regiment consisted of remnants only, while the *223rd* had been seriously hurt. The 2nd Battalion of the 20th Infantry had only 200 combat effective men left at the end of June 25th and the 3rd Battalion was little better off. The losses and the exhaustion of the 20th Infantry Regiment prompted General Sibert to call forward the last of the 6th Division's infantry regiments, the 63rd.

From June 27th to 30th the 3rd Battalion, 63rd Infantry mopped up around Lone Tree Hill. Supported by the 3rd Battalion, 1st Infantry, and with the 1st Battalions of both the 1st and 20th Infantry Regiments mopping up the beach area and approaches to Lone Tree Hill, the area was totally secured by nightfall, June 30th. Over 1,600 American soldiers had been killed, wounded or evacuated sick in the 10 days between June 20th and June 30th. Yet the Japanese still held several hills overlooking Maffin Bay and until these were captured the bay would not be secure for shipping. General Sibert ordered the 63rd Infantry Regiment, supported by the 1st Infantry, to capture Hill 225 and Mount Saskin.

When these units advanced on July 1st, they were pleasantly surprised. Although both hills were well prepared for defense with caves, pillboxes and dugouts, the Japanese had abandoned them completely. Cautiously examining the positions, both units moved in and occupied their objectives without opposition. Moving further west under General Sibert's orders, the 1st Battalions of the 1st and 63rd Infantry Regiments encountered opposition at Hill 263, and spent July 8th and 9th clearing the *224th Infantry* remnants from their defenses on the hill. The brief fight was as difficult as the ones for Lone Tree Hill. First Lieutenant Eugene R. Dean added his name to the division's list of Silver Star winners when he made a solo patrol under heavy enemy fire after the rest of his men had been pinned down by the same fire. Private Howard A. Gregg, already wounded twice, aided a fellow wounded soldier, then returned to his position in time to repel an enemy counterattack. He, too, lived to receive his Silver Star. With the capture of Hill 263 the battle to secure Maffin Bay ended for the 6th Infantry Division. The Division was ordered to halt and await relief. It was destined for the invasion of the Philippines, where General Sibert would be promoted to command of X Corps, to be replaced by General Patrick, another veteran of Lone Tree Hill in command of the 6th Infantry Division. General Patrick would lead the division into the Philippines where he would later be killed in action.

Although there were still active Japanese forces around Sarmi, General Krueger needed the now experienced 6th Infantry Division elsewhere, specifically a place called Sansapor. Like the 158th Regimental Combat Team before it, the 6th Division was pulled out for a quick rest and recuperation period, before starting its next operation. General Krueger called forward the 31st Infantry Division, a unit new to the 6th Army, to relieve the 6th Infantry Division.

Major General John Cecil Persons commanded the 31st Infantry Division. General Persons was not a career military man. A graduate of the University of Alabama, class of 1910, he was a lawyer by profession. During the First World War he had accepted a commission in the Alabama National Guard, won a Distinguished Service Cross in France, and left federal service in 1918 as a major of infantry. He remained in the Alabama National Guard between wars, rising through the officer ranks while at the same time pursuing a successful business career in banking and insurance in his native Alabama. By 1940 he was a brigadier general in the National Guard, and was given command of the 31st Infantry Division when it was called into federal service in 1940.

The 31st Infantry Division had been drawn from the National Guards of the states of Alabama, Florida, Louisiana and Mississippi. It had spent its wartime career so far in training at home and in New Guinea. Maffin Bay would be its first combat operation. One of the Division's regimental combat teams was already committed at Aitape, but the rest of the division arrived at Maffin Bay between the 14th and 18th of July. The 6th Infantry Division immediately began departing, with the last units of the 20th Infantry leaving Maffin Bay in mid-August.

As events turned out, however, the 31st Infantry Division saw little heavy combat at Maffin Bay. Much of its time was spent in helping load the 6th Division and its supplies, and by the end of that time, it was itself scheduled to move westward. Nevertheless some heavy patrol action did occur during the six weeks the

Division held Maffin Bay. Under Dutch liaison officers, who brought armed native police and guides with them, the 31st Infantry units consistently engaged the enemy holding positions along Maffin Bay. They also encountered and intercepted many fleeing Japanese from the *Hollandia Garrison*, now trying to reach safety in Western New Guinea with the *2nd Area Army*. Another 42 Americans were killed and 229 hospitalized during these mopping up operations. No major action developed because neither side wanted one. The Americans were anxious to move on to their next operation, while the Japanese had little fight left in them. The 31st Infantry Division was relieved on September 1st by the 123rd Infantry Regimental Combat Team, drawn from the 33rd Infantry Division.

After the 31st Infantry Division left Maffin Bay, Tornado Task Force was dissolved, and headquarters, 123rd Regimental Combat Team, assumed responsibility for the area until October, when Headquarters, 8th U.S. Army under the command of Lieutenant General Robert L. Eichelberger, took over. General Eichelberger's newly created command relieved the 123rd Infantry with a battalion of the 93rd Infantry Division, a unit of black Americans. The 93rd Infantry Division was one of three all-black divisions raised by the United States during World War II. One, the 2nd Cavalry Division, was sent to North Africa, but was disbanded before entering combat. The second, the 92nd Infantry Division, saw extensive combat in northern Italy. The last was the 93rd Infantry Division which was the only one sent to the Pacific. It never saw combat as a complete division, with its units farmed out in regiment or battalion strength, usually for mopping up operations.

The battalion of the 93rd Infantry Division patrolled for security purposes, but their main duty was to expedite and protect the withdrawal of all supplies from Maffin Bay. The division, commanded by Major General Harry Hubbard Johnson, a graduate of Texas Agricultural and Mechanical College who had risen in the Texas National Guard to command the 2nd Cavalry Division and then the 93rd Infantry Division, sent its 368th Infantry Regiment to remove all trace of American presence from the shores of Maffin Bay. In January and February of 1945, the 368th Infantry supported by the 594th Field Artillery Battalion removed all remaining supplies and equipment from the mainland. The American cemetery was even removed to Wakde. The Americans were finished here, and they were leaving nothing to the starving enemy sheltering in the jungle. The airstrips on Wakde were designated as emergency fields and all American troops left the mainland on February 6th. Wakde was occupied by an infantry company of the 93rd Infantry Division until the end of the war.

The cost to the Americans for the Wakde-Sarmi operation was totaled at 400 killed, 1,500 wounded and 15 missing. In exchange the *36th Japanese Infantry Division* was rendered harmless, a staging base was secured for moving a few hundred miles closer to the Philippines, and the flanks of both the Southwest Pacific and Central Pacific Theaters were secured. Additionally, several inexperienced units, notably the 158th Infantry, the 6th Infantry Division, and the 31st Infantry Division were exposed to combat conditions. Each of these units would go on to future battles, including the Philippines, which had been the main reason that all this hardship had been undertaken.

Education Of The Generals

One of the most neglected aspects of the study of the Second World War has been the educational background of the leading personalities of the war, particularly the commanding generals of the major military formations. It is widely assumed that the leaders of the army combat forces in all theaters of war were graduates of the United States Military Academy at West Point. There have been some studies done on the so-called "West Point Protection Association," which many believed arose in the Second World War and went on to damage the American effort in Vietnam.

This was certainly not the case in the Southwest Pacific. While the Military Academy was well represented, it did not produce the overwhelming majority of leaders during the New Guinea campaign. Of eighteen leaders of major units serving in New Guinea in 1944, just seven were graduates of West Point. These were corps commanders Robert L. Eichelberger (1909) and Charles P. Hall (1911). Division commanders from West Point were Jens A. Doe (1914), Horace H. Fuller (1909), Frederick A. Irving (1917) and Franklin Cummings Sibert (1912). Regimental or Task Force commanders who graduated West Point included Oliver P. Newman (1922).

The next most productive method of enlisting generals in the Southwest Pacific was the direct commission. At the pinnacle of the hierarchy in the Southwest stood General Walter Krueger, a result of this process. Others who entered the army this way were Edwin D. Patrick (Indiana National Guard), Leonard F. Wing (Vermont National Guard), Harry H. Johnson (Texas A & M College/Texas National Guard), William H. Gill (V.M.I./Virginia National Guard) and John C. Persons (University Of Alabama/Alabama National Guard). Probably the highest ranking non-West Point officer in the Southwest Pacific was General MacArthur's senior Army Air Force commander and advisor, George C. Kenny, a graduate of the Massachusetts Institute of Technology (1911) and recipient of a direct commission. Other schools represented in this area were Virginia Military Institute which graduated, in addition to General Gill, his assistant division commander, Clarence A. Martin (1917) and George Washington University which graduated Julian W. Cunningham (1916).

Whatever the circumstances of the source of generals in other theaters of war, the Southwest Pacific Theater was certainly well rounded in terms of drawing its leaders from many sources.

CHAPTER IV

The Schouten Islands

While the battle for Lone Tree Hill progressed, the campaign westward continued. The next step in General MacArthur's plan was the seizure of Biak Island. This was a crucial step because it was an integral part of the coordinated plan between General MacArthur's Southwest Pacific Theater and Admiral Nimitz's Central Pacific Theater. A part of the agreement made in March had been that the Schouten Islands, of which Biak was the only one with enemy airfields, would be seized in time for General MacArthur to support Admiral Nimitz's amphibious assault on Saipan, in the Mariana Islands.

Biak Island is the largest of the group of islands known as the Schouten Islands. It is a coral outcropping with thick rain forest jungle-type vegetation. Much of the terrain is made up of coral outcroppings, ridges and shelves. The largest portions of flat land, suitable for airfields, lay on the southeastern part of the island. Here also were the main population centers, the villages of Bosnek, Sorido and Opiaref. Only two other areas contained noticeable populations, the villages of Korim to the northeast and Wardo to the northwest. Coral reefs fringed much of the island. Off to the southeast were a small group of islands, known as the Padaido Islands, which would briefly become involved in the coming battle for Biak. Soepiori Island, smaller sister to Biak, lay immediately off the northwest corner of Biak, separated only by a narrow strait.

As usual in the Western New Guinea Campaign, the objectives which made Biak important were airfields. The Japanese had built two on Biak, both on the southeastern plain. One had been built near the village of Mokmer and was known to the Americans as Mokmer Drome. A short distance away was Sorido Drome, near the village of the same name. A third field, known as Borokoe Drome, was just coming into operation, while the Japanese had planned a fourth field which was not yet under construction.

Sixth Army's objective was to secure these fields for two purposes. First, these airfields had been selected to provide the air support promised by General MacArthur to Admiral Nimitz for the Navy-Marine invasion of Saipan, scheduled for June 15th. Second, the Southwest Pacific's own air support would be advanced by the seizure of these airfields, giving the Sixth Army air cover to the western end of New Guinea. Once squadrons from the 5th and 13th Army Air Forces had been established on Biak, the Sixth Army could proceed knowing that air cover would be available until New Guinea had been secured. Air cover from Biak would also prevent any enemy attempt at an attack on the flanks of either General MacArthur's or Admiral Nimitz's forces. The seizure of Biak would give the Americans control of the seas between New Guinea and the Mariana Islands using air power. It would also eliminate the possibility that the Japanese based on Biak could counterattack either advance by air.

The Japanese forces on Biak were known as the *Biak Detachment*. The major unit of the *Biak Detachment* was the *222nd Infantry Regiment*, from the *36th Infantry Division*, the balance of which was fighting the 6th U.S. Infantry Division on the mainland. The regimental commander, Colonel Naoyuki Kuzume, was also the commander of the *Biak Detachment*. Reinforced by a company of divisional light tanks, field and anti-aircraft artillery, three *Field Airdrome Construction Units* and some 1,500 naval troops, Colonel Kuzume had about 11,400 soldiers and sailors available to oppose an American attack. About 4,000 of his soldiers were trained combat troops.

Colonel Kuzume had some serious problems in planning his defense. Warned by his superiors that an American attack was likely, he had to defend the airstrips, the obvious objective of the enemy. Yet he had an inadequate force to accomplish that goal.

He did not have enough troops to defend the entire coastline, nor enough to defend in strength the coast along the airfields. So he decided to defend in depth the cliffs and high ground which overlooked the airfields. From here he could prevent the enemy from using the airfields long enough to allow reinforcements to arrive on Biak and destroy the American invasion force. When he received word of the American attack on Wakde, he ordered all airfield construction work stopped, and all troops were ordered into the hills to prepare defensive positions. All his artillery and anti-aircraft weapons were hauled into these hills and ridges and sited to cover both the airfields as well as the coastal road which connected them. From here Colonel Kuzume reasonably assumed he could hold the Americans until his promised reinforcements could arrive. The commander, *Biak Detachment*, had considered well, and except for the poor state of the *Imperial Japanese Navy*, he might well have succeeded.

Colonel Kuzume still had to prepare for other eventualities. He detached one company of infantry to Korim Bay and held his *3rd Battalion, 222nd Infantry* with the *36th Division Tank Company* in reserve. Apparently unsure of American intentions, or perhaps fooled that the Americans were fully engaged in the ongoing battle for Lone Tree Hill, he had not ordered his men into their defense positions when the Americans began landing on Biak. Ironically, the effect of his indecision was to work to the Japanese benefit, because when the Americans first landed they received a false impression of Japanese unpreparedness. It was an impression that was soon forcefully corrected.

General Krueger had selected the 41st Infantry Division for the amphibious assault on Biak. One regimental combat team of the division, the 163rd, was seizing the Wakde Islands. The balance of the division, reinforced with artillery, engineers and service troops was directed to land and seize Biak Island. The Biak invasion force was codenamed Hurricane Task Force, and as usual the task force was directly responsible to Alamo Force, the Sixth Army under General Krueger. Naval support and transportation was under the command of Rear Admiral William M. Fechteler, U.S.N. and consisted of 2 heavy cruisers, 3 light cruisers and 21 destroyers protecting 5 attack transports, 8 Landing Ships Tank and 8 Landing Craft Infantry along with

Captured Japanese antiaircraft gun on Biak. Note nearby shell hole made by pre-invasion bombardment. (National Archives)

numerous support ships. Air support would be flown by 5th Army Air Force planes from Hollandia and the Wakde Islands. Thirteenth Army Air Force and Australian and Dutch aircraft would perform long range reconnaissance and strategic bombing missions.

Major General Horace Hayes Fuller was a native of Fort Meade, South Dakota and a graduate of the United States Military Academy at West Point, class of 1909. Commissioned into the cavalry, he served in a number assignments in cavalry regiments, including two years in the Philippines. Transferring to the field artillery, he served in France in World War I with the 108th Field Artillery Regiment of the Pennsylvania National Guard's 28th Infantry Division in the Meuse-Argonne and Ypres-Lys offensives. Major Fuller then served at Fort Benning, attended the Command and General Staff School which he

General MacArthur with Maj. Gen. Horace H. Fuller after inspecting 41st Division in New Guinea.

graduated as a Distinguished Graduate, and later attended the Army War College. Interwar assignments included duty as a military attaché in Paris, France, service on the War Department General Staff, and promotion to major general and command of the 41st Infantry Division in December of 1941. He commanded the 41st Infantry Division throughout the New Guinea campaign.

General Fuller commanding, in addition to his duties as divisional commander, Hurricane Task Force, selected his 186th Infantry Regiment to make the initial assault. It was to land in column of battalions on the beaches near the village of Bosnek. The 2nd Battalion, supported by Company D, 641st Tank Destroyer Battalion and the 121st Field Artillery Battalion, would secure the beaches. The balance of the Task Force would then come ashore and exploit the beachhead. The attack was to be preceded by a heavy air and naval bombardment. The date of the attack was set for May 27th.

Initial operations went well. The air and naval shelling found their targets and received little Japanese fire in return. The 2nd

Lt. Gen. Robert L. Eichelberger confers with Col. Oliver P. Newman (center) of the 186th Infantry at Mokmer Airdrome.

Battalion formed up in boat waves and crossed the line of departure on schedule. Then nature took a hand in the form of a strong sea current which pushed both the transports and the landing craft well west of their intended path. Smoke and fire caused by the pre-invasion bombardment prevented the navy crews from seeing their objectives, with the result that the first assault waves landed nearly two miles west of their assigned beaches. Worse still, they faced a mangrove swamp which impeded progress inland and hampered vehicles. Confusion reigned on the beach for some time, until officers could sort out the units and determine their locations. The 3rd Battalion, 186th Infantry, came ashore to the east of the 2nd Battalion, but they were also well west of their assigned positions. Colonel Oliver P. Newman, commanding the 186th Infantry Regiment, asked permission of General Fuller to change missions with the 162nd Infantry Regiment, which was to have advanced west from the beachhead. Colonel Newman, a West Point graduate with the class of 1922 and commander of the 186th Infantry since March of 1942, felt that since his units were inadvertently where the 162nd Infantry was supposed to be in a few hours, they could exchange roles. General Fuller denied Colonel Newman's request, requiring considerable marching and counter-marching by the two infantry regiments. In effect, General Fuller's refusal to switch the missions of his two regiments required them to cross each other's line of march, causing additional confusion and delay.

Fortunately for the Americans, the Japanese did not take advantage of their confusion. The 2nd and 3rd Battalions, 186th Infantry, moved east, while following waves were landed correctly. This delay did not prove immediately decisive. It probably reinforced the impression held by the Americans that the Japanese were themselves disorganized. By mid-morning most of the 186th Infantry were in their planned positions for the dawn landing. By noon the regiment had secured the originally planned beachhead area. Supporting units now began to come ashore. Patrols sent into the interior of the island reported scattered Japanese resistance, including finding empty enemy defensive positions, but no organized enemy resistance.

The 162nd Infantry had landed without difficulty at the correct landing areas. The Task Force plan called for this regiment to secure the division's objectives, the Japanese airfields. This plan required the regiment to move west from the beachhead in column of battalions, overcome the Japanese and secure the field as soon as possible. If the Japanese attempted to flank the operation, then the 162nd Infantry would detach one battalion to guard its inland flank while advancing along the coast. The flank battalion was to seize the high ground behind the coastal track leading to the airfields. However, the lack of Japanese resistance caused the commanders in the 162nd to reconsider the plan and make adjustments. The regiment would advance in column of battalions, 3rd Battalion leading, followed by the 2nd. The 1st Battalion would bring up the rear, stringing out its companies to maintain a line of communication with the beachhead. Instead of the originally planned full battalion to cover the inland flank, only one company of the 2nd Battalion was detached to move into the ridges above the coastal road.

The 3rd Battalion, 162nd Infantry, moved west along the coast, preceded by the regimental Intelligence and Reconnaissance Platoon. The advance continued unopposed for nearly two hours, when the leading units discovered that at the village of Ibdi the coast road passed through a defile between the sea and coral cliffs which came to within one hundred yards of the sea. This narrow passage between sea and cliff continued for about two thousand yards before opening to a series of ridges and the village of Parai. This position, soon to erupt in flame, was marked on American maps as the Parai Defile.

Only a few Japanese were in evidence, but the nature of the terrain was such that tanks had to be called forward to offset the advantage the terrain gave the Japanese. Using tank fire from a platoon of the 603rd Tank Company and rocket fire from offshore LCI's the 162nd Infantry pushed its way through the Parai Defile after some four hours of combat.

The 2nd Battalion, following the 3rd down the road, had ordered its Company E into the hills above the road to provide flank protection. This unit quickly found that the jungle and general terrain features made keeping up with the main force next to impossible. Faced with difficult terrain and finding no Japanese on the regiment's flank, the company was recalled to the main body, arriving at the time the 2nd Battalion was passing through the Parai Defile. After the resistance at the Defile itself, the 162nd did not encounter any Japanese opposition, although Japanese were occasionally sighted in the distance. Nightfall was now approaching and the two battalions began to prepare positions for the night. The 1st Battalion settled for the night at Ibdi, east of the Defile. "Supporting the infantry were the 205th and 146th Field Artillery Battalions, the 121st Field Artillery of the 32nd Infantry Division, and the 947th Field Artillery Battalion, a Sixth Army battalion of 155mm Howitzers, which had been attached to the Task Force for this operation." The artillery was located with Division Headquarters near the village of Bosnek.

Enemy aircraft had been active in the general area, but no determined attack took place before nightfall. After dark four Japanese bombers with fighter escort flew over the beachhead. The planes approached from beyond the northern part of the American position, using the hills as a shield from the radar set up at the beach. They found an unusually lucrative target. Four LST's tied up at the beachhead were unable to maneuver to avoid a bombing attack. The Japanese attacked determinedly both the ships and the beaches stacked with supplies vital to the task force's success. In addition to bombing, each plane strafed the area. Remarkably, for all the effort expended by the Japanese aircrew, no ship was hit and personnel casualties were light. The bombs dropped on the beach failed to explode, while none aimed at the ships hit their targets.

The strafing attack was more successful, wounding two soldiers and killing one. All the bombers were shot down by anti-aircraft fire from both ships and beachhead defenses. One of the enemy bombers fell onto a small naval auxiliary, killing two sailors. Nine others were wounded. The auxiliary had to be towed away for repairs. Damage ashore to supplies and equipment was minor.

Unloading proceeded after the Japanese had been driven off. By the end of the daylight hours over 12,000 troops had been landed, twelve tanks and numerous other vehicles were ashore, and nearly all the supplies needed to maintain the Task Force's attack were on the beach at Bosnek. The 542nd Engineer Boat and Shore Regiment, reinforced by units of the 41st Infantry Division, had met all objectives for the day. Meanwhile the 116th Combat Engineer Battalion worked at the roads and bridges needed within the beachhead. Equally important, the engineers established water points within the beachhead. Water was known to be scarce on Biak, and the Task Force would need much of it just to satisfy its troops' and vehicles' normal needs. Heavy combat would require a lot more. General Fuller, reviewing the day's activities, had reason to be pleased. Despite serious initial confusion, the Hurricane Task Force had landed on an enemy held island, secured a beachhead, landed both follow up troops and supplies, and was close to securing the objectives of the operation. Losses were negligible, and enemy opposition appeared disorganized. Tomorrow looked like another easy day.

May 27th had been an unhappy day for Colonel Kuzume. He had been caught out of position by the landings, and the initial reaction of his troops had been less than expected. Positions which had been prepared for defense were unmanned, and in their few contacts with the enemy some of his troops had performed poorly, retreating as soon as they were fired upon. One platoon of the *2nd Company, 222nd Infantry* had committed suicide while the Americans were landing and the few survivors had fled into the jungle. Colonel Kuzume had not done well, nor had his *222nd Infantry Regiment*. Fortunately for the Japanese, the Chief of Staff of the *2nd Area Army* happened to be on Biak inspecting the defenses. This officer, Lieutenant General Takazo Numata, took command and ordered the defenses properly manned. One of his first actions was to order a counterattack by the *3rd Battalion, 222nd Infantry* which fell upon Batteries B and C of the 146th Field Artillery Battalion which had settled near Ibdi for the night. The attack was driven off by rifle and machine gun fire, but not before 5 Americans died and another nine were wounded. A small action, it did not reveal to the commanders of the 41st Infantry Division that things on Biak were about to change. That they would discover the following day.

Armor In The Pacific

An often overlooked aspect of the Pacific War was the use of armor by both sides. Initially, each side believed that the use of armor was impractical due to conditions of jungle and terrain. The Japanese did land and use tanks during their conquest of the Philippines, but they contributed little. The first successful use of armor by the Allies was by the Australians during the Buna Campaign. Looking for a way to save Australian lives while attacking entrenched enemy positions, they tried their light tanks. These proved highly successful and very frustrating to the enemy, who had no tanks. Complaints to Imperial Headquarters in Tokyo were too late to affect the Buna Campaign, but future campaigns did feature Japanese use of tanks.

The first tank versus tank battle of the Pacific War took place on Biak. Within days of the destruction of the 36th Infantry Division's Tank Company by the 603rd Tank Company another tank versus tank battle took place on Saipan, where the 2nd Marine Division was attacked by Japanese tanks while still struggling to secure its beachhead. Sherman tanks from the 2nd Marine Tank Battalion, a unit organic to the 2nd Marine Division, ended the attack but not before some bloody fighting took place. The largest tank

battle of the Pacific War took place on Luzon. Here the Sixth Army encountered the Japanese 2nd Armored Division. During a counterattack the bulk of the Japanese division's armor was destroyed by the 710th Tank Battalion, attached to Sixth Army. Some tanks from this unit continued to turn up in the Luzon Campaign until the end of the war, but the armored might had been destroyed by the American tank battalion and the infantry's attached anti-tank weapons.

The most common use of tanks in the Pacific by all Allied forces was in combination with infantry assault teams against entrenched Japanese defenses. So common was this procedure that it came to be regarded as essential for success in most American units. Nor was the tank inviolate because of its armor protection. The Japanese became adept at picking off the tank commanders, who had to keep their heads out of the tank to direct operations. Suicide attacks by Japanese soldiers carrying demolition charges destroyed many tanks and damaged many more. Mines, artillery and terrain also contributed to allied tank casualties. Like most other aspects of the Pacific War, the armored forces had a difficult job made even more difficult by a determined enemy.

CHAPTER V

Fight for the Airfields

*T*he first night ashore on Biak was a quiet one for most of the assault force. Only Companies B and I of the 186th Infantry reported harassment from Japanese patrols. With daylight, the 162nd Infantry moved forward, resuming its easy advance of the previous day. Supported by the 146th Field Artillery and the 603rd Tank Company, the regiment planned to seize Mokmer Village as a prelude to seizing the airfield nearby.

Just past the Parai Defile "the coral ridge and cliff turned sharply north just east of Mokmer Village and widened into a coastal plateau. A sharp coral cliff approximately twenty feet high ran diagonally across the coastal corridor, forming a terrace."

Here Japanese, now reorganized under Lieutenant General Numata's direction, began their defense of the airfields. As the 3rd Battalion, 162nd Infantry, moved forward it assigned Company L, reinforced with heavy machine guns and crews from Company M, to move along the high terrace. The rest of the battalion moved along the coastal road toward the airfields. At first Japanese resistance remained negligible, but as the Americans approached the airdrome, shortly after passing the village of Mokmer, the *2nd Battalion, 222nd Infantry Regiment* counterattacked heavily, using heavy mortar and machine gun supporting fires. American supporting artillery fire from the 146th Field Artillery Battalion failed to suppress the Japanese fire, and the 3rd Battalion, 162nd Infantry, withdrew some 600 yards to reorganize.

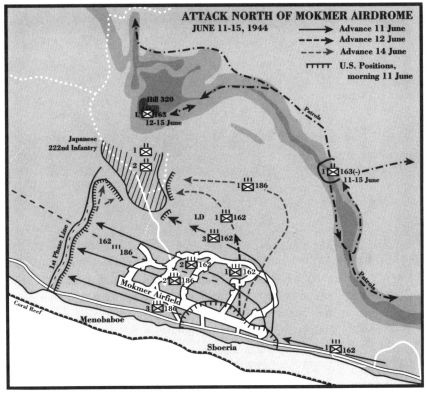

The Japanese of the *2nd Battalion, 222nd Infantry* did not let the Americans rest or regroup. Continuing their attacks and devastating supporting fires, the Japanese increased the pressure felt by the Americans. Committing more troops to the battle, the Japanese circled the 3rd Battalion and finally drove a wedge between it and the rest of the 162nd Infantry. Before noon on May 28th the 3rd Battalion was cut off from the rest of its Task Force and fighting to survive.

The 3rd Battalion found itself trapped in the plateau area some 500 by 200 yards in depth. The 2nd Battalion, which was to have supported the 3rd from the coral cliffs above, had been stopped earlier and was unable to move onto the cliffs from which most of the devastating enemy fire was coming. Nor could the 2nd Battalion advance along the coast, now that the Japanese had moved down from the cliffs and occupied positions between the two American units. American return fire and supporting fires were doing little to reduce Japanese fire, largely because "small secondary growth covered the area and was thick enough to prevent good observation from the ground but was open enough to allow excellent observation from above." In other words, the Japanese could easily observe the Americans, who could not see them.

The troops on the terrace, above the Japanese positions, Company L and part of Company M, quietly withdrew when the Japanese attacked. These two companies managed to skill-fully withdraw to the main battalion position along the coast road, but had lost one platoon which had been cut off but managed to fight its way to the 2nd Battalion's position, north of Mokmer Village. The arrival of the two companies did little to relieve the 3rd Battalion's situation. Company G of the 2nd Battalion had been attempting to get on the terrace as well, and had been briefly cut off before fighting its way back to the 2nd Battalion. Casualties had been heavy, and there was no immedi-ate prospect of any American unit gaining the top of the terrace, which would have given the Americans some advantage. All American units were now accounted for in one of three areas. The 3rd Battalion, less its lost platoon, was in defensive posture along the beach west of Mokmer Village. The 2nd Battalion was along the beach north of the village, and the 1st Battalion had begun to move to reinforce its sister battalions.

The Japanese could probably feel victory within their grasp. One American battalion was pinned down and surrounded. Another was under heavy attack and had withdrawn its leading units. Clearly the Americans were on the defensive. Twice the Japanese launched ground attacks against the 3rd Battalion, and twice they were repulsed. But these attacks were having their effect. "The cut-off 3rd Battalion was suffering heavy casualties and communication was difficult since all wire lines had been cut and all but one radio failed to function. The position of the 3rd battalion forward elements was untenable, and further advance was impossible until the enemy on the ridge and in the face of the cliff could be dislodged either by action from the north or by naval fire from the seaward side."

The U.S. Navy tried to help. A rocket carrying landing craft, LCI-34, moved in along the coast to contribute her rockets for support. Before she could fire, however, Japanese coast defense

119

guns, silent until now, opened an accurate fire and chased her away. Her supporting destroyers, the USS *Stockton* and *Reid*, moved in to destroy the enemy guns which had attacked the LCI-34. In the following exchange of fire *Reid* silenced the Japanese who had hit the *Stockton* just above the waterline, injuring one sailor and killing another. This gun was not destroyed, however, and would open fire again later that day when the Reid returned to provide supporting fire to the hard pressed infantry. *Reid* was obliged to withdraw. The ground troops would have to hold on by themselves for a while longer.

About mid-afternoon the Japanese made their major attack against the 3rd Battalion, this time employing tanks in the assault waves. Supported by the 3rd Platoon, 603rd Tank Company, and gunfire from the destroyers offshore, the tank attack was repulsed. The American tanks were slightly damaged in the exchange of fire, but none were lost. Japanese losses could not be determined. The spirited Japanese effort to destroy the 3rd Battalion, 162nd Infantry, had caused General Fuller to rush reinforcements forward. Only tanks could get past the curtain of fire between the 2nd and 3rd Battalions, so the 1st Platoon, 603rd Tank Company was sent forward in support. Supplies and ammunition, which had reached critical levels at 3rd Battalion, were increased using the small craft of the 542nd Engineer Boat and Shore Regiment. These played a cat and mouse game with the Japanese gunners, waiting for a chance to dash in to shore, dump supplies, load critically wounded, and escape. While all this was going on the Naval Gunfire Officer attached to the 162nd Infantry was killed and naval fire support ceased for the rest of the day. By late afternoon General Fuller had no choice but to order the 3rd Battalion to withdraw to the positions held by the 2nd Battalion.

It took nearly an hour for General Fuller's withdrawal order to reach the 3rd Battalion, so bad were communications at this point. Using tanks as an advance and rear guard force, the 3rd Battalion moved out along the coast road. Moving in small groups to make smaller targets for enemy gunners, the men of the 3rd Battalion moved towards their comrades in the 2nd Battalion. Some of the troops used the waterline as their withdrawal route, hoping to further avoid Japanese fire. Within two hours all elements of the 3rd Battalion had reached the safety of the 2nd Battalion's perimeter. Nearly one hundred men had been wounded and sixteen known killed in the day's fighting. Worse yet, there was no indication that tomorrow would be any better.

While the day had been a disaster for the Americans, the Japanese seemed to get their fighting spirit back. Encouraged by the successful day's action, the Japanese command moved the *1st Battalion, 222nd Infantry* forward, to an area known as the West Caves. *Biak Detachment Headquarters* also moved into this area. This force would be the reserve while the *2nd* and *3rd Battalions, 222nd Infantry* continued to repulse the American attacks. Early on the morning of May 29th the Japanese renewed their attack. This time their effort was directed at the 2nd Battalion, 162nd Infantry. This unit, supported by the 2nd Platoon, 603rd Tank Company, was in defensive positions along the coast road half a mile east of Mokmer Village. The first attack was a joint effort by the *2nd* and *3rd Battalions, 222nd Infantry*, which was thrown back by the Americans. One hour later these Japanese troops came back, this time with tanks from the *36th Division Tank Company*. The first tank versus tank battle of the Southwest Pacific campaign was about to occur.

The Japanese tanks were light by American standards. Known as the Model 95, they were first manufactured in 1935, weighed about nine tons, and carried a crew of three men. They were armed with one 37mm cannon and two 7.7mm machine guns. While they could be quite effective against infantry who did not have their own armor or artillery support, they were no match for the standard American battle tank of the war, the M4A1 Sherman Medium Tank. This tank carried as its main armament a 75mm cannon and two heavy machine guns. Both in weight and depth of armor it was superior to the Japanese Tank. Results of the battle were predictable. The Japanese infantry, supported by their tanks, advanced. The infantry was shattered by the combined weapons of the 2nd Battalion, 162nd Infantry, while each Japanese tank was destroyed in turn by the Sherman tanks of the 603rd Tank Company. Hits on the Shermans by the Japanese tanks had little effect, while the American tankers' biggest problem was the need to fire two rounds to

Japanese tanks made a rare appearance during the Biak fighting.

destroy one enemy tank, since the first invariably went through the enemy tank without exploding, so light was its armor. A second round was necessary to ensure destruction of each Japanese tank.

But the Japanese remained determined. A second wave of tanks and infantry assaulted the American perimeter. This time the Japanese managed to get one effective hit on an American tank, temporarily preventing it from traversing its turret cannon. Despite this modest success, the attack ended as had the first. The Japanese withdrew. They had accepted the fact that a frontal attack on an American defensive perimeter which had armor support was impractical. A new strategy was needed.

Having failed to destroy the American positions by direct assault with tanks and infantry, the Japanese changed their tactics and began to encircle the positions of the 2nd and 3rd Battalions. By midday the Japanese had moved completely around the two units, again cutting the coast road linking them with the rest of Hurricane Task Force. The Japanese established a roadblock at Parai. The 1st Battalion, 162nd Infantry, dispatched the regimental cannon company and Company B to open the road, which they did after a successful counterattack. Clearly, the resources of the 162nd Infantry were now insufficient to accomplish its mission, given the renewed vigor of the Japanese defense. Colonel Harold Haney, a native of Brazil, Indiana who had enlisted in the army in 1914 and three years later received a direct commission as a second lieutenant of infantry, commanded the 162nd Infantry Regiment. He asked for permission to withdraw his regiment to Ibdi for rest and reorganization. He hoped to be able to plan a new approach to the airfields while reorganizing. General Fuller granted permission for the withdrawal. Shortly after the 1st Battalion broke the Japanese roadblock, orders were given to begin the withdrawal and join the 186th Infantry near Ibdi.

The 1st Battalion, holding secure positions near Parai, was to cover the withdrawal, while the remainder of the combat team passed through their lines to safety. The withdrawal was to be along the coast and by sea using the amphibian craft of the same 542nd Engineer Boat and Shore Regiment that had done such a superb job of keeping the surrounded units supplied. After nearly three hours preparing the withdrawal, it began. The majority of the 2nd Battalion moved by water to Bosnek while the 3rd Battalion moved overland, supported by the tanks of the 603rd Tank Company. A platoon of Company D, 641st Tank Destroyer Battalion, attached to the combat team, remained behind to cover the withdrawal with heavy mortar fire. Once the infantry had departed safely, the Tank Destroyer men disabled their weapons and left with the last tanks. As a final measure to ensure a safe withdrawal, Company D of the 542nd Engineer Boat and Shore Regiment went ashore armed with rifles and machine guns and defended the Parai Defile while the infantry passed safely under their guns. Then they joined the rear guard of tanks and mortarmen. By nightfall the entire 162nd Infantry Regimental Combat Team was safely back at Ibdi, Mandom and Bosnek. It had lost 16 killed, 96 wounded and had 3 non-battle casualties. More importantly, it had lost the initiative to the Japanese who followed the regiment to Parai and dug in along the cliffs overlooking the road.

It had become clear to General Fuller even before May 29th that his force was inadequate to accomplish its assigned missions. With only two regiments available he could not secure the island of Biak against the enemy forces known to be defending it. He was also concerned about the enemy armor. Although he knew that American tanks were superior, he did not know how much armor the enemy had available. General Fuller contacted General Krueger at Sixth Army headquarters, explained his concerns, and requested additional infantry and armor support.

The immediate result of this request was the recall of the 41st Division's third regiment, the 163rd Infantry, from Wakde-Sarmi to its parent division. General Krueger also alerted the Southwest Pacific's reserve force, the 503rd Parachute Infantry Regiment, for a possible rush airborne reinforcement operation to Biak. He then ordered the advancement of the scheduled movement of the 6th Infantry Division to Wakde-Sarmi in order to free forces which could be used to reinforce the attack on Biak.

While awaiting his reinforcements General Fuller established his defensive positions. The 162nd Infantry was established in a semi-circle perimeter around the village of Ibdi, with its back to the sea. The 1st Battalion, 186th Infantry, protected Task Force headquarters in a perimeter at the village of Mandom. The 3rd Battalion, 186th Infantry, moved into defensive positions in the ridges above the village of Bosnek, to protect the main beachhead. The 2nd Battalion of the 186th, reinforced with part of the 3rd Battalion, remained at Bosnek as Task Force Reserve. General Fuller planned that when the 163rd Infantry arrived, the 186th Infantry would become his assault force while the 163rd assumed responsibility for the beachhead defenses. Meanwhile both units on Biak would patrol extensively to discover what they would be facing when they returned to the attack. Harassment on the ground in the form of Japanese patrols and in the air by daily hit and run bombing attacks continued.

"The 162nd patrols found that what was thought to be a single ridge was actually a series of seven sharp coral ridges, which apparently had been caused by an upheaval in the earth's surface. this entire ridge arrangement was honeycombed with small caves, holes, and crevices and, though there was practically no soil covering the coral, the area was covered with a dense growth of rain forest. Two native tracks crossed the ridges just east of Ibdi, but the enemy had strong positions blocking both trails." When the 163rd Infantry began to arrive on June 1st, the reorganization planned by General Fuller was put into effect. In learning about its future battleground the 162nd Infantry had lost an additional 6 killed, 17 wounded and had 3 non-battle casualties in skirmishes with the enemy.

While the 162nd Infantry was patrolling around Ibdi, the

186th Infantry had been doing the same around Bosnek. Little in the way of Japanese opposition was found and the 186th Infantry patrols moved as far as Opiaref, some four miles from the beachhead, without difficulty. But when patrols from this regiment went to assist in the patrolling of the Ibdi-Mandom area, they too were heavily opposed by the Japanese. Clearly, the main enemy force lay in front of the 162nd Infantry, and between the 41st Infantry Division and its main objectives on Biak.

During this period when the Americans were reorganizing themselves to resume their attack, the Japanese were doing the same. The entire *3rd Battalion, 222nd Infantry*, still some 800 men strong, moved into the Ibdi area and prepared it for defense. They were the reason for the losses suffered by the American patrols in this area. The *2nd Battalion, 222nd Infantry*, was withdrawn to rest and reorganize. Colonel Kuzume moved the *1st Battalion, 222nd Infantry*, forward to replace them. Naval troops and the *Mortar Company, 2nd Battalion, 222nd Infantry*, moved into the defensive positions north of Mokmer Airfield. By the time of the 163rd Infantry's arrival on Biak, the Japanese had made their adjustments and were ready to receive the renewed American attack.

The June 1st arrival of the 163rd Infantry on Biak permitted the Task Force to resume its attack. This was made more urgent by the order from General Krueger to General Fuller that he was expected to regain the initiative and quickly secure his objectives. The airfields, the purpose of the entire operation, were still not in American hands, and the Central Pacific operations were quickly arriving at a climax at which the air support promised by General MacArthur would be expected. That air support was supposed to come from the Biak airfields.

General Fuller structured his attack along the lines of the original assault, except that he would now use regiments where earlier he had used battalions. The 162nd Infantry would move along the coastal road to the airfields. The 186th Infantry would move into the hills and ridges above the coastal plateau and also direct its advance on the airfields, supporting the 162nd Infantry. The 163rd Infantry would secure the rear areas, including protecting the beachhead and headquarters areas. Every available supporting unit was included in this plan, including tanks, artillery and naval gunfire. The initial moves began early on June 1st.

The 3rd and 2nd Battalions, 186th Infantry, moved to the surveyed airstrip near Bosnek Village, where they established defensive positions. Engineers of Company B, 116th Combat Engineer Battalion, worked to prepare a motor road from the beach to the strip and by midafternoon had succeeded to the extent that military vehicles could travel to the Bosnek area. The Japanese, observing this activity, attacked. Men of the *1st Battalion, 222nd Infantry* attacked Company K, 186th Infantry defending the engineers near the proposed airstrip. Using mortars and machine guns, the Japanese attacked throughout the afternoon until repulsed by a flanking movement made by Company K. This action caused the reinforcement of Company K with Companies I and L and elements of the regimental antitank company. The Japanese withdrew, but returned under cover of darkness heavily reinforced and attacked the defensive positions of the 3rd Battalion. Again the attackers were from the *1st Battalion, 222nd Infantry*. Four hours of confused hand-to-hand fighting resulted in heavy casualties to the Japanese, including the battalion commander, while American losses were light. Worse yet for the Japanese, the American attack was not delayed, and the 1st and 3rd Battalions, 186th Infantry, moved towards the Japanese positions on the morning of June 2nd.

Both the 186th and 162nd Infantry Regiments attacked on that morning. For the 186th the advance was a series of skirmishes with small parties of Japanese, armed with rifles and machine guns, which hindered but did not stop the advance. The 162nd, on the other hand, fought terrain as much as it did the Japanese. Movement into the coral ridges was time consuming, and the need to clear each ridge of Japanese slowed the advance even more. By darkness of June 1st the regiment had secured only three ridges and had outposted a fourth. The attack of June 2nd made better progress and all seven ridges had been taken by mid-afternoon, although many Japanese positions had been bypassed in order to continue the advance. Contact was made between the two attacking regiments at this time, one of the objectives for the day's attack.

41st Division troops and a Sherman tank on a ridge north of Mok-mer Airdrome.

June 3rd was a better day for the 186th Infantry. Japanese resistance was especially light, but supply problems became acute. Water, an essential commodity in combat conditions, especially in the tropic conditions found on Biak, was nowhere to be found in the hills despite every effort by the 116th Engineers. The supply road, following behind the advancing infantry, could not keep pace, and so most supplies including water had to be hand carried at some point. On June 3rd the 2nd Battalion, 186th, was assigned to help the 41st Division Quartermaster Company and the engineers bring supplies forward to the infantry. Even this was not enough and "Troops caught rain water in ponchos and, in many cases, this prevented heat exhaustion." Nevertheless, the infantry appreciated the absence of the enemy and the advance continued.

While this movement was continuing on the mainland, Company A of the 163rd was making progress offshore. On June 2nd this unit had been assigned the mission of securing the offshore Padaido Islands, which lay close enough to Biak to be a threat if occupied by enemy units. First landing on Owi Island, and then on Woendi, the Americans found no enemy present. These islands were found to be suitable for airstrips and supply bases, and Army Air Corps troops moved ashore to begin development of the islands.

June 4th began with General Fuller ordering Colonel Newman to push his battalions forward over the main ridge and on to Mokmer Airfield. Colonel Newman objected, citing terrain and enemy opposition problems. While this discussion was going on, General Fuller received word from Sixth Army headquarters of a major enemy reinforcement attempt from the sea. All action beyond resupply was suspended pending the outcome of the expected attack from the sea. The day was spent waiting and patrolling. The 41st Infantry Division looked over its collective shoulders to see what the outcome at sea would be before making any deeper commitment to the attack in progress. For the next 24 hours, the Hurricane Task Force would feel itself surrounded, by the *222nd Infantry* to its front and the *Imperial Japanese Navy* to its rear.

The Intelligence Question

When the United States entered the Second World War it entered that war with a major advantage over its opponents. In the European Theater its ally, Great Britain, had developed a system to read the enemy's codes. Using what was termed the "Enigma," a codebreaking machine which was provided to Great Britain by her ally, Poland, Britain gave the Western Powers access to much of Germany's highest priority coded signals. Great Britain, and her allies, kept this secret for thirty years after the war, so important was it considered by their intelligence services. Not only was it a secret from all outsiders, very few insiders knew of its existence. Only Army commanders and higher could see the decoded signals from the enemy they fought, and even they could not copy anything down. A special intelligence officer was stationed at each headquarters and his sole duty was to safeguard what came to be called the "Ultra Intelligence."

In the Pacific, naval code breakers had actually broken the Japanese codes before Pearl Harbor. The situation in the Pacific was different from Europe. Here there was no one codebreaking machine doing the work. The Japanese codes were broken manually, using primitive computer equipment and large amounts of manpower. Another problem for Pacific commanders was that the Japanese changed their codes at regular intervals, as a security measure. Each time the enemy changed the code, the Americans had to break it again. This often caused gaps during times between the code being changed and the time it took to break it.

The most classic case of codebreaking in the Pacific would result in the decisive battle of Midway, in June 1942. The Americans had broken the Japanese Naval code, and could tell that the Japanese were planning another attack somewhere in the Pacific. The problem was that the Japanese kept referring to their objective by a code name. Admiral Nimitz was approached by his intelligence officers and asked to send an official message from Midway, which the intelligence department believed was the enemy's objective, to Pearl Harbor claiming that Midway's supply of fresh water was running low due to faulty equipment. Admiral Nimitz made the arrangements for the false message, and shortly afterwards his intelligence officers were delighted to read a decoded message from the Japanese that their objective was short of fresh water. Such successes were also largely responsible for the successful interceptions by American submarines of enemy forces on the high seas, and may have contributed to the success of the U.S.S. *England* in her successful destruction of the Japanese scouting line of submarines off the coast of New Guinea in 1944.

One theater in the Pacific which seemed to have problems with handling this intelligence coup was General MacArthur's Southwest Pacific headquarters. Reading the enemy's "mail" had shown General MacArthur the enemy's complete disposition of his forces in an intercept dated March 28th, 1944. From this General MacArthur deduced that his most profitable target, and the one with the least opposition, would be Hollandia. One month later his forces landed there. The intelligence proved precise, in fact more so than had been believed before the operation was launched. The small garrison and low supply levels were fully borne out by the landing. Nevertheless, the intelligence officer for Southwest Pacific Headquarters, Major General Charles A. Willoughby, greatly overestimated the number of enemy troops defending Hollandia, and so two reinforced infantry divisions were committed to the assault. As we have seen, the opposition was handled by less than one regiment of the 24th Infantry Division. Terrain was more of a problem than the reported strong enemy garrison.

Another problem arose over Hollandia resulting from a lack of sharing of the available intelligence information. Hollandia was the only one of General MacArthur's operations in Western New Guinea in which main force U.S. Navy units were to take part. The U.S. Navy jealously guarded its aircraft carriers, fully conscious of the fact that the Japanese Imperial Navy was still a formidable opponent. Rear Admiral Marc A. Mitscher commanded the Fast Carrier Task Force, loaned to General MacArthur for Hollandia. So tight was Southwest Pacific Headquarters with their intelligence information that Admiral Mitscher had to risk the life of his Chief Of Staff, Captain Arleigh Burke, in a flight over Hollandia shortly after the landing to determine for himself how much opposition Sixth Army was facing at

Hollandia. He found no Japanese ground forces, but he did nearly get killed when his plane was hit by one burst of antiaircraft fire and had to crash land on the deck of his aircraft carrier.

The success at Hollandia, despite the difficulties in making the intelligence more useful, did result in cutting off General Adachi's *18th Army*. Ultra continued to provide Southwest Pacific headquarters with intelligence on General Adachi's strength and intentions. One of these intercepts which was dated June 25th said without disguise that an all out attack by *18th Army* on Aitape was to begin on July 10th. So detailed was this intercept that it gave the locations of the command posts of the Army and its divisions. With this knowledge, it is difficult to understand the continued reluctance of General Krueger to believe in the coming attack. Certainly his subordinate commanders, Generals Gill and Martin, believed the attack was coming. Yet another puzzling aspect is the lack of insistence by General MacArthur or General Willoughby to General Krueger to make at least preparations for the possibility of such an attack.

Certainly there were problems with the intelligence. While General Adachi was bent on attacking Aitape, he had not been ordered to do so by his superiors. They had ordered him to bypass Aitape on his way further west. They then promptly wrote off the *18th Army*, and continued to assume that General Adachi was doing as he had been ordered. Their signals to him, based upon that assumption, confused the issue for intelligence interpreters. Another factor making things difficult was the need to disguise the source of the intelligence, in the event the enemy captured documents or otherwise learned of the Americans' advance knowledge of their intentions. Southwest Pacific used the disguise of referring to the information as being obtained from prisoner interrogations. When one remembers how accurate General Patrick's prisoner had proved to be on Noemfoor, it is not surprising that less than full credence was placed in this information by some officers. General Willoughby would later claim that his lack of belief in the coming attack was based also on Ultra, but he concentrated on the Japanese supply problems, which

General Willoughby believed would prevent them from carrying out the attack, whatever they intended to do.

Ultra even today has yet to be fully appreciated. Clearly in the Southwest Pacific Theater it was instrumental in giving General MacArthur the information he needed to make his celebrated "hops" between major Japanese forces. Yet it had its limitations as well, especially when not correctly interpreted, as at Biak and Aitape. Without it, the battles for places like New Guinea would have been much more difficult, if not impossible.

CHAPTER VI

Sea Chases

While the fighting on Biak continued, the *Imperial Japanese Navy* was in a desperate quandary. The Japanese High Command was certain that the pressing need at this time was for the long-sought "decisive battle" which would decide the fate of the Pacific War. The Japanese had been seeking this battle since 1942, when they had decided that they had achieved all their goals in the Pacific, and that now they had to create conditions which would result in a negotiated peace with the Allies, particularly the United States. That had been the purpose behind the battle of Midway in June of 1942. That battle, however, had gone decisively against the Japanese and, if anything, had strengthened the resolve of the United States to continue the war to a successful conclusion.

Since Midway the Japanese had sought another decisive battle, one that they could win. Guadalcanal had proved another disappointment. Now, with Allied forces moving closer to the Japanese homeland, the pressure for the decisive battle was greater than ever before. But there were problems within the Japanese High Command as to where and when this battle should take place. In order to prepare for the decisive battle, the Japanese needed to know with certainty where and when the Americans would attack in order to allow them time to assemble their forces for the battle. However, opinion was divided between the Japanese as to where the next allied attack would occur, and whether the Central Pacific or the Southwest Pacific drives were the main enemy effort. The Japanese Army did not favor a strong defense of Biak, but the Japanese Navy did favor a confrontation.

The first reaction the Japanese had was to send air reinforcements to New Guinea. The *23rd Air Flotilla* was ordered on May 28th to fly 50 fighter planes from Japan to the Philippines. An additional 20 fighters and 20 bombers were transferred to New Guinea from the Marianas. Later, 48 fighters, 20 bombers and 8 reconnaissance planes were brought in from the Caroline Islands.

Japanese submarines were sent into the area in strength to warn of Allied Task Forces and to harass attempts to advance along the New Guinea coast. This effort availed the *Japanese Navy* little in the way of positive information, since Allied antisubmarine measures by this stage of the war were honed to such a fine degree that not one of the eight submarines accomplished anything of importance. This attempt to aid the defenders of New Guinea was costly, as well. Unfortunately for the *Imperial Japanese Navy*, these submarines ran into the champion submarine killer of the war, the U.S.S. *England*. Recently commissioned, in December of 1943, the destroyer escort U.S.S. *England* was one of a new class of warships created expressly to address the submarine menace of the Axis powers. Basically a small destroyer with less firepower but additional antisubmarine equipment, it was serving in all theaters of war by 1944.

Under the command of Lieutenant Commander Walton B. Pendleton, the U.S.S. *England* was on her first combat assignment off the New Guinea coast. Allied intelligence had learned, from reading broken enemy naval codes, that the Japanese were sending several submarines into the area. Accompanied by destroyer escorts U.S.S. *George* (Lieutenant Commander Fred W. Just, USNR) and U.S.S. *Raby* (Lieutenant Commander James Scott, II) the *England* was ordered to investigate.

Proceeding to the reported estimated position of the enemy, the three destroyer escorts sailed along in a scouting formation. There was little excitement expected, for at this stage of the war the Japanese submarine menace was too often discounted by many U.S. Navy officers. Suddenly, on May 19th, *England* made contact with an underwater object. Identified as an enemy submarine, Commander Pendleton attacked. Five runs over the submarine destroyed the *Imperial Japanese Navy*'s submarine *I-16*. Continuing to proceed as ordered, the group was next alerted by a radar contact from the USS *George*. Attacking at once, the USS *George* forced the *RO-106* to dive beneath the sea. Commander Just made the first attack but missed. *England* made the next two attacks and sank the submarine. The next day, May 23rd, *Raby* made first contact, all three American ships attacked, and *England* killed *RO-104*. The following day the *England* contacted and sunk unaided *RO-116*. Again, on May 26th, *Raby* contacted and *England* sank *RO-108*.

Five confirmed kills in seven days was certainly unique. But the U.S.S. *England* was not quite finished. After refueling and taking on more antisubmarine ammunition, *England*, *George* and *Raby* reinforced by an escort carrier with additional destroyers and destroyer escorts returned to the open sea. Once again contact was made with a submarine, this time by destroyer U.S.S. *Hazelwood* (Commander V. P. Douw) which attacked immediately. *Raby* and *George* attacked as well. The three ships spent the night alternately tracking and attacking the enemy submarine. The following day, warned by intelligence of a possible air attack, *England* and the U.S.S. *Spangler* (Lieutenant Commander D. J. McFarlane, USNR) were ordered to attack. *Spangler* missed. *England* didn't. The sixth enemy submarine, *RO-105*, was destroyed.

The Japanese Navy's first attempt to influence the battle for Western New Guinea had ended disastrously. Six of eight submarines sent to intercept the Allied naval force had fallen to one American destroyer escort supported by two others. The surviving two enemy submarines, *RO-108* and *RO-109*, warned by Japanese Naval Headquarters of the disaster overtaking their comrades, quickly left the area around New Guinea. Another submarine, not a part of the scouting group, was seriously damaged by air attacks. The *I-44* managed to return to its base.

The *England* and her accomplices had done more than merely destroy six enemy submarines. They had greatly added to the confusion running rampant in the headquarters of the *Imperial Japanese Navy*. It appeared obvious to them that there must be a great enemy naval force off the coast of New Guinea destroying

U.S.S. **Nashville** *(CL-43) standing off the beaches at Biak to cover the landing of U.S. troops. Her observation plane is about to fly over Biak. (U.S. Navy)*

their submarines. The only purpose of such a force would be for another invasion along the New Guinea coast. And as always in major invasions, the supporting forces must contain the main force vessels of the United States Navy. Those who argued that the main effort would come in the Central Pacific had nothing to point to for proof. The *Combined Fleet* staff had prepared a detailed plan for the relief of Biak. This plan, called "Operation Kon" called for 2,500 troops of the *2nd Amphibious Brigade* to be transported from Mindanao to Biak supported by major surface units of the fleet. Since transport was scarce for the Japanese at this stage of the war, the troops would be transported on the same warships expected to protect their movement to Biak. The force was commanded by Rear Admiral Naomasa Sakonju from his flagship, the heavy cruiser *Aoba*. light cruiser *Kinu*, destroyers *Shikinami, Uranami* and *Shigure* would carry the troops while screened by the battleship *Fuso*, heavy cruisers *Myoko* and

Haguro with five additional destroyers. Air cover was to be provided by the newly reinforced *23rd Air Flotilla*. Additional troops were to be sent to Biak by barge from Manokwari.

Operation Kon began with the air attack of June 2nd on the Biak beaches. The attack was unopposed because of a weather front which kept the Allied aircraft at Wakde and Hollandia grounded. Despite these ideal conditions, the enemy pilots only managed to damage one LCT while losing twelve of their planes to American antiaircraft gunners. There were no Allied personnel casualties.

Late on May 31st the transport unit embarked most of the *2nd Amphibious Brigade* at Zamboanga in the Philippines. The balance of the soldiers, about 800 troops and their equipment, were embarked at the same time in minelayers *Itsukushima* and *Tsugaru*. The only true transport in the force, *Transport Number 127*, also took aboard troops and sailed with the minelayers. The transport and covering forces sailed separately for Biak. After a few hours at sea the transport unit saw a periscope and heard what was interpreted as an Allied submarine sending a contact report to its headquarters. This was the U.S. submarine *Ray*, under the command of Lieutenant Commander Brooks Harral. This episode alarmed the Japanese, who had hoped to get much closer to the objective before being discovered. Actually, they had been shadowed by U.S. submarines *Gunard* (Lieutenant Commander Herbert Andrews), *Bluefish* (Lieutenant Commander Charles Henderson) and *Cabrilla* (Lieutenant Commander William Thompson) since they had left Tawi Tawi on the night of May 30th. None of the U.S. submarines had been able to get close enough to launch an attack, and only *Ray* properly identified the ships, although all sent off contact reports.

Admiral Sakonju was unhappy about being observed, and immediately after the submarine sighting he received additional disturbing news from headquarters. It was believed that the Allied forces covering Biak included an aircraft carrier. This report may have originated from the Allied attack on Surabaya in which U.S. and British aircraft carriers took part. In any event, this additional bit of news was enough to make Admiral Toyoda, commander of the *Combined Fleet*, order the operation

U.S.S. **Gurnard** *(SS-264) underway. She later alerted Allied naval forces to the coming attack of "Kon Force." (U.S. Navy)*

postponed. Admiral Sakonju ordered the ships back to Tawi Tawi and Davao, where destroyer *Kazagumo* was sunk by U.S. submarine *Hake* (Lieutenant Commander Chester Nimitz, Jr.). American submarines harassed the ships at Davao for the next few days, but no more sinkings resulted.

At the time that *Kon Force* withdrew before what it believed to be superior enemy forces, the Allied forces at sea around Biak consisted of only U.S. destroyers *Reid, Mustin* and *Russell.* Covering the landings at a distance were Allied cruisers H.M.A.S. *Australia,* U.S.S. *Phoenix, Boise* and *Nashville* with twelve American and two Australian destroyers in escort. This force, under the command of Rear Admiral V. A. C. Crutchley, Royal Navy, was roughly equal to the force which withdrew before it because of poor intelligence evaluation.

The *23rd Air Flotilla* continued to attack Biak whenever weather permitted and the Japanese apparently felt that this activity was softening up the naval opposition. In addition, returning pilots of the *23rd Air Flotilla* reported no enemy aircraft carrier near Biak. With this information, *Combined Fleet* ordered a new reinforcement attempt for Biak.

The second attempt at getting troops to Biak was scheduled for June 8th and 9th. This time destroyers *Shikinami*, *Uranami* and *Shigure* would carry 600 troops escorted by destroyers *Harusame*, *Shiratsuyu* and *Samidare*. Each escorting destroyer would also be towing a barge of troops, which inhibited its fighting ability. These were experienced ships and crews, however, and the Japanese still believed themselves better sailors than their enemies. The *Shigure*, for example, had fought from the first days of the war, and had survived the murderous battles of the Solomon Islands campaign without a scratch. Grouped together with *Shiratsuyu* and *Samidare* for most of those difficult days, *Shigure* had acquired a reputation as an unsinkable ship due to the skill of her captain, Captain Tameichi Hara, and her crew. Captain Hara was back in Japan preparing to assume command of a light cruiser, but the crews of all the ships had been with them for years of heavy combat. Rear Admiral Sakonju, still in command and sailing in the destroyer *Shikinami*, had reason to expect success. Cruisers *Aoba* and *Kinu* were standing by at a distance. Air cover remained the responsibility of the *23rd Air Flotilla*. This force left for Biak at midnight, June 7th.

For once American submarines did not sight the Japanese sortie. Nevertheless, they made their presence known. One who especially struck heavy blows was the U.S.S. *Harder*, under the command of Lieutenant Commander Samuel David Dealey. *Harder* was on her fifth war patrol when she was ordered on some special missions. The first required her to pick up Allied guerrillas on Borneo. Their route to Borneo passed Tawi Tawi where they encountered one of the many convoys which supplied the Japanese fleet units there. Dealey attacked and found himself attacked in turn by an enemy destroyer. Usual procedure was for American submarines to avoid combat with their traditional enemy, the destroyer. Commander Dealey, armed with a new directive placing enemy destroyers high on the target priority list, decided to stand and fight. Waiting with remarkable coolness, *Harder* fired three torpedoes at only 1,000 yards range and blew destroyer *Minatsuki* out of the water.

U.S.S. **Hake** *(SS-256), which later sank one of the "Kon Force's" ships, at her launching on July 17, 1942. (U.S. Navy)*

Dealey returned to the enemy convoy, but he could not get an opportunity to attack. Returning to his mission, he set course for Borneo. However, on the morning of June 7th another destroyer crossed his path. Dealey attacked, this time waiting until the enemy had closed to within 700 yards before firing. Three torpedoes sank the *Imperial Navy's* destroyer *Hayanami*. The Harder didn't escape unscathed this time, however. A sister ship of the *Hayanami* attacked with depth charges for the next two hours. When Commander Dealey came up to periscope depth for a look around, he found more enemy destroyers arriving on the scene. Believing discretion the better part of valor, the *Harder* discretely withdrew and headed once again for Borneo.

The *Harder* successfully picked up its passengers at Borneo and then returned to Tawi Tawi to observe enemy movements, another of its assigned missions. On June 9th another Japanese destroyer crossed *Harder's* path, and down went the I.J.N. *Tanikaze*. The same fight seriously damaged another enemy destroyer. Later in this patrol Commander Dealey attacked and believed he had destroyed another enemy destroyer, but post-war records failed to confirm this sinking. In recognition of this incredible cruise, Commander Dealey was awarded the Medal of Honor, while the crew of the *Harder* received a Presidential Unit Citation. Tragically, the *Harder* and Commander Dealey failed to return from their sixth war patrol.

The second reinforcement attempt also contributed to the attrition of the Japanese fleet. Alerted again by Allied intelligence, Fifth Army Air Force sent additional planes forward to the Wakde airfields in preparation to repel the incoming attack. These planes did not get into the action, however, for the 63rd Bombardment Squadron reportedly attacked the force and sank a transport. Fifth Army Air Force relaxed its alert status for the time being. During the night of June 5/6, the Japanese made a heavy air raid on the allied airfields on Wakde, damaging a considerable number of aircraft. Then came word that the Japanese second attempt was still in progress. The only available aircraft, ten B-25 Bombers of the 17th Reconnaissance Squadron and an escort of P-38's found and attacked the enemy reinforcement force on June 8th. Identifying the ships as two cruisers and four destroyers, the attack was unusually successful and *Harusame* went under while *Shiratsuyu*, *Shikinami* and *Samidare* were damaged. The attack was costly to the Americans, however, with three crews including that of the squadron commander, Major William G. Tennille, Jr., shot into the water. The remaining B-25's were so badly damaged that the squadron was temporarily withdrawn from combat.

Rear Admiral Sakonju was not to be easily deterred. Pausing to recover survivors of *Harusame*, the reinforcement force then continued on to Biak. The next eight hours were uneventful and then came a report from a scout of the *23rd Air Flotilla* that an enemy task force had been sighted. The report included the information that this task force was headed at high speed towards the Japanese. Still, perhaps influenced by past false reports of enemy forces around Biak, Admiral Sakonju continued towards Biak. Withdrawing a second time without contacting an actual enemy was unthinkable.

Just before midnight on June 8th Admiral Sakonju received the word he had hoped to avoid. One of his own destroyers reported sighting an enemy force. Now the Japanese had little choice but to withdraw. Admiral Sakonju ordered a reversal of

U.S.S. Fletcher *(DD-445) underway at sea. She led the pursuit of the "Kon Force" off Biak, June 1944. (U.S. Navy)*

course and his force cast off the towed barges to enable them to run for safety.

The task force sighted first by the Japanese scout plane and then by the destroyer was Rear Admiral Crutchley's force which now consisted of the heavy cruiser H.M.A.S. *Australia*, light cruisers U.S.S. *Phoenix* and *Boise*, with 14 allied destroyers. Admiral Crutchley knew that the Japanese were in the vicinity from intelligence reports. He also knew that his own force had been sighted by enemy scout planes. His task force had spent the preceding hours searching for the Japanese, determined to prevent reinforcements from landing on Biak. It wasn't until two hours before midnight that Navy scout planes reported the size and course of the Japanese to Admiral Crutchley. He immediately set an interception course which resulted in the two forces meeting shortly before midnight.

Admiral Crutchley was aware that he outnumbered the enemy force and he immediately set out in pursuit of the retreating Japanese. Admiral Crutchley's leading destroyers, Destroyer Division 42 under the command of Commander Albert E. Jarrell, U.S.N. immediately went in to attack. Commander Jarrell noticed that the Japanese ships appeared to have made a turn and correctly interpreted this as a sign that they had launched torpedoes at the Americans. Commander Jarrell's warning to the ships of the task force prevented any Allied losses. Admiral Crutchley, deciding that his cruisers would only hinder the pursuit, and knowing his destroyers could handle the enemy destroyers, pulled his cruisers out of the pursuit. He sent his entire escorting force, twelve American and two Australian destroyers, after the Japanese. The three cruisers followed at a distance in case more enemy ships appeared.

The Japanese ships had a long lead and the Allied ships struggled to get within range. As time passed it became clear to Admiral Crutchley that only the leading eight American destroyers had a chance of catching the enemy. Accordingly, he ordered the destroyers H.M.A.S. *Arunta* (Commander A. E. Buchanan, R.A.N.) and H.M.A.S. *Warramunga* (Commander N. A. MacKinnon, R.A.N.) to find and sink the enemy barges. The remaining four U.S. destroyers would return to screen the cruisers.

After nearly two hours of chasing, destroyer *Fletcher* (Lieutenant Commander J. L. Foster) was the only ship within range. She immediately opened fire. She continued to fire while chasing the enemy, even though only her forward guns could reach the enemy. Commander Jarrell, still in the lead, decided to try and fool the enemy into changing course, which could close the gap between the two forces. He ordered all the destroyers of his Division 42 to turn and open a heavy broadside on the retreating enemy, even though they were out of range. The ruse worked only in part. One of the two Japanese columns did turn, actually to launch torpedoes, and this act closed the gap enough to put all eight pursuing American destroyers in range. Shortly after their turn, the destroyers *Shiratsuyu, Shikinami* and *Samidare* were slightly damaged by American gunfire. No damage resulted from Japanese fire.

The Allied ships were now approaching an area of ocean where allied planes and submarines were free to fire on all ships without stopping to identify them, a "free-fire zone." Admiral Crutchley ordered all ships to return rather than risk a fight between allied forces. While the Allies could return having successfully prevented the reinforcement of Biak, the Japanese once again disembarked their soldier passengers at their starting point. The Japanese were not through with Biak, however. Having failed twice with local forces, the Japanese High Command now sent in some of its heavy main force units.

Reports of the Japanese Navy's attempts to reinforce Biak had filtered down to the troops fighting to take the island. Reported on June 4th as two battleships, eight cruisers and many destroyers, it caused General Fuller to alert his artillery battalions to be prepared to fire seaward. Engineers were diverted to dig new emplacements for the artillery to allow for protection from naval gunfire. Division headquarters selected an alternate site for itself and had new communications prepared. For the 41st Infantry Division the day is recorded as "very hot" with "excitement and trepidation" running high. Many of the infantry and engineers were on the beach when Admiral Crutchley's force steamed past and they cheered at the sight. Then they returned to the fight at hand. It must have seemed to some that the desperate conditions of the early days on Guadalcanal were about to repeat themselves. When the second attempt to reinforce Biak was turned back, the 41st Infantry Division could stop looking over its shoulder, and concentrate on the situation on Biak.

The repeated failure of the reinforcement attempts to Biak and the loss of so many submarines in the same area caused serious concern at Japanese Naval Headquarters. These events suggested to those who believed that General MacArthur's drive on the Philippines was the main American effort that this drive had to be stopped, and that in stopping the drive the decisive battle so long sought might be found. Admiral Toyoda ordered a major effort to reinforce Biak. This time enough firepower would be made available to repulse any Allied effort to turn his ships back. The *Mobile Fleet* was ordered to release the two monster battleships *Yamato* and *Musashi*, light cruiser *Noshiro* and eight destroyers. This force would be added to the ships already assigned to reinforce Biak. The only U.S. force in the area, the Seventh Fleet, had little to stop such a force.

A new commander, Vice Admiral Ugaki, was assigned to command the combined force. He organized it into an attack division consisting of the battleships *Yamato* and *Musashi*, heavy cruisers *Myoko* and *Haguro*, light cruiser *Noshiro* and destroyers *Shimakaze, Okinami* and *Asagumo*. The second unit, *Transport Unit Number One*, consisted of the cruisers *Aoba* and *Kinu* with destroyers *Shikinami, Uranami, Yamagumo* and *Mowaki* as escorts. This unit was under the command of Admiral Sakonju. A third unit, *Transport Unit Number Two*, was made up of *Itsukushima* and *Tsugaru, Transport Number 127* and several smaller patrol craft and freighters. Admiral Ugaki's plan was to transport the troops to Biak, bombard enemy positions on Biak and Owi, and destroy any allied naval forces found in the area. Although he did not know it, there was nothing to stop him.

All of Vice Admiral Ugaki's force was assembled by midnight of June 11th in the harbor at Batjan. Boarding troops and making detailed plans was expected to take a couple of more days. The force was scheduled to sortie for Biak on June 15th. In the meantime, however, mixed intelligence reports kept the Japanese in confusion. Allied warships bombarded Japanese positions in the Mariana Islands on June 11th and 12th. Submarines were being destroyed regularly off New Guinea, indicating a large enemy task force in that area. Opinion remained divided among Japanese naval staff as to where and when the main American effort would reveal itself. Finally, with the American strikes in the Marianas continuing and growing in intensity, Admiral Toyoda suspended Operation Kon pending the outcome of events in the Marianas. It was never resumed.

Japanese reinforcement attempts at Biak now resorted to the same inefficient and dangerous methods employed when Japan had lost naval and air superiority over an area where Japanese troops remained. Know as the "ant transport," it consisted of barges and submarines and even native canoes being used to move men and material into bypassed areas. It was as it had been in the South Pacific and eastern New Guinea, too little too late. The Japanese at Biak were on their own.

There was a parting shot from the *23rd Air Flotilla*, however. This unit, which had been reinforced for Operation Kon, had been whittled down more by the deadly New Guinea mosquito than by the Americans. Barely effective, its survivors were moved north when Biak was left to its own resources. But before departing four of its aircraft attacked the U.S. destroyer *Kalk* at the Biak beaches. Hit by one bomb amidships, the destroyer lost 30 men killed, including 4 officers. An additional 4 officers and 36 sailors were wounded. The ship was out of action for several months. Ironically, given the amount of effort the *Imperial Japanese Navy* had expended for Biak, the U.S.S. *Kalk* was the only allied warship to suffer major casualties and damage there.

Seeing the Enemy

One of the most recognizable differences between the War in the Pacific and the War in Europe was the attitudes of the men fighting each war. The U.S. Army sponsored a study of the reactions of its soldiers which was conducted during and immediately after the war. Some of the results of this study, conducted by civilian specialists, clearly show the feeling of the American soldiers towards their enemies.

Two groups of infantrymen, one from the Pacific and the other from Europe, were asked what their reactions were after contact with enemy prisoners. The difference is striking. The Pacific soldiers answered forty two per cent of the time that they felt more like killing the enemy now than before, while only 18 per cent of the soldiers serving in Europe had the same reaction.

Another survey asked what the soldiers of two veteran Pacific divisions thought should be done to the Japanese people after the war had been won. Here again an overwhelming majority, fifty six per cent, wanted to "wipe out the whole Japanese nation." In European divisions, the answers resulted in an al-most opposite per cent in favor of a peaceful solution to postwar Germany, with fifty four per cent of those soldiers expressing regret that they had to fight Germany. In one Pacific division hatred for the enemy was the second most popular response to a question of how they overcame their fear of combat, with only fear of letting their friends down being more important.

The soldiers in the Pacific were also more prone to believe the enemy they fought was uncivilized. When veteran infantrymen in Pacific and European divisions were asked if they had personally witnessed an atrocity, the percentages were identical, but when these same men were asked if they had heard of atrocities, twice the number of Pacific veterans claimed to have been told of atrocities as European veterans. When infantrymen serving in the Pacific and European theaters were asked about their vindictiveness towards their enemy the Pacific theater soldiers more than twice as often replied that they would like to see the Japanese people destroyed. Surprisingly, when this same issue was asked of sol-

146

diers who had not yet left the United States, their answers were even more against the Japanese than the soldiers who had already fought the enemy.

This type of attitude was not the exclusive property of the American soldier. The Japanese soldier, for the most part, had a low opinion of his enemy. Sergeant Ogawa's views when he first arrived in New Guinea was that his enemy, at that time the Australians, were inferior and weak. After some time in combat, he considerably revised his opinion of the Allied military might. Yet that attitude persisted among the Japanese as it did among the Americans. Some of the atrocities committed, for example the bayoneting of prisoners, had been carried over from the war in China, were a superior attitude over the

Chinese had made that a normal practice in some Japanese units. Many Japanese continued to believe that the material might of the Allies, and not their soldiers, was defeating them, a rationalization they shared with the Germans.

These shared attitudes towards each other by the American infantrymen in the Pacific and their Japanese opponents resulted in a war without quarter. We have seen how prisoners surrendering were killed under a white flag, how prisoners were tied to a tree and bayonetted to death, and how fearful small groups of soldiers were when surrounded and out of support range. All of these factors resulted from a conditioned hatred of the enemy. The final result was one of the most brutal campaigns in American military history.

CHAPTER VII

Fireman of the Pacific

The excitement on Biak over the threat posed by the Japanese reinforcement attempts had delayed resolution of the argument between General Fuller and Colonel Newman as to how the 186th Infantry was to proceed over the ridges above the airfields. Colonel Newman, thinking it over while awaiting the outcome of the events at sea, decided on June 5th that his three battalions would push over the ridges in strength before trying to secure Mokmer Airfield. Once again the luck of the 186th Infantry held and by mid-afternoon the 3rd Battalion had secured the main ridge which overlooked the task force objective, Mokmer Drome. Supported by its sister battalions and the 2nd Battalion, 162nd Infantry, the 3rd Battalion prepared to clear the ridgeline the next morning.

Before operations could begin on June 6th, however, Colonel Newman again received a call from General Fuller, ordering all battalions under Colonel Newman's command, including the 2nd of the 162nd, to advance directly upon Mokmer Drome and also to establish a beachhead directly opposite the airfield. Clearly General Fuller was under great pressure to seize at least one of the airfields which were the Task Force's objectives, and as soon as possible. The operations in the Central Pacific were to begin is a very few days and it would take that long to get the airfield in shape for American operations. General Fuller was trying to speed up operations, perhaps at the risk of securing properly the approach to the objective. This is what Colonel Newman and the assistant division commander, Brigadier General Jens A. Doe, argued. Despite the arguments, General Fuller ordered his plan put into effect.

It took nearly all day on June 6th to get adequate supplies, especially water, up to the advance elements of the 186th Infantry, even using the 2nd Battalion as porters once again. Faced with this fact, General Fuller granted a one day postponement of his planned attack. This delay proved fortunate, for before dark patrols discovered a route to the airdrome from the top of the ridge, and at the same time sufficient supplies arrived to permit the advance to begin the following day.

Colonel Newman planned for his 3rd Battalion to lead the attack, followed by the 1st Battalion. The 2nd Battalion of the 162nd, still attached to Colonel Newman's command, would follow in support while his own 2nd Battalion continued to act as porters to the advancing infantry. A heavy supporting fire program was planned for this advance, including artillery from the 121st, 146th, 205th and 947th Field Artillery Battalions. Fifth Army Air Force bombers would add their support in bombing Borokoe Drome.

Once again, the luck of Colonel Newman and his regiment held, and before noon on June 7th his entire force had moved across Mokmer Drome, established a beachhead, and gone into defensive positions to protect their objectives. There was no Japanese opposition. Initial satisfaction quickly turned to concern, for even as the Americans were settling into their new positions, Japanese fire from three sides poured into them. Japanese artillery, antiaircraft and mortar fire pounded the American positions. Weapons usually directed against tanks and aircraft were now directed against the infantrymen of the 186th and 162nd Infantry Regiments.

Colonel Newman and his officers quickly called for supporting fire from their own artillery. The afternoon of June 7th turned into an artillery duel, with the infantry in the middle, as the Japanese and American artillery fought it out. The 121st Field Artillery Battalion alone fired over 2,000 rounds that day, and both the 205th and 947th Field Artillery Battalions were equally involved. As darkness approached the Japanese began to stand down, anxious to move their artillery to new, undetected, positions in preparation for the next day's battle. The

Men of 205th Field Artillery demonstrate difficulties of New Guinea terrain.

186th Infantry continued to improve their defenses around the airfield and beach. An initial attempt to resupply the regiment by sea failed when undetected Japanese along the beach opened fire and turned back the landing craft. The 186th moved to clear these Japanese out of the area, and later that evening, under cover of darkness and not without some confusion, supplies and tanks were landed and wounded were evacuated. Fourteen men had been killed and another 65 wounded, nearly all by the artillery duel of the afternoon. Except for the few Japanese near the beach, no enemy infantry had been encountered during the day. The first of the three main objectives of the 41st Infantry Division had been taken, but there was little cause for congratulations.

At the end of June 7th the 41st Infantry Division had one reinforced regiment on Mokmer Airfield, trapped against the sea and with an extremely tenuous supply line. Another regiment, the 162nd, was strung out along the coastal track, trying without success to open a supply and evacuation route for the

186th. The third regiment, the 163rd, was holding the main headquarters and supply positions and protecting the right flank of the assault force. The Japanese had not committed their main force yet, and clearly their main defenses had yet to be breached. Worse still, there were two more airfields to seize. The Japanese had made at least one major effort to reinforce their *Biak Garrison*, and might make another. Central Pacific operations which required support from Biak airfields were due to begin within a week, and other Southwest Pacific Theater operations had been altered to speed troops to Biak. Clearly, things were not going well despite outward appearances.

Exactly why the 186th Infantry met so little in the way of opposition on the way to Mokmer Drome has never been clarified. The Japanese had the entire *2nd Battalion, 222nd Infantry*, heavily reinforced with service and supply troops available either to block the advance of the Americans or to counterattack. They did neither.

The Japanese command also permitted the 186th Infantry to slip between its two main defensive positions in reaching Mokmer Drome. By passing over the main ridge without clearing it, the 186th Infantry passed between the East Caves and the West Caves defensive positions. While the result of all this was to place the reinforced American regiment directly under the heaviest guns of the *Biak Garrison*, this could not have been planned as the Japanese could not have known in advance where the 186th Infantry intended to go when they first approached the cliffs. So it appears that a combination of luck and circumstance, as so often happens in war, combined to place the airfield in American hands while at the same time giving the Japanese the best possible opportunity to deny its use to the Americans.

It was clear that the battle for Biak had only just begun, despite the seizure of Mokmer Airfield. By dawn of June 8th the Americans were still planning on clearing the area quickly and moving on to the other fields. The 186th Infantry continued to clear its immediate area of scattered resistance, while the 2nd Battalion of the 162nd was ordered to move east to effect a junction with its parent regiment still trying to clear the coastal track. Reinforced by Company G, 186th Infantry, the battalion moved barely 600 yards before being stopped for the day by Japanese fire. The Japanese had now brought the *2nd Battalion, 222nd Infantry*, into action and they attacked throughout the night in small groups. Supported by mortar fire the Japanese attacked the 2nd Battalion, 162nd Infantry and the 3rd Battalion, 186th continually during the night. During these attacks, the battalion commander of the *2nd Battalion, 222nd Infantry*, was killed. Nevertheless these counterattacks and the fire from the Japanese defensive positions kept the Americans from making any progress during the next few days. The American aviation engineer battalions, who had been brought forward to work on the airfield, sat idly while the battle raged. Every attempt to move the Japanese beyond the range of the airfield failed. Even the departure of the Japanese commander, General Numata, on June 9th, failed to change anything. Colonel Kuzume continued the defense as before.

East of the airfield, the 162nd Infantry less its 2nd Battalion, had been making repeated attempts to force a passage of the coastal track. Every effort had met with failure. Each was turned back by the Japanese entrenched in the Ibdi Pocket and the East Caves. By June 7th General Fuller had decided to try an overwater approach, since all land approaches were blocked. Companies I and K were loaded into landing craft and proceeded to Parai, where they were landed. A heavy fire from the Japanese on the cliffs inspired an urgent call for immediate reinforcements. The regimental cannon company, fighting as infantry, and six tanks of the 603rd Tank Company landed, after which a firm beachhead was established. The following day, reinforced by Company C, the force pushed west under continued fire from the East Caves. Progress was slow due to that fire and to enemy mines laid to impede the armor. The mines, which were actually six inch naval shells converted for the purpose by the enemy, made things slow and dangerous, but they did no damage. It was not until mid-day on June 9th that contact was finally established between the 186th and 162nd Infantry Regiments, and the rest of the 41st Infantry Division. Even then, the coast road was under constant fire from the East Caves and useless for supply purposes. The 1st Battalion, 162nd Infantry, came forward on June 10th to clear the area around Parai of

Japanese so that a supply route could be made secure. With this done, General Fuller could now look again towards securing Mokmer Airfield and seizing the remaining airfields.

General Fuller prepared a new plan of attack for clearing Mokmer Drome and securing the coastal track. The 162nd and 186th Infantry Regiments would advance in line abreast northwest to clear the remainder of the airfield and the heights from which the enemy continued to prevent the Americans from using the field. The 163rd Infantry Regiment would continue to protect, by active patrolling, the beachhead and supply areas. In addition, the 3rd Battalion, 163rd Infantry, would move into the jungle north of the field and patrol to determine enemy strength in that area. This plan was to go into effect on the morning of June 11th.

General Fuller was by this time well aware of the higher command's displeasure at his progress on Biak to date. Several days earlier, on June 3rd, General MacArthur issued one of his famous communiques saying the campaign on Biak was in its final stages, and that he expected to secure the island swiftly. General Fuller and his Hurricane Task Force were not keeping up with General MacArthur's press releases. Repeated urging from Sixth Army headquarters for more speed had become daily occurrences. As early as May 30th General Krueger had inquired of General Fuller if he thought that the surveyed airstrip could be quickly developed, making the capture of the completed airstrips less urgent. An engineer report to General Fuller on the surveyed area prompted him to reply that it would take some three weeks to establish an airstrip there, and that he would have Mokmer Drome in hand and operational sooner than that. Two additional weeks had now passed, and with Mokmer captured but still unusable, it was too late to begin work on the surveyed airstrip now.

General Krueger next ordered the reconnaissance of the offshore islands, hoping to find another suitable airfield site. One was found on Owi Island, secured by Company A, 163rd Infantry on June 1st. As soon as the site was identified, the 860th and 864th Aviation Engineer Battalions were moved to Owi, where construction started on June 9th. The engineers had the field adequate for fighter planes by June 17th. Finally, on June

Knee-deep in mud, engineers work to construct a P.T. Boat base along the coast of New Guinea. (National Archives)

21st fighter squadrons from the 8th Fighter Group, Fifth Army Air Force, were based on Owi. At the same time, U.S. Navy Construction Battalions built and established a Patrol Torpedo Boat base at Mios Woendi, and Seventh Fleet PT Boats began operations there by June 8th. Yet, despite this remarkable progress by the army and navy construction units, there was no air support available to fulfill General MacArthur's promise to Admiral Nimitz that air cover from the Schouten Islands would support his landings on Saipan.

General Fuller was also becoming something of an embarrassment to General MacArthur. By the time General Fuller had reorganized his forces for the drive to clear Mokmer Drome, General MacArthur had issued several communiques announcing progress on Biak, none of which were now close to reality. As early as June 1st, before any Americans had set foot on the first objective and while General Fuller was asking for more troops, Southwest Pacific Headquarters had announced that Japanese resistance on Biak was "collapsing." Again on June 3rd came the communique announcing that operations were in the "mopping up phase." Equally severe in the view of General MacArthur, was General Fuller's failure to fulfill MacArthur's promise about air support to the Navy. General MacArthur was in competition with the Navy, for whichever drive succeeded in getting closer to the Philippines, that commander would have more influence in deciding the course of future campaigns. General MacArthur knew that the navy favored bypassing the Philippines in favor of a strike at Formosa or a landing on mainland China, neither of which spared any troops for a reconquest of the Philippines. Such strategy was anathema to the General. Despite all his urging, there were no airfields available to allow the Army Air Forces to fulfill General Mac-Arthur's promise of air support for the U.S. Navy's Marianas Campaign. When the Navy's 2nd and 4th Marine Divisions landed on June 15th, they were supported only by Naval air support.

General Krueger had been equally unhappy with progress on Biak. When on June 5th he received an inquiry from General MacArthur's headquarters asking for an explanation as to the slow progress, he acted immediately. His first step was to contact General Fuller and direct the speeding of operations, specifically to seize the airfields and directing General Fuller to pressure his subordinates to move faster. This was undoubtedly why General Fuller overruled General Doe and Colonel New-man when they protested moving on Mokmer Drome without first clearing the ridges which overlooked it. General Krueger next laid the groundwork for his next move, when he replied to General MacArthur that he felt progress on Biak was too slow and that he was considering replacing General Fuller with a new commander. He added that only reports from an observation team he had sent from his headquarters to observe Biak operations had kept him from taking this step already. His observation team had relayed how overextended the 41st Division was and how difficult the terrain made operations. General

Krueger, not satisfied with his first team's report, now sent a second team to Biak.

General Krueger's new observation team reported back to him on June 6th. Their report was critical of leadership in the 41st Infantry Division down to company level. They cited inadequate reconnaissance, poor intelligence gathering, and troops permitted to group together rather than dispersing to avoid enemy fire. Their report also stated that the command and staff group of the division had failed to visit the front lines often enough to obtain a clear picture of the situation. Yet, as General Krueger was reviewing this unfavorable report, he received news of the capture of Mokmer Drome. This welcome news was quickly relayed to General MacArthur's headquarters, with the notation that General Fuller would be retained in command pending further developments. Shortly before the next attack was scheduled to begin, General Krueger again reminded General Fuller of the need for a speedy victory.

General Fuller and his staff, however, saw things differently than did General Krueger. Ironically, they were as critical of the Sixth Army handling of the operation as was the Sixth Army staff of their own operations. Colonel Kenneth Sweany, the chief of staff of the 41st Infantry Division recorded his criticisms of the visiting inspectors, specifically Colonel Clyde Eddleman, the operations officer of Sixth Army and a close personal friend of General Krueger. Colonel Sweany claimed that Colonel Eddleman "saw only what could be seen from the beach, couldn't have the vaguest notion of this hellish terrain" and yet reported critically on activities of the 41st Infantry Division of which he did not have first hand knowledge. The staff of the 41st Infantry Division also felt that a visit by either General Krueger or General MacArthur was long overdue. It was also believed that neither was showing any loyalty to the men of the 41st Infantry Division.

Colonel Kuzume and the men of the *222nd Infantry Regiment* were not the least bit interested in the schedule of General MacArthur, General Krueger, or the 41st Infantry Division. When the attacking regiments of the 41st Infantry Division moved forward on June 11th, the 186th on the right and the 162nd on the left, it was once again the 162nd Infantry Regiment which received the heaviest fire even before leaving the line of departure. The 186th was forced to wait while the 162nd could come forward to the jump-off line, which they seemed to be doing by mid-day. The 2nd and 3rd Battalions, 186th Infantry moved along the beach and over the airstrip to reach the day's objective. Resistance had been light in this zone, mostly long range fire coming from enemy positions within the area of the 162nd Infantry.

There the Americans faced the *2nd* and *1st Battalions, 222nd Infantry*. Although enemy fire was heavy and constant, the 2nd Battalion of the 162nd managed to keep pace with the 186th Infantry on its left. The 3rd Battalion, 162nd, faced the low cliffs which ranged along the coast and included those which formed the Parai Defile. This battalion fought all day long against pillboxes, bunkers, caves and automatic weapons pits. The Japanese, as before, had excellent concealment while the Americans had little. Support from the 947th Field Artillery Battalion could not break the enemy defenses. By dusk the battalion had advanced only some 500 yards and was still nowhere near the day's objective.

During the day escaped Javanese slave laborers had come into the lines of the 162nd Infantry. They reported the existence of the large caves directly in front of the regiment, holding Japanese troops, positions, and supplies. This was the first indication to the Americans of the Japanese stronghold known as the East Caves. Colonel Haney ordered his 1st Battalion to patrol the area the following day.

The 186th Infantry remained in place the following day, although there was no opposition to its front, in order to allow the 162nd to finish its reduction of the Japanese positions attacked the previous day. The 3rd Battalion, 162nd, had sent Company L around the ridge to the north in an effort to outflank the Japanese. This effort was unsuccessful, as was an attempt made by the regiment's heavy mortars from Company M to suppress the enemy's fire. However, a second attempt later that day found that the earlier efforts did have some effect. The mortars had reduced a few enemy positions, and the pressure from Company L had reduced the enemy's ability to deny the ridge to the 3rd Battalion. Yet the fight remained a difficult one, with one set of positions after another facing the infantry. Still, progress continued to be made.

Bad news arrived from the 3rd Battalion, 163rd Infantry at mid-day. Company L of that battalion had established an observation post inland of the cliffs under attack by the 162nd Infantry. From this observation post the Americans observed and reported that the Japanese had a number of antiaircraft guns in position to fire upon the attacking infantry. Fearing heavy casualties in the event these weapons opened fire, Colonel Haney withdrew all his units from the north side of the ridge, facing the enemy. American artillery fired upon the reported positions of the enemy guns, after which the 162nd Infantry regained the ridge. There were gaps in the line, and many Japanese in front of it, but the main Japanese defensive position was at last under direct attack by the Americans. Equally important, the engineers had been able to begin work on the captured airstrip. Protected by the 186th Infantry, and under sporadic Japanese mortar and artillery fire, progress remained slow.

June 13th was a repetition of the day before. The 162nd Infantry continued its attacks along the ridge. The 186th Infantry patrolled its front and protected the engineers working on the airstrip. On this date the first American plane landed on the island, but the airfield was still only available for emergency landings. Japanese still occasionally fired upon the strip. General Fuller, concerned about the condition of his troops and alarmed about new reports of reinforcements arriving for the enemy on Biak, asked General Krueger for additional troops to augment his Task Force. General Krueger ordered the 34th Infantry Regiment from the 24th Infantry Division to Biak. General Fuller's request, however, prompted General Krueger to take the action he had postponed earlier. Feeling that the command of the Task Force and the 41st Infantry Division were too much for General Fuller, General Krueger decided that a new Task Force commander would be appointed. This would allow General Fuller to devote himself fully to the command of his division. It is likely that reports appearing in the Australian press, less friendly to MacArthur than their American colleagues, which highlighted the American failure to keep pace with the reports emanating from Southwest Pacific Headquarters encouraged a decision at this time. General Krueger made his decision known the following day, June 14th.

General MacArthur chose Lieutenant General Robert L. Eichelberger to assume command of Hurricane Task Force. Still commanding I Corps at Hollandia, General Eichelberger was not very familiar with the situation at Biak. He had met briefly with General Fuller, a fellow West Point classmate and lifelong friend, when the 41st Infantry Division had departed Hollandia for the Wakde-Biak operations. He remembered that "Fuller expressed some apprehension" over the speed required to mount one operation so soon after another. After that, General Eichelberger heard only the official communiques, citing the "mopping up the enemy" stories. On June 14th he was ordered to Sixth Army headquarters. General Eichelberger had a premonition that this was no ordinary summons, coming near dark and requiring his immediate presence. Once before, during the Papuan Campaign, he had received a similar summons and found himself appointed the commander of the faltering American effort at Buna-Gona. General Eichelberger's premonition was, of course, correct. Arriving at General Krueger's headquarters, General Eichelberger found himself appointed commander of Hurricane Task Force, and together with his entire I Corps Headquarters was ordered immediately to Biak to take charge of that operation.

General Eichelberger and his staff arrived at Bosnek Bay by air on June 15th. He spent his first few hours learning the history of the Biak Operation. That afternoon he went out to survey the terrain, while his staff officers compared notes with General Fuller's staff. General Eichelberger was immediately impressed by the terrain over which his task force was fighting, especially the cliffs towering over the coast road, where the 162nd Infantry had first met disaster. On his return to Hurricane Task Force Headquarters, he was "solemn and reflective." Clearly the situation was nothing like that portrayed in General MacArthur's press releases. He assumed command of the Task Force at midday, and found General Fuller angry and upset with General Krueger for his action in replacing him. General Fuller told General Eichelberger that he had sent a letter to General

*Lt. Gen. Robert L. Eichel-
berger, commanding I Corps,
aboard ship enroute to another assault in New
Guinea. (National Archives)*

Krueger at Sixth Army asking to be relieved of command of the 41st Infantry Division as well as Task Force commander. He also asked to be assigned to duty outside of the Southwest Pacific Theater Area of Operations. General Eichelberger tried to dissuade his friend from such a drastic step, but General Fuller remained adamant, and his request was quickly granted. Relieved on June 18th, General Fuller was subsequently to serve with distinction in the China-Burma-India Theater of Operations. His departure was noted by his command, but they were in the middle of a battle, and they knew and trusted his successor, Brigadier General Jens A. Doe, the former assistant division commander. Biak was now completely General Eichelberger's problem.

Lieutenant General Robert Lawrence Eichelberger was a native of Ohio and a graduate of West Point, class of 1909. The son of a Union officer and Southern mother who had witnessed the siege of Vicksburg during the Civil War, he had grown up fascinated by the military, particularly things connected with the Civil War. Appointed to West Point, he was an average cadet, and was commissioned into the infantry upon graduation. His first active duty assignment with the 10th Infantry Regiment on the Mexican Border put him in contact with two men who would be central to his future career, Captain Douglas MacArthur and Lieutenant George C. Marshall. Married with no children, he and his wife were devoted to each other throughout their lifetimes. His letters to her form a personal record of the General's career. First seeing combat, as a neutral observer, during Pancho Villa's raids in Mexico, he later taught military science at Kemper Military School in Missouri. At the entry of the United States into the First World War, Major Eichelberger served on the General Staff in Washington, D.C. before being appointed assistant Chief of Staff to General William S. Graves, who was destined to lead the American Expeditionary Force into Siberia at war's end. Here, as assistant chief of staff and intelligence officer, Major Eichelberger again witnessed combat close up, observing the tactics of foreign military units, investigating atrocities, and evaluating America's allies. He worked his way home after the war, serving briefly in China, Japan and the Philippines. After returning home, he attended the Command and General Staff School and graduated behind Dwight D. Eisenhower. He remained to teach for three years, attended the Army War College, and then taught at West Point.

His next assignment was as secretary to the War Department General Staff. The chief of staff at that time was Major General Douglas MacArthur. Eichelberger, now a colonel, and MacArthur seemed to work well together, each with a mutual respect for each other's abilities. Staying on while MacArthur went to serve in the Philippines, he eventually requested duty with the infantry, as the conditions in Europe deteriorated. After attending the Infantry School at Fort Benning, Georgia, he was given command of the 30th Infantry Regiment in California. Here he earned a reputation as a complete soldier, familiar with all aspects of his trade and even acquiring some knowledge of amphibious warfare. In 1940 he was promoted Brigadier General and named superintendent of West Point. With the entry of the United States into World War Two, he was appointed commander of the 77th Infantry Division, a New York army reserve division then forming in South Carolina. Successful in establishing this division as combat ready, he next was assigned to organize the XI Corps, and shortly thereafter given command of the I Corps. This command was originally destined for the amphibious assault scheduled for North Africa, but Eichelberger and his command were suddenly called to report to General MacArthur in the Pacific. General George S. Patton took command of the North African assault, while Eichelberger and his corps went to the South Pacific, presumably due to his earlier association with MacArthur and his knowledge of amphibious assault tactics.

Lieutenant General Eichelberger and his staff arrived in Australia, and was told by General MacArthur that I Corps would lead the American effort about to begin in Papua, New Guinea. These plans were canceled, apparently by General MacArthur's irascible Chief of Staff, General Richard K. Sutherland, and General Eichelberger's role became little more than an observer. He was in fact ordered to keep a distance from the Australian military, and at the same time not permitted to observe the American forces in New Guinea, for which he was technically responsible. When he did receive permission to visit New Guinea he was ordered by General MacArthur not to go forward, and on the same day of his arrival he was ordered back to Australia by General Sutherland. His mission, he decided, was strictly a training one.

All that changed abruptly when General MacArthur called him forward once again on November 29th, 1942. It was at this meeting with General MacArthur that he was told to "take Buna, or not come back alive," an unusually stringent command from an American General. Fortunately for the future American effort in the Southwest Pacific, General Eichelberger both prevailed and survived. His arrival at the front was described by one Australian commander as "a very pure breath of fresh air." Stopping all offensive action, he reorganized and resupplied the exhausted and dispirited American troops now under his command. After a month's bitter fighting, the enemy positions around Buna were reduced and the success demanded by General MacArthur had been achieved. General Eichelberger was what is often know as a "soldier's general" in that he listened to his troops, visited them often, and went to the front to see things for himself whenever necessary. Back in the United

States, his wife found out where he was serving when one reporter, who was not permitted to identify him, included in his article the fact that the general visiting the front line troops called them "my lads," a term she knew only her husband used.

General Eichelberger's success at Buna earned him the sobriquet "Fireman of the Pacific," or "MacArthur's Fireman." It was for this reason, General MacArthur's confidence in him, that he was given command of the Hollandia operation. And now, with events at Biak calling for redemption, MacArthur's Fireman once again took hold.

Displeased with the situation he found on Biak, he promptly visited the 186th and 162nd Infantry Regiments where he discovered "that their colonels were almost as much in the dark as I was." Apparently no officer he spoke with knew the location of the main enemy positions, nor the strength of the enemy. Nobody knew what lay beyond the ridges currently under attack. Yet as more information came to him, he realized that the intelligence estimates of enemy strength and intentions were grossly inaccurate. Rather than the originally predicted four thousand troops including service troops, expected on the island they could now identify the entire *222nd Infantry Regiment*, with supporting troops numbering more than eleven thousand soldiers and sailors. Reports had come in from the Navy that supplies and reinforcements were being filtered in by barge and small craft, the "any transport" at night. "Ordinarily, considering the hazards of attack, a 3 to 1 advantage in troop strength for the invaders is set up by the military textbooks as a fair and equal fight. The 41st Division had not, in (Eichelberger's) opinion, done badly."

General Eichelberger continued his survey of the forward areas, coming under fire on more than one occasion. It became clear to him that the advance was seriously disorganized. He found, for example, that one battalion of the 162nd Infantry had gotten lost and turned up in the American rear instead of the Japanese rear, the intended destination. On another occasion he was moving forward to examine a ridge taken by the division, when American tanks began firing in his direction. He learned quickly that the ridge was back in Japanese hands, although no report of the recapture had arrived at his headquarters.. He concluded that "this battlefield was a confused scramble" and ordered all attacks to cease immediately.

General Eichelberger was disturbed that reconnaissance was so inadequate. The 41st Infantry Division "did not definitely know the locations of the major caves which hid the main enemy forces and some of their mortar and mountain batteries." He ordered all forward units to use their time in reorganizing and patrolling extensively. Before General Eichelberger sent the 41st Infantry Division against the Japanese again, he wanted to know everything there was to know about them.

June 18th was spent in reorganizing and preparing for the next attack. General Doe, now commanding the Division, proposed a plan that would send the entire 162nd Infantry Regiment against the now identified West Caves, while the entire 186th Infantry Regiment moved to the ridgeline above the caves. General Eichelberger vetoed this plan for one of his own. The 34th Infantry Regimental Combat Team had now arrived on Biak, and General Eichelberger planned to make immediate use of them. His plan called for the 41st Division units to seal off the West Caves from all sides while the 34th Infantry moved west and secured the remaining airfields. And this is exactly how things went.

Starting on June 19th the infantry regiments, supported as always by the engineers and artillery, moved as directed by the new Task Force commander. Moving quickly ashore, the 34th Infantry by June 20th had secured Borokoe and Sorido Airfields while the 186th and 162nd Infantry Regiments moved against the West Caves and the ridges beyond it. The attack, which had for so long stalled in or around Mokmer Drome, had at last moved into the final stages.

General Fuller left Biak on June 18th, and since the attack moved quickly at about the time of his relief there was some speculation that his relief was premature. At the time of his relief he had seized one airfield, had a secure beachhead, and the enemy threat to push the Americans off the island had been negated. Patrols had learned that the other two airfields were not defended and could be easily seized. General Fuller preferred to secure his lines of communications before seizing them, and this required a secure road past the West Caves, something not easily accomplished. However, General Fuller had failed, in the opinion of his commanders, to push his subordinates hard enough. His early planning was inadequate, and his efforts at intelligence gathering were seriously deficient. General Krueger particularly cited his failure to secure the ridges along the coast road on the first days of the invasion, when they were lightly defended, as a serious deficiency. Too often his troops stumbled into the Japanese, rather than finding them by patrols. Most importantly, he had failed General MacArthur. He had not secured the airfields in accordance with the Southwest Pacific commander's promised schedule. He had failed to keep pace with the progress reported by the communiques issued by General MacArthur's headquarters. Any delay, however small, threatened to endanger General MacArthur's cherished desire to lead the liberation of the Philippines, and would not be tolerated. This determination, which "frequently reached the level of obsession" and General Fuller's failure to advance it past Biak may have been the final reason for his relief. Now it was up to General Eichelberger, "Fireman of the Pacific," to see if he could improve on his classmate's performance.

Robert L. Eichelberger

Of all the U.S. Army commanders who served in the Pacific theaters of operation none has received more praise for his performance than Lieutenant General Robert Lawrence Eichelberger. On some occasions thrust into a difficult situation on a few hours' notice, notably at Buna and Biak, he never failed to deliver to General MacArthur a victory. He has been called the "Fireman of the Pacific" and "MacArthur's Fireman." He is also the only one of the Southwest Pacific generals who was complimented by MacArthur by a comparison with how General MacArthur would have himself conducted a campaign.

Born March 9th, 1886 in Urbana, Ohio, he was the youngest of five children, and one of four brothers. His family had a history going back to the Civil War, with his father a former Union Army officer and his mother a native of Vicksburg, Mississippi. His father made his living as a lawyer, but the children were raised on a farm outside Urbana where the family lived. Steeped in the history of the Civil War, he jumped at the offer of an appointment to West Point from his father's law partner, a local judge. He had already completed his freshman year at Ohio State University, but Bob Eichelberger was destined for the U.S. Army.

Graduating 68th in a class of 103, he was commissioned into the infantry and appointed to the 10th Infantry Regiment stationed in Indiana. His regiment was sent to the Mexican border the following year, 1910, to keep an eye on events in Mexico.

While on this assignment he met briefly two officers who would later have a major impact on his career, Captain Douglas MacArthur and Lieutenant George C. Marshall. The following year his regiment was transferred to the Canal Zone in Panama, where Lieutenant Eichelberger met and married Miss Emma Gudger, daughter of the Chief Justice of the Canal Zone. In later years the two, devoted to each other in the absence of children, would correspond regularly and Eichelberger's letters to "Dear Miss Em" would provide a valuable historical record of his service in the Pacific.

Eichelberger first witnessed combat in 1915, when while serving with the 22nd Infantry on the Arizona-Mexico border, he observed a raid by Pancho Villa on a town just across the border. He also came under fire for the first time as stray bullets flew across the border into his observation post. One of the things which impressed the young officer was the fact that his fellow professional officers ignored the ongoing battle, preferring to socialize instead. This left a lasting impression on Lieutenant Eichelberger, and in the future he took every opportunity to observe battle conditions. This would be a crucial factor in his success in the Pacific. He was one of the few higher commanders who personally viewed his battlefields, preferring personal observation to staff reports which were often in error or misleading.

After a brief tour as a Professor of Military Science at Kemper Military School in Missouri, he returned to the infantry, this time as a major commanding a battalion of the 43rd Infantry Regiment, the result of the American military's expansion in preparation for the First World War. Later he would serve in staff positions in Washington and under the command of Major General William S. Graves. When General Graves took command of the 8th Division, Captain Eichelberger went with him as his Operations officer. Although originally scheduled for the Western Front, General Graves and his division were sent instead to Siberia to aid isolated Allied troops in that area. Here Major Eichelberger observed at every opportunity the troops of all the different nations located in the area, learning how they conducted their operations, their tactics, and motives.

After several staff and observer appointments at the end of the war, the newly promoted Colonel Eichelberger was assigned to the adjutant general's department in Washington. In part as a result of this appointment, he was sent the following year to the Army's Command and General Staff College, where he graduated on a list of Distinguished Graduates, a list headed by Dwight D. Eisenhower.

He next spent four years as an administrator at West Point, followed by an appointment as secretary to the War Department General Staff, another prestigious appointment. The chief of staff for whom he worked was General Douglas MacArthur. Colonel Eichelberger found working for his new boss difficult but pleasant. General MacArthur worked long hours, and often required the same of the staff. Yet Eichelberger found him friendly, courteous and interesting. When

General MacArthur left to take command of the Philippines, Colonel Eichelberger continued to work for his successor, General Malin Craig. General Craig was one who influenced Eichelberger very positively. They had a friendly relationship, and General Craig looked after his secretary's career. During the Second World War, General Craig exchanged letters with General Eichelberger, which the latter found very reassuring.

One of General Craig's strongest recommendations to his protege was that in time of war service with the infantry was essential to an officer's career. Accordingly, as it became more and more apparent that another war was coming, Colonel Eichelberger requested duty with the infantry. He attended the Infantry School at Fort Benning, a creation of General George C. Marshall, and then took command of the 30th Infantry Regiment. For the next two years he learned all over again the needs of a commanding officer in the infantry. In 1940 he was promoted brigadier general and appointed to command the Military Academy at West Point. His success there earned him another promotion to major general.

After Pearl Harbor, General Eichelberger requested duty with combat troops. He was given command of the 77th Infantry Division, a unit drawn from the Army Reserve units of New York State. He organized and trained this division before moving on to new commands. So effective was General Eichelberger with the 77th Infantry Division that it was one of the outstanding divisions in the Pacific theater. During the invasion of

Guam, when assigned to and fighting alongside the Marines, it earned the highest accolade ever given an army unit by the Marines when it was described by a Marine officer as "almost as good as the Marine Divisions fighting alongside it."

General Eichelberger had moved up to command the I Corps. His first assignment was to plan and conduct the planned invasion of North Africa. Yet suddenly and without warning, in a forecast of other such calls, he and his corps were rushed to Australia. Called for by General MacArthur, now commanding the Allied efforts in the Southwest Pacific, he was rushed to New Guinea to take command of the faltering Allied effort to crush the Japanese at Buna-Gona. As his wife, Miss Em, wrote to him, during a war he always seems to be sent to the strangest places. It was during this assignment that General MacArthur ordered General Eichelberger to win or "not come back alive." As an added inducement for success, however, General MacArthur offered to "release your name for publicity" should General Eichelberger succeed.

Succeed he did. He then led his I Corps into Hollandia and later saved the reputation of General MacArthur at Biak. Upon returning to Hollandia after the fall of Biak, General MacArthur rewarded him with command of a new army in the Southwest Pacific. The Eighth Army became General Eichelberger's. Sent from the United States where it had

formed and trained, General Eichelberger added only his old chief of staff and a few selected staff officers to the existing staff of Eighth Army. His first operation as an Army commander was on Leyte, once again mopping up an operation left unfinished by General Krueger. General Eichelberger had some adverse feeling about General Krueger, even though it was General MacArthur's directive which sent the Sixth Army onto the Philippine island of Luzon while delegating the Eighth Army to finish Leyte.

Once again General Eichelberger finished the job in swift and economical fashion. Next came a series of amphibious attacks on dozens of other Philippine islands while Sixth Army faced the main enemy defense force on Luzon. General Eichelberger and his Eighth Army conducted thirty five amphibious operations in just over a month. Most were lightly opposed, but others such as Mindanao required the conquest of some 50,000 enemy troops. It was after these operations that General Eichelberger received his highest praise from General MacArthur when he was told by his commander that "You run an Army in combat just like I would have done it."

After serving in the occupation of Japan, still in command of the Eighth Army, General Eichelberger and Miss Em enjoyed a well earned retirement, ending some forty years of outstanding service to his nation.

CHAPTER VIII

Mopping Up Biak

*J*une 18th was the day General Eichelberger had ordered for Hurricane Task Force to rest and reorganize. Dissatisfied with the way things had gone thus far, the new Task Force Commander wanted all troops and supplies in order before making any more costly attacks against the entrenched *Biak Garrison*. He ordered the entire 162nd and 186th Infantry Regiments to prepare for a new attack the next day, which would not be simply another frontal attack against entrenched enemy troops, but would include an effort to encircle the main enemy force in the West Caves. As General Eichelberger would comment later, "We now had the airfields, but still did not have the Japanese." Without the airfields, the entire operation remained unsuccessful.

While the infantry rested and reorganized, the engineers worked. Colonel David W. Heiman, commanding the 1112th Combat Engineer Group had the responsibility for base development under Hurricane Task Force. Divided between Wakde and Biak Islands, the engineer group had to develop the bases needed on those islands with speed. Problems arose even before the landings, when the engineers discovered that no plans had been drawn up describing exactly what was expected of them. The operational instructions issued by General MacArthur's Headquarters on May 10th had no engineer annex, the place where base development was usually covered and explaining to the engineer commanders what they were supposed to create once the base had been seized. Colonel Heiman contacted Sixth

Army Headquarters and learned that he was to create two airdromes, one for fighters and one for bombers, and that additional instructions would follow. Preparing tentative plans from aerial photographs and estimates based on meager intelligence, the engineers went into battle as poorly prepared as the infantry. It was the 542nd Boat and Shore Regiment of Colonel Heiman's command that put the 41st Infantry Division ashore on Biak, less its Company A which had just won a Presidential Unit Citation for its work at Wakde. After the landings, most of the engineer units engaged in supply missions and mine clearing.

Lieutenant Colonel E. L. Griggs' 864th Engineer Aviation Battalion was the first to reach Mokmer Airfield, on May 30th. Enemy fire prevented them from doing any work on the strip, so they went to work building jetties to speed supply operations, widened the road along the beach, unloaded ships and carried water to the front line troops. It wasn't until June 4th that General Fuller ordered the battalion to Owi Island to construct an airfield there. Two additional battalions, the 860th Engineer Aviation Battalion and Lieutenant Colonel Raymond J. Harvey's 863rd Engineer Aviation Battalion, landed on Biak on June 8th. Lieutenant Colonel Benjamin E. Meadows' 863rd was ordered immediately to Owi, to assist the engineers already engaged in airfield construction there. The 863rd was directed to Mokmer, and given 36 hours to make it serviceable. Because the enemy still harassed the supply road to Mokmer, General Fuller had directed that the engineers go to Mokmer by sea. Boarding an LST, Company A of the battalion set out during the darkness of June 9/10. During the landing in pitch darkness the equipment so necessary to the construction of an airfield was landed, and within minutes was swamped by an incoming tide. The morning was spent pulling the equipment up on the beach to dry. As Colonel Heiman later explained, "We had to work fast and in the darkness on a strip of beach that was strange to all of us, we were lucky." Despite these extreme measures, enemy fire on Mokmer kept the engineers from working on the field for another few days. Progress on Owi Island by the 864th Engineer Aviation Battalion was moving as planned, but ominous signs began to appear within the ranks of the engineers as 64 officers

Supported by infantrymen of the 32nd Division, a tank destroyer struggles through the difficult terrain always present in New Guinea operations. (National Archives)

and enlisted men came down with Scrub typhus, which in the first days killed one officer and two enlisted men.

General Eichelberger's plan was now ready for action. It called for the 162nd Infantry to hold its positions facing the Japanese in the West Caves. The 186th Infantry, relieved of guarding the airfields by the 34th Infantry, would encircle the West Caves, assisted by the 3rd Battalion, 163rd Infantry. All available support would be given the attacking infantry, including the artillery from the 121st, 167th, 205th and 947th Field Artillery Battalions. Included in the opening barrage were the heavy mortars of the 641st Tank Destroyer Battalion and the tanks of the 603rd Tank Company.

Although delayed by rough terrain and climate conditions, the attack went nearly as planned. Colonel Newman's 186th Infantry circled behind the West Caves and cut them off from flight or reinforcement. The 162nd Infantry was now free to attack the next day with the knowledge that the enemy was trapped. The 34th Infantry had secured all three airfields. Again on June 20th, the attack would begin with a much better chance of success than ever before.

Later that evening as the I Corps staff officers sat down to dinner under the large tents serving as a mess hall, conversation centered on two main topics. The first was the relief of General Fuller while the second concerned the Japanese defenses. The caves in particular were known to be a serious problem. No amount of artillery, mortar or small arms fire seemed able to eliminate them. During the conversation General Eichelberger turned to his chemical warfare officer, Colonel Harold Riegelman, and asked "How about it, Chemical officer? What do you do with those caves?" Colonel Riegelman, believing his general to be joking, replied "We got a lot of Jap gas that isn't being used, sir." There was no response, and Colonel Riegelman went on with his meal. He had already visited with his counterparts at the 41st Infantry Division and discussed with Lieutenant Colonel Frank Arthur the problems facing Hurricane Task Force. Stopping to pay his respects to General Fuller, who he reports felt that had he received the 34th Infantry when he first asked for reinforcements he never would have had the difficulties he experienced in securing the airfields, he saw the general leave with his "grey eyes filled and a tear streaked the weathered cheek."

Colonel Arthur had recommended the use of the enemy gas, mostly in the form of poison smoke candles. When Colonel Reigelman raised the question of flamethrowers he was told that they could not effect the deeper caves, where most of the enemy sheltered. While flame throwers and demolitions could, and did, eliminate enemy caves, there were not enough flame throwers to go around. Casualties among trained flame thrower operators also increased the difficulties encountered by Hurricane Task Force. The Corps Chemical Officer was left with his questions and no solutions.

After dinner Colonel Reigelman strolled back to his tent, thinking over his earlier conversation with Colonel Arthur. There seemed no easy solution to the problem of the caves. Suddenly, it struck the colonel that perhaps his general had not

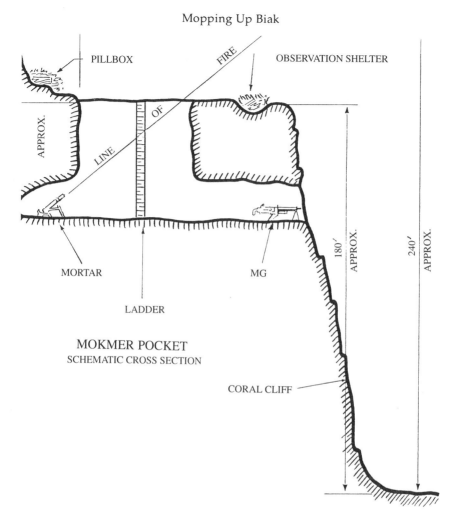

PILLBOX

FIRE

OBSERVATION SHELTER

APPROX.

LINE

OF

MORTAR

MG

180' APPROX.

240' APPROX.

LADDER

MOKMER POCKET
SCHEMATIC CROSS SECTION

CORAL CLIFF

Japanese cave emplacement.

been joking when he asked him to come up with a solution for the cave problem. Stopping dead in his tracks, the colonel hurried to General Eichelberger's tent where he met the general just walking up to his sleeping quarters. Colonel Riegelman inquired "Sir, it just came to me that you might not have been joking when you popped the caves at me." The general's reply supported Colonel Riegelman's worst fears. "Harold, I was never more serious in all my life." Knowing what was expected of him, the colonel spent a sleepless night.

For the next three days Colonel Riegleman and his staff

investigated every cave they could find that was not occupied by the Japanese. Many had been taken along the beach and in the interior areas already secured by the infantry. Colonel Riegleman went into as many as he could reach to learn how best to destroy them as defensive positions. Joined by Colonel Arthur, he found and investigated one of the outlying West Caves. Colonel Arthur explained how his troops had set off a group of white phosphorous mortar shells inside the entrance to the cave, and stood by while the smoke came out of several different entrances hundreds of yards away. Colonel Reigelman supervised and then watched as 850 pound of TNT was placed within the entrance to one of the West Caves. Pulling his troops and tanks back to safety, the explosion detonated successfully. Poisonous fumes delayed briefly the Americans' entrance into the cave, during which Colonel Riegleman took pictures and notes for his report to General Eichelberger.

That report was delivered that evening. Colonel Riegelman detailed the successful attempts at destruction of various caves, including flame throwers, demolitions, and white phosphorous shells. Colonel Reigelman's report was quite detailed, citing different methods for different size and type caves. Even the use of war dogs to bring explosives into the deeper caves was considered, although Colonel Riegelman did not recommend that method.

Shortly after dark that same evening Colonel Reigelman was summoned to the tent of General Eichelberger's chief of staff, Brigadier General Clovis Byers. When he arrived he found all the staff officers and General Eichelberger present. Obviously to Colonel Reigelman, a serious discussion was under way. General Eichelberger's first question to Colonel Reigelmen confirmed his impressions. Asked "How much Jap gas do you have?," Colonel Reigelman replied "Plenty Sir, we have taken great quantities, mostly poison smoke." The questioning continued, with the possible use of the Japanese poison smoke candles obviously under serious consideration. Finally, General Eichelberger put the question to his chemical warfare officer, "Harold, there is a disagreement between me and my staff. I believe we should use that gas. My staff differs. I shall follow your judgement." Colonel Reigelman considered quickly and re-

Japanese cave-mouth, typical of many cleared by 41st Division on Biak.

sponded "Sir, in my opinion the staff is right. And I believe you'd be relieved in twenty-four hours after you used gas. In the end that would cost us more in time and casualties than if we keep on as we are." Colonel Reigelman was then dismissed and left the meeting. General Eichelberger did not use gas against the *Biak Garrison*.

Dawn of June 20th had brought the Hurricane Task Force into the true mopping up phase of the battle for Biak. With the main enemy forces trapped in the West Caves, elimination of each position could begin methodically. Tanks, demolition charges, gasoline and small arms fire added to the effort to destroy the enemy entrenched within the caves. Few attempts succeeded. As proof of the American's inability to effectively neutralize their defenses, during the night of June 20th the Japanese counterattacked, hitting the 1st Battalion, 162nd Infantry and shelling Mokmer Drome with mortars and light artillery. Before any American fire could locate and destroy this enemy force, the

Japanese returned safely to their caves. Clearly, the Japanese had to be totally eliminated before the airfields would be truly secure. Incidents such as this only increased General Eichelberger's frustration and caused him to seek out solutions such as the possibility of gas warfare.

Once again, on June 21st, the infantry, armor, artillery and engineers set about the task of conquering the West Caves. Once again every available weapon was used to little avail. By the end of the day all outpost positions had been eliminated and some of the smaller openings had been conquered, including the one supervised by Colonel Reigelman. While all this effort without noticeable result frustrated the Americans, Colonel Kuzume was making his own decisions about his defenses. Now that the West Caves were cut off from supply, and the tightening perimeters of the 162nd and 186th Infantry Regiments prevented him from doing more than harassing operations at the airfields, he felt he could no longer conduct an effective defense. Apparently, on the night of June 21st, Colonel Kuzume instructed his remaining troops to flee to the north and conduct a guerilla warfare campaign. After issuing these instructions Colonel Kuzume burned the regimental colors of the *222nd Infantry Regiment* and committed suicide in the West Caves. The survivors of the *1st* and *2nd Battalions, 222nd Infantry*, burst out of the West Caves that same night and fell upon the lines of the 186th Infantry. Several waves of attackers hit the American lines. Others attacked the 162nd Infantry. Supported by machine guns and mortars, the Japanese succeeded in reaching the American foxholes and engaged in hand-to-hand combat. Infantrymen of Company G, 186th Infantry, found the Japanese so close they could not call for their own supporting fires. Time after time the Japanese attacked, until the coming of daylight brought an end to the fighting.

American commanders hoped that the attack had broken the back of Japanese resistance. The attack of June 22nd proved this a vain hope. Although it was noted that resistance was less intense than previously, there was still considerable strength left to the enemy holding the West Caves. Apparently Colonel Kuzume had ordered recently arrived reinforcements from the *221st Infantry Regiment* to defend the West Caves in order to

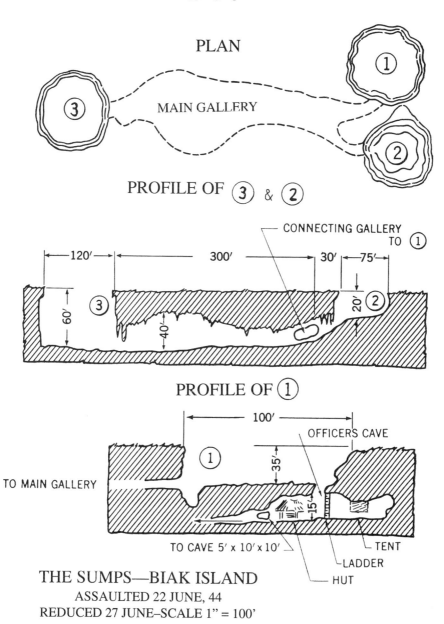

PLAN

MAIN GALLERY

PROFILE OF ③ & ②

CONNECTING GALLERY TO ①

PROFILE OF ①

OFFICERS CAVE

TO MAIN GALLERY

TO CAVE 5' x 10' x 10'

TENT

LADDER

HUT

THE SUMPS—BIAK ISLAND
ASSAULTED 22 JUNE, 44
REDUCED 27 JUNE–SCALE 1" = 100'

cover the withdrawal of his regiment. The 1st Battalion, 186th Infantry, supported by the 116th Combat Engineer Battalion spent the day attacking the West Caves, with notable success now that the garrison was reduced in strength. At the end of the day Colonel Newman reported the West Caves secured. That night, June 22/23, once again the 162nd Infantry was counterattacked by Japanese from inside the West Caves. Yet in fact the caves were finished. No organized enemy remained to hold the defenses, although there were many stragglers in the area. After more mopping up operations, the 1st Battalion, 162nd Infantry joined by the 41st Counter Intelligence Detachment entered the caves on June 25th, and by June 27th could report with authority that there were no living Japanese in the West Caves. Exactly one month after the landings on Biak, the airfields were free of enemy fire.

Nevertheless there were still Japanese in caves harassing the Task Force. Although the Japanese had been eliminated from the West Caves, and the 863rd Engineers had the airfields operational, there was much left to be done on Biak. There were still thousands of enemy troops roaming the island, and these had to be eliminated as a cohesive force. The 163rd and 186th Infantry Regiments were to patrol north and west to find and destroy these enemy remnants. Japanese positions were discovered in several locations, including an artillery position with five 75mm artillery pieces. These were attacked and captured by Companies K and L of the 186th Infantry. At another location called the "Teardrop" for its shape on the map, coordination between 41st Infantry Division units broke down. The 2nd Battalion, 186th Infantry, had to wait three days for the 3rd Battalion, 163rd Infantry to get into position to reduce the enemy positions at the "Teardrop." It turned out that the 163rd Infantry units did not realize how far it was from its starting point to the attack position, and that delayed things by several days. By the time the attack could be mounted, the Japanese had slipped away.

The fall of the West Caves and the withdrawal of the Japanese from the area around the airfields had satisfied General Eichelberger that his mission had been accomplished. Although aware that there were many live Japanese at large on Biak, and that there was much left to do, he had other duties awaiting him, including future invasions to plan. So, on June 27th, he and his I Corps staff left for Hollandia. General Eichelberger went on to command a new field army, the 8th U.S. Army, which he would lead with distinction in the liberation of the Philippines. General Doe took command of Hurricane Task Force while retaining command of the 41st Infantry Division. He, too, would lead the division into the Philippines. Orders came down for the 34th Infantry Regiment to rejoin its parent division. So, the battle for Biak would end with the same forces which had begun it a month earlier, the 41st Infantry Division versus the *Biak Garrison*.

There was still plenty of combat left in the *Biak Garrison*. The 1st Battalion, 34th Infantry, ran into a detachment of the *219th Infantry* on June 26th, before they left Biak. This enemy unit, another of the reinforcing forces which arrived at Biak safely, ambushed Company C and later attacked the battalion's command post. These troops disappeared, apparently the result of new orders from General Anami to withdraw north and form guerilla units.

Another troublesome position, known to the Americans as the East Caves, had existed all along above the coastal road. Because they had been quiet, and because they did not directly threaten the airfields, they had been observed throughout the campaign to conquer the West Caves, but not directly attacked. Now, with only mopping up left, these positions were to be reduced. The Japanese garrison was mixed, consisting of troops from the *222nd Infantry*, the *17th Field Airdrome Construction Unit*, and stragglers from many other Japanese service units. Artillery, mortar and naval gunfire had been used to neutralize the caves and keep the coast road open. The Japanese had managed to close the road several times, but never after June 13th. The enemy remained quiet until Company E, 542nd Engineer Boat and Shore Regiment, began construction of a jetty near Mokmer Village. This work directly under them proved too much for the East Caves garrison, and they opened fire. A call went out for troops and artillery.

Between June 29th and July 3rd, mortars, artillery and infantry patrols from Company E, 542nd Engineers and Company I, 163rd Infantry, eliminated Japanese positions in the East Caves.

41st Division war dog helps flush out Japanese defenders during Biak fighting.

With harassing fire continuing to come from the East Caves after the clearing operation, an infantry attack by Company E, 163rd Infantry, was prepared. However, when the Americans attacked on July 5th, they discovered the East Caves had been evacuated. The Japanese had left behind much equipment and food, but the survivors had made a successful escape.

There was one last pocket of Japanese resistance remaining in the original beachhead sector. This pocket, the Ibdi Pocket, also overlooked the Coast Road, and had caused problems since the early days of the landing. It had been contained throughout June, and occasionally attacked by the 163rd Infantry. Continually bombarded by artillery and air strikes, it had not been a threat to the invasion since early June. Now, however, it was the last position held by the enemy within the Americans' perimeter. As such, it had to be eliminated. At the end of June, the 163rd Infantry had made a concerted effort at reducing the size of the pocket. The 1st and 2nd Battalions had attacked the fringes and eliminated all outlying positions. The operation was slow and costly. Already understrength from the Wakde-Sarmi operation and weeks of combat on Biak, the American units had difficulty mustering enough strength to accomplish their mission. By the end of June, for example, Company F had only 42 effectives and

Company G only 65 able bodied men. But the enemy was known to be weak as well, so the attacks continued.

They continued throughout July. By July 28th the Ibdi Pocket, and with it the *3rd Battalion, 222nd Infantry*, had been eliminated. The positions of the enemy were now thoroughly examined. Here were the first signs of the type of defenses the Americans would face in the near future on Palau, the Philippines, and Iwo Jima. Caves, pillboxes hidden at ground level, connecting tunnels from one position to several others, all were found on Biak.

While the Ibdi Pocket was being reduced, the other units of the 41st Division were patrolling far and wide to eliminate remaining organized enemy groups on the island. Using infantry patrols, supported by amphibious patrols, the division covered as much of the island as possible. Landings were made at places along the coast where it was believed the Japanese would try to establish bases or attempt to escape from the island. The 41st Reconnaissance Troop and the infantry of the 186th and 162nd Regiments all participated in these patrols, some of which were guided by Netherlands officials, part of the returning Netherlands East Indies Civil Administration. Occasional clashes resulted in some American casualties and in further dispersing the Japanese. These patrols continued throughout August, when General Krueger officially ended the Biak Campaign. In actual fact, they continued until early January, when the 41st Infantry Division left for the Philippines.

Other units chased the Japanese stragglers as well. During the month of November, 1944, the 369th Infantry Regiment's detachment guarding a radar site at Wardo had several sharp skirmishes which resulted in 38 Japanese killed and 1 captured. When this regiment left Biak, leaving behind its 2nd Battalion as a security and labor force, it had killed an additional 74 enemy troops and captured 34 with no loss to themselves. The regiment, less the 2nd Battalion, rejoined its parent 93rd Infantry Division on Morotai.

Official records indicate that the Hurricane Task Force lost some 400 men killed in action, 2,000 wounded and 150 injured in action, and had 5 men missing in action. Most of these casualties were, of course, within the 41st Infantry Division. In addition to combat casualties, some 7,234 men were brought down by illness. Most of these were service and engineer troops who were engulfed in the scrub typhus epidemic which began on Owi Island and spread quickly. Thus, the cost of taking Biak Island, including all causes, was about 9,800 men. This is not a low figure, and does not include those few additional casualties which occurred after August 20th, the official end of the campaign. At this cost, some 5,000 enemy soldiers had been killed and three airfields had been secured.

Perhaps the best epitaph for the battle of Biak was written during General MacArthur's only visit to the island, after the war ended. It was written not by the General, but by his personal pilot who was flying him back to the Philippines after a visit to Australia. Stopping to refuel on Biak in November, 1944, he recorded "This island, which cost many American lives to capture and which once was a beehive of activity, is now practically deserted. Dozens of buildings stand unoccupied, and the jungle is rapidly edging up to the roads and the fine airstrips. In a very few years, I daresay, it will be difficult to find traces of this once tremendous airbase." The airstrips may be overgrown, but for those men of Hurricane Task Force and the *222nd Infantry Regiment* who survived, the battle of Biak remains etched in their memories.

CHAPTER IX

Noemfoor

*I*t had become apparent early in the Biak Operation that things were not going well, and that additional operations would be needed to ensure the success of the plan to secure Geelvink Bay as a base for future operations. If the Biak fields were not operational in time, then other sites would have to be secured. Further, if these fields could not be operational for any length of time then the planned operations to secure the rest of New Guinea would be seriously delayed. They could not be conducted without air support. With no aircraft carrier support permanently assigned to the Seventh Fleet, Southwest Pacific operations continued to be limited to the extreme range of the air support provided by the Fifth and Thirteenth Army Air Forces. Accordingly, General MacArthur's headquarters began, on June 4th, preparations to ensure uninterrupted progress towards the Philippines.

Planners at Southwest Pacific Headquarters decided that the island of Noemfoor, about midway between Biak and the tip of New Guinea's western end, would be the next operation. Army Air Force aircraft could easily reach it from the now secure fields on Wakde. The island had an airfield or two, was known to be a staging area for reinforcements on the way to Biak, and once seized it would provide additional security for the Allied bases in and around Geelvink Bay.

Like Biak, Noemfoor is a coral and limestone island, with heavy jungle covering. It is circular in shape and much smaller than Biak. Again like Biak, the terrain is rugged, with little or no road development. Noemfoor was also surrounded by a coral reef. Its only appeal to the allies was its strategic location and its Japanese airfields.

The Japanese on Noemfoor were there for two reasons. Originally they had established airstrips there, as on Biak. Two were complete, a third still under construction. With the invasion of Biak, Noemfoor became a staging base for the reinforcement of the *Biak Garrison*. Elements of the *36th Infantry Division* were passed through Noemfoor, arriving and departing by small craft and hiding ashore by day to avoid Allied sea patrols. It was by this method that the battalion of the *221st Infantry Regiment* had landed on Biak in time to reinforce the West Caves. Allied intelligence had little confirmed knowledge about the enemy on Noemfoor, but in view of their error on Biak, they overestimated the enemy force, claiming over 3,000 troops on the island and declaring most of them to be combat troops.

Actually, there were only some 2,000 enemy troops on Noemfoor at the time of the invasion. Only about half of these were trained combat troops. The only combat experienced unit available was the *3rd Battalion, 219th Infantry*. Passing through Noemfoor on its way to Biak was a part of the *2nd Battalion, 219th Infantry*. There were also a few soldiers from the *222nd Infantry* who had not been on Biak at the time of the American invasion there. A Colonel Shimizu commanded the garrison. He was well aware that he was a likely target for the next allied amphibious assault, and correctly estimated that the landing would come over the beach near Kamiri Drome, one of the completed airstrips. His conviction about the allied landing area was reinforced when his troops discovered signs of an allied reconnaissance in progress in the area of Kamiri Drome. These scouts, known as the Alamo Scouts, were a special group of intelligence gatherers formed earlier in the campaign for use by Sixth Army headquarters to conduct clandestine landings for the information needed for amphibious assaults.

While Colonel Shimizu made his preparations, General Krueger was doing the same. Because the 6th Infantry Division was still engaged at Lone Tree Hill, and because his long range plans called for that unit to participate in an already scheduled invasion later in the campaign, he substituted the 158th Infantry

Regimental Combat Team for the originally suggested 6th Infantry Division. Planning between the services began on June 16th, when General Krueger called his first meeting dealing with Noemfoor. Naval planners missed the conference, called at short notice. Yet this meeting did determine that no carrier based air support would be available. The fast Carrier Task Forces were all fully engaged in the Central Pacific campaign. Because Biak was still not operational as an air base, and because a recent Japanese air attack on Wakde had knocked out some sixty allied aircraft and damaged the base, the operation had to be postponed. The delay in relieving the 158th Regimental Combat Team with the 6th Infantry Division also postponed matters. In the meantime, another conference on June 20th settled all matters pertaining to interservice cooperation.

For the now experienced soldiers of the 158th Infantry, the necessary decisions were made rather casually. Major Boysie Day suggested that since the bulk of the enemy opposition could reasonably be expected to be at or near Kamiri Drome, the main field, that the regiment should land east of the field and attack from the rear of the suspected enemy defenses. Colonel Sandlin rejected Major Day's plan and ordered the assault to land directly at the airfield. When asked why he wanted to land where enemy opposition could be expected to be the heaviest, Colonel Sandlin replied, "because it's too damn far to walk." Obviously, "planning Noemfoor was as hectic as its code name, Tabletennis."

The assault force was designated Cyclone Task Force, and was commanded by Brigadier General Edwin D. Patrick, still commanding the 158th Regimental Combat Team. The troops were mounted in Landing Vehicles, Tracked, known to the troops as LVTs, sometimes called Alligators. These caterpillar landing vehicles had been developed at the request of the U.S. Marine Corps before the war, but were only now arriving in sufficient numbers in the Pacific for general use. Produced in several models during the war, the transport type which carried the men of the 158th Infantry mounted one 12.7 machine gun in front and two 7.62 machine guns in the rear. Often additional weapons were added by the individual crews. Capable of speeds from ten to twelve miles per hour in the water, and

Jeep convoy brings sup-plies along improvised road in New Guinea jungle.

twenty to thirty miles per hour on land, they carried troops in a sheltered compartment which would protect them from any-thing other than a direct hit by an artillery or mortar shell. The task force managed to get one rehearsal on June 28th, and then loaded for the combat assault on Noemfoor. Pre-invasion bom-bardment began on June 20th and continued until the actual assault. Some 800 tons of bombs dropped in and on Kamiri Drome, and Allied cruisers and destroyers added their weight to the bombardment. The Allied naval support force, under Commodore John A. Collins, Royal Australian Navy, began their attack at first light, July 2nd.

The day was partly overcast and conditions were exactly right for an amphibious assault. The Japanese did not at first respond to the Allied attack, only anti-aircraft fire at naval spotting planes which quickly ceased. The 1st and 2nd Battal-ions, 158th Infantry, landed without opposition and crossed Kamiri Airdrome still in their assault craft. They reached a coral ridge on the far side of the airstrip and then dismounted, preparing to carry their attack further. No Japanese had yet been seen nor enemy fire received. It was in all respects an ideal landing against an enemy held beach. When Japanese were finally encountered, 500 yards east of Kamiri Airfield, they were confused and disorganized. The 2nd Battalion used automatic weapons and rifles to eliminate some 40 Japanese who were apparently shell shocked, too shaken by the pre-invasion bombardment to fight or flee. Some distance from this encounter, reinforced by the 1st Platoon, 603rd Tank Company, the battalion encountered enemy troops in solid defensive positions. These presented some resistance and the battalion with its tank support reduced them carefully. Moving west, the 1st Battalion encountered only sporadic resistance, and quickly seized the riverbank which was its beachhead objective.

The last of the combat troops came ashore while the assault units were moving inland. The 3rd Battalion went to the assistance of the 2nd Battalion, although not called for by that unit. With the additional strength in the line the beachhead perimeter was secured well before nightfall. Somewhat less than hoped for, due to the careful mopping up operations within the perimeter, it was more than adequate to secure the airfield. Problems soon arose on the beach, however. Here reef conditions and soft sand caused delays in unloading until the engineers used their bulldozers, tanks, and tracked amphibian vehicles to pull all other types of vehicles ashore. Naval demolition parties and the Shore Battalion, 593rd Engineer Boat and Shore Regiment blew holes in the reef while constructing temporary causeways leading from the reef to the shore. Some random Japanese artillery fire fell on the beach, destroying two vehicles, but it was not enough to hinder the landing of troops and supplies.

The end of the day found Cyclone Task Force in complete control of the beach, with a defensible perimeter and all supplies and follow-up support troops ashore as planned. The first airstrip was secure. The only thing missing was the enemy. No sizable Japanese force had been encountered, and from a prisoner taken evidence reached General Patrick that he may have to face more than he expected. The prisoner reported that on June 25th, some 3,000 more Japanese combat troops had landed on Noemfoor. This would bring the garrison to well over 4,000 troops, with most of them classed as combat troops, according to General Patrick's information. Fearing a repetition of Biak, General Patrick did not attempt to halt the planned landing of reinforcements by air the following day.

The follow-up assault force for the Noemfoor operation was the 503rd Parachute Infantry Regiment. Planners had decided that it would be flown to Noemfoor and parachuted in as reinforcements when Kamiri Airfield had been secured. This had been accomplished on the first day. The plan had an alternate scheme should Kamiri Airfield not be taken on the first day. In that case the 34th Infantry Regiment, still on Biak, would come by water. Because the paratroopers could get there faster, and because of his new information on enemy strength, General Patrick allowed the paratroopers to land according to the original plan.

The 503rd Parachute Infantry Regiment, under Colonel George M. Jones, had been in the Southwest Pacific theater for more than a year. It had participated in the seizure of Nadzab Airfield in September of 1943, after which it remained in Australia as a sort of general reserve for the entire theater. It was difficult to find a suitable mission for paratroopers in the kind of terrain found throughout the Southwest Pacific. At Nadzab they had landed by parachute on an airfield, a rare clear spot to use airborne forces. Unopposed at Nadzab, seized by Australian troops before the arrival of the Americans, they were still relatively combat inexperienced. With the seizure of Hollandia they had been sent forward to gain some combat experience in patrolling against the enemy stragglers in the area. While planning the Noemfoor operation, it was decided to use them as the support force since once again there was an opportunity to use them. This also helped to alleviate the concern at General MacArthur's Headquarters that if they couldn't find uses for the airborne force, it would be assigned to other theaters of operations.

At the time of the Noemfoor operation, the 503rd was still conducting combat patrols against enemy stragglers at Hollandia. Due to an inadequate number of C-47 transport planes, the regiment would have to jump at the rate of one battalion a day, the first jump scheduled for July 3rd. Major Cameron Knox's 1st Battalion, accompanied by Colonel Jones as observer, departed early on the morning of July 3rd. Shortly after they took off, General Patrick advised General Krueger's headquarters that he recommended the planes fly over the airstrip in single file and drop their paratroopers one planeload at a time. He made this recommendation based on advice from a Canadian paratrooper officer who was observing Noemfoor operations. This officer pointed out that the Kamiri Strip was made of a hard coral surface, had many large pieces of equipment parked along it, and had jungle close alongside. General Patrick's message reached General Krueger, who forwarded it to the aircraft carrying Major Knox's battalion. Unfortunately, it never reached the pilots flying the 503rd to Noemfoor.

The 503rd Parachute Infantry encountered other difficulties. For reasons never explained, the transport pilots, who had no experience with airborne operations, flew much too low. Most flew below the 400 feet minimum altitude necessary for the paratroopers to drop safely. Further, Colonel Jones had been told by reconnaissance photograph interpreters that Kamiri Airfield was 260 feet wide. Actually it was only 170 feet wide. The result of all this lost and confused information was disaster for the 1st Battalion of the 503rd Parachute Infantry Regiment.

At 10 A. M., the C-47's began crossing the strip in pairs. During the next half hour the battalion jumped, a total of 739 paratroopers landing all over the area. Some 72 men were injured during these landings. These injuries resulted from low jump altitude, from hitting the hard packed coral surface, and from landing on the many pieces of equipment parked along the airfield. Colonel Jones himself, jumping from one of the lead, low flying, planes "crashed into the coral runway, incurring a sharp blow to his head. Had Jones not been wearing his steel helmet, his skull would have undoubtedly been crushed." Nearly ten per cent of the paratroopers were out of action before they had even formed up. Assigned responsibility for airstrip defense, Colonel Jones, who spent the rest of the campaign with a splitting headache, called immediately for his 3rd Battalion to jump on July 4th.

The 3rd Battalion, 503rd Parachute Infantry, landed on Kamiri Airfield on July 4th as ordered. This time all precautions had been taken and confirmed. General Patrick cleared the strip of all equipment. Planes dropping the troopers stayed above 400 feet, in single file. Despite all these steps, Major John Erickson's 3rd Battalion suffered 56 jump casualties while landing. Colonel Jones had enough. He asked General Patrick to bring in Lieutenant Colonel John Britton's 2nd Battalion by sea. The 503rd

Troops use improvised grease rack for vehicle maintenance.

Parachute Infantry had lost 144 men before ever seeing a Japanese soldier on Noemfoor.

Little was accomplished by rushing the 503rd Parachute Infantry to Noemfoor. Allied intelligence had overestimated the Japanese garrison's strength, and the report General Patrick had received from the enemy prisoner was false. However, now that the 503rd was guarding the airfield, the 158th could advance to locate and eliminate the enemy. On July 4th, the 3rd Battalion, 158th Infantry, moved east toward the second airstrip. Although they found much evidence to indicate the enemy was present, there was no opposition. Minefields and defensive positions were located along the coast road between the two airstrips, but no Japanese. By the end of July 4th the second airfield, Kornasoren Drome, was in American hands.

The 1st Battalion occupied Kamiri Village at the opposite end of the beachhead perimeter. Here again there were no Japanese. However, as the battalion proceeded beyond the village, scattered rifle fire began to be received. Directly ahead lay an area known as the "Japanese gardens" and Hill 201. Here the main Japanese force waited to be discovered. Approaching Hill 201 the leading scout saw a group of Japanese, heavily armed, moving towards Hill 201. Alerted to the presence of the enemy on Hill 201, the battalion commander decided upon a double envelopment. Sending one infantry company around each flank, with his heavy weapons company in support, the battalion commander surrounded the hill before dark. The battalion settled down for the night, registering artillery and heavy mortar fire in the event of a night attack on their positions.

The precaution was well taken. At 4:30 a. m. on the morning of July 5th, the Japanese attacked the American positions. As the attack began, the battalion requested that all supporting fires begin, and artillery from Lieutenant Colonel Fred Shurr's 147th Field Artillery Battalion, mortars of the 641st Tank Destroyer Battalion and the 1st Battalion's own heavy mortars combined to smash the enemy attack. The attacking force, about 400 men of the *10th* and *12th Companies, 219th Infantry*, were severely mauled by this barrage. Only small groups managed to reach the American lines, where they were cut down with rifle and automatic weapons fire. Lieutenant Colonel Shoemaker had observed that the enemy tended to use the most obvious avenue of approach to American positions, and he had placed his automatic weapons accordingly. Digging into the coral had been difficult, but now paid dividends as the Americans were in the ground, as at Sarmi, while the Japanese were exposed. Sergeant William Hardy's heavy machine gun from Company D was in the direct line of advance for the Japanese, and he was kept busy all morning, but never once in danger of being overrun. At no time did they threaten to break the American perimeter. After some two hours of fruitless assault, the survivors withdrew, leaving over 200 dead behind. The back of the Japanese defense of Noemfoor had been broken.

So quick and concentrated had been the Japanese attack that some of the men of the 1st Battalion did not even realize that there had been a full scale counterattack. Lieutenants Herbert Erb and Gustave Green had been talking about their prewar occupations, insurance salesman and sheep shearer, respectively, when they noticed the fire of heavy weapons coming from the other side of Hill 201. Curious, they wandered over to find scores of enemy bodies in front of Sergeant Hardy's machine gun, including one actually draped over the weapon.

Lieutenant Erb was later told that the actual count of enemy dead was over 300, but only 201 were officially reported.

While the 1st Battalion mopped up around Hill 201, the 2nd Battalion, relieved at the airstrip by the 503rd Parachute Infantry, moved against the last airfield. This was done on July 6th, when the battalion boarded amphibious assault craft and landed on the west coast. The battalion seized Namber Drome without firing a shot, with no casualties, and had the strip operational by lunchtime. All objectives originally set for Cyclone Task Force had now been accomplished. Vigorous patrolling over the next several days failed to reveal any Japanese force of threatening size, and so General Patrick divided the island into two sectors, southern and northern. Each of his regiments was assigned one sector to clear of remaining enemy groups. When, on July 11th, the 2nd Battalion of the 503rd arrived, the plan went into effect.

The 158th Infantry had been assigned the northern sector, and for them combat on Noemfoor was largely over. Mopping up continued within their sector. Captain Clarence Fennell, still in command of Company L, was preparing his company's position for the night when he heard movement in the bushes to his front. Expecting enemy, he was surprised to see "a column of nearly naked Asians." They were Javanese forced laborers who had been used by the Japanese. In order to prevent them from escaping, each had a spike put through their ankles. Captain Fennell and his men rescued some 22 people, including women and children that day, part of the 403 survivors of the original 3,000 Javanese brought to the island by the Japanese Army. Also captured on the island were some Formosan laborers. These individuals usually fought alongside the Japanese regular soldiers, but were quicker to surrender than the Japanese. In one instance on Noemfoor, a dozen Formosans, surrendered and under a white flag, were killed by an American infantryman. In the Pacific war there was little quarter given or expected.

As the Japanese survivors had decided to concentrate in the west central part of the island, it fell to the 503rd Parachute Infantry to finish the conquest of Noemfoor. For three days, July 13-16, the 1st Battalion attacked Hill 670. This was Colonel Shimizu's command post. On the night of July 15/16, the

Japanese evacuated the area, and once again the 503rd sent out patrols to find the remnants of the Noemfoor garrison.

It was the 2nd Battalion, 503rd, which found the Japanese next. Company D ran into a Japanese position near the village of Inasi. The Japanese attacked by surprise, and one platoon of the company was cut off. The company commander ordered Sergeant Roy E. Eubanks to take his squad forward and relieve the trapped platoon. Sergeant Eubanks moved his men to within 30 yards of the Japanese, ordered them to provide covering fire, and then with two scouts advanced on the enemy. Halfway to the enemy the small group was pinned down by enemy machine gun fire. Sergeant Eubanks, armed with an automatic rifle, jumped forward and advanced standing in full view of the Japanese. All enemy fire was concentrated on him. Just before he reached the enemy he was struck by a burst of enemy fire which destroyed his weapon. Despite serious wounds, Sergeant Eubanks continued his attack into the enemy position and killed four more of the enemy, using his rifle as a club, before he himself was killed. His actions, which saved the trapped platoon, also resulted in 45 enemy casualties. Sergeant Eubanks was posthumously awarded the Medal of Honor.

July turned to August, and still the remaining Japanese could not be eliminated. Days would be spent in locating a group of Japanese. Then an attack would be mounted. Sometime during the night the surviving enemy soldiers would slip away, starting the whole process all over again. The American patrols had discovered some disturbing signs during their searches. First, the rest of the Javanese slave laborers were rescued. They were in as poor condition as the earlier ones rescued by Captain Fennell and his men. Shortly afterwards, patrol reports began to indicate the possibility of cannibalism by the Japanese. On August 11th, the 158th Infantry regimental headquarters received a report forwarded by the paratroopers that they had over fifty enemy dead after a skirmish, and that two of their own dead, who had lain behind enemy lines during the night, had been cannibalized. This report also stated that four of the Japanese, who had apparently been dead prior to the skirmish with the paratroopers, had also been cannibalized. At first higher authority felt that these bodies had suffered from concentrated artillery fire, but it soon became apparent that this was not the case. Late in August a captured Japanese medical officer admitted surgically removing portions of dead bodies for food.

Not all the Japanese fought to the bitter end. One young Japanese pilot, in his early 20's, decided that he had enough of this war. Piloting his fighter plane to Noemfoor, he crash landed on the beach right in front of an observation post manned by Private Joseph Palma and his squad of the 158th Infantry. Climbing out of his plane, the pilot quickly surrendered to the Americans. It turned out the pilot was a graduate of the University of Southern California and that he intended to survive this war. Private Palma and his comrades marched their unique prisoner directly to regimental headquarters. The following day Private Palma and his squad captured 60 naked Japanese with many officers who had stripped to ensure that the Americans didn't misunderstand their intentions. The officers kept their insignia of rank in their hands, to ensure treatment due officers under the Geneva Convention, an agreement to which Japan was not a party. Clearly, the battle for Noemfoor was over.

General Krueger agreed, and decided to officially end the Noemfoor campaign on August 31st. Total casualties for the Cyclone Task Force operations to that date totaled 63 men killed, 343 wounded and 3 missing. Over 1,700 Japanese had been counted dead, and 180 had been captured. Once again the mopping up of Japanese stragglers was left to the native police under the Netherlands Indies Civil Administration. For Cyclone Task Force, the battle of Noemfoor was officially over.

CHAPTER X

The Driniumor River Line

While Southwest Pacific Theater forces moved steadily westward, ever closer to the Philippines, things were not static to their rear. The ease with which the Sixth Army had seized Hollandia was deceptive. Within days of securing the airfields, intelligence officers began to evaluate information coming in from a variety of sources. Much of this data indicated that the mass of Japanese troops bypassed by the Hollandia operation, nearly the entire Japanese *18th Army*, was on the move, heading west. Reports from natives and aerial photography indicated that the enemy was organizing and moving towards the American perimeter at Aitape. Combined with Ultra intercepts, the reading of the Japanese military codes, this information clearly indicated that a major movement of the enemy force was in progress. Most assumed that it would be directed against the American eastern perimeter at Aitape.

It would be some time before such a large force could be expected to arrive at Aitape. This time was used by the Americans to reorganize their forces in and around Hollandia. The 41st Infantry Division was moving west, and so it was relieved by the 32nd Infantry Division. Major General William H. Gill, commanding the 32nd Infantry Division, assumed command of Persecution Task Force on May 4th. The 41st Infantry Division was relieved by the 32nd Infantry Division the same day and took over responsibility for the eastern defense perimeter at Aitape and Hollandia. The division's regiments were assigned roles for the coming defense of Hollandia. The 126th Infantry

Regiment was assigned to defend the western perimeter, while the 127th Infantry took over the eastern sector. The division's third regiment, the 128th Infantry, was held in reserve.

Major General William Hanson Gill was born in Loudon County, Virginia in 1886. He began his military career at the Virginia Military Institute as a part of a continuing family tradition. Entered in the class of 1907, he was a classmate with future General George S. Patton, who later went on to West Point. Cadet Gill had also planned to go on to West Point despite his grandparents' strenuous objections to his wearing a blue uniform, the color of their most recent enemies in the Civil War. His plans were thwarted, however, when his father could only provide him with the alternate appointment from his Congressional District, and the young man who had the principal appointment accepted it. Ironically, many years later, he would visit West Point as a guest speaker during the annual reunion of the Class of 1904, the one he would have been in had the West Point appointment been his. During the festivities the now retired Major General Gill was made an honorary member of the West Point Class of 1904.

Graduating VMI with an engineering degree, he tried his luck in private industry with a friend in Spokane, Washington. After a number of years, he returned to Virginia to help his father out in business. While there, he organized and trained a local militia company of volunteers. Still interested in a military life, Gill studied for an examination which would provide him a commission in the regular army from civilian life. Passing successfully, he was commissioned a second lieutenant of engineers and posted to Fort Leavenworth, Kansas, to brush up on his military knowledge. After this initial schooling Lieutenant Gill was assigned to the infantry, and after some years in the northwest, was ordered to the Philippines. While there, he made the acquaintance of another lieutenant, George C. Marshall. Promoted to captain, he returned to the United States at the time it entered the First World War. Serving in France with the 5th Infantry Division as a battalion commander, he earned a Silver Star by scouting ahead of his battalion during an intense artillery barrage, saving his command from suffering numerous casualties.

After the war Captain Gill served as the Inspector-Instructor of the Virginia National Guard. Later he took the Advanced Infantry Course at Fort Benning, Georgia where he did so well he was then sent on to the Command and General Staff School, where again he did so well he was kept on as an instructor. One of his students was future General of the Army Dwight D. Eisenhower. After four years teaching, he was sent on to the Army War College to complete his military education. After this, he commanded various infantry units in the United States. Here, as a young major commanding an infantry battalion, he first met General Douglas MacArthur while acting as an honor guard for the visiting dignitary. Four years on the Army's General Staff was followed by a return to infantry duty in Hawaii. Finally, before the entry of the United States into World War II, he served as the Reserve Officers Training Corps commander at the University of California at Berkeley. By now a colonel and well regarded in the Army, Colonel Gill was assigned as Chief of Staff to the newly forming 8th Infantry Division. Later he would serve with the Pennsylvania National Guard's 28th Infantry Division where he was promoted to brigadier general and assistant division commander. Shortly afterwards, he became division commander with the rank of major general of the 89th Infantry Division. General Gill created the 89th Infantry Division from scratch, and was looking forward to leading it into combat when he received an unexpected telephone call from Washington. It seems his immediate presence was required in Australia, to take command of the battered 32nd Infantry Division, whose previous commander had just been relieved of command after the disastrous Papuan campaign. General Gill protested to no avail. Told that General MacArthur, who barely knew him, had personally requested him, General Gill had no choice but to take command of the battered 32nd.

General Gill was interviewed by General MacArthur, and then sent on to the 32nd Infantry Division. He found over 8,000 of its men down with malaria. The troops were tired and equipment in bad condition. Supported by General Eichelberger, who had been his classmate in some of the staff schools, General Gill set about rebuilding the division, almost repeating exactly what he had just done for the new 89th Infantry Division he had left behind in Colorado. Several months were needed to rebuild the shattered division. After jungle and amphibious assault training, the division moved back to New Guinea, and landed at Saidor, where other American units had largely cleared the area of the enemy. For the 32nd Infantry Division Saidor was largely a defensive operation. One problem investigated by General Gill, how the enemy continued to get supplies although bypassed, included his participating in a PT boat raid well behind the enemy lines. Then, in April of 1944 the 32nd Infantry Division was ordered to land at Aitape.

Having landed and seized the main objective, the Tadji airstrips, the Persecution Task Force's next priority was the protection of those facilities. Having created the Eastern Sector using the 127th Infantry Regiment, General Gill made the regimental commander, Colonel Merle H. Howe, the sector commander. Colonel Howe's troops soon discovered that there were enemy troops facing them across the Nigia river. These troops, members of the enemy's *20th* and *41st Infantry Divisions*, were concentrating in villages along the coast and inland as well. Clearly, the intelligence reports had some substance. Colonel Howe distributed his regiment to keep contact with the Japanese, while at the same time putting blocking positions in their path. His 1st Battalion was to block and patrol the Dandriwad River, the 2nd Battalion was to cover the inland territory from the villages of Chinapelli and Afua, while the 3rd Battalion was to block and patrol the Driniumor River between the coast and Afua. These dispositions began to take effect by May 7th.

Some of the planned positions in Colonel Howe's scheme required his units to move beyond the established perimeter. The first to move east was Nyaparake Force, Company C and a part of Company D, under Captain Tally D. Fulmer. After crossing the Dandriwad River, they encountered a well organized Japanese force which opposed their advance. The Americans withdrew and spent the following day reorganizing. Reinforced by troops from Company A, the Nyaparake Force recrossed the Dandriwad River on the 9th. Additional support was available from Seventh Fleet PT boats offshore. Resistance continued all day, and all troops withdrew to the village of Babiang, where Captain Fulmer reported to Colonel Howe that he had encountered large and aggressive groups of enemy troops. Colonel Howe ordered Captain Fulmer to attempt to push east, for it was imperative that the enemy be kept at a distance from the airfields. Supported by air strikes from Number 78 Wing, Royal Australian Air Force, Captain Fulmer again sent out platoons of his Company C, this time without opposition. For the next two days the Nyaparake Force fought their way east, against continuing but uneven Japanese resistance. During the night of May 14th, a counterattack by elements of the *20th Infantry Division* indicated that the Japanese were no longer content to remain on the defensive. This attack, although it did no serious damage to Nyaparake Force, did alert Colonel Howe and General Gill that things had changed to the east. Although Captain Fulmer was willing to proceed on his mission, General Gill decided that such a course was unwise given the aggressiveness of the enemy and their suspected strength. He ordered Captain Fulmer to withdraw, while Company A under Captain Herman Bottcher established a defensive position along the banks of the Dandriwad River.

Before Captain Fulmer's force moved west, however, Japanese forces moved between it and the Dandriwad River. During the 14th, these Japanese also began harassing Captain Bottcher's force which had taken up positions at Ulau Mission. General Gill ordered both units evacuated by sea, which was successfully accomplished on May 15th. Clearly there were strong and aggressive enemy forces just to the east of the Americans' defensive perimeter. General Krueger believed at this time that the sudden aggressiveness of the enemy was intended to cover their withdrawal of their main force around the American positions at Hollandia. He believed that their true destination was Sarmi, where they could rejoin the main enemy forces and regroup and resupply. The Americans believed that the Japanese were moving the *20th Infantry* and the *41st Infantry Divisions* around the inland flank of the Hollandia perimeter, while covering forces harassed the Americans and kept them within their perimeter. The remaining division of the *18th Army*, the *51st Infantry Division*, had not been identified, and was believed to have been left behind at Wewak to delay pursuit by the Australian infantry. Based upon these assumptions, Brigadier General Clarence A. Martin, assistant division commander of the 32nd Infantry Division, was ordered to take command of the eastern defense sector and to "maintain contact with and delay enemy units moving eastward." General Martin withdrew the original Nyaparake Force for rest and replenishment and substituted Company A, 127th Infantry and the division's Reconnaissance Troop. Captain Bottcher was transferred to the command of the Reconnaissance Troop and also given overall command of the new force. His orders were to keep contact with the enemy.

The Japanese, who had plans of their own, did not cooperate. Instead of trying to bypass Captain Bottcher's position, they continually attacked in small groups. Reconnaissance patrols were similarly harassed and prevented from completing their missions. By nightfall on May 22nd, Captain Bottcher's force was obliged to fight its way out of encirclement and withdraw some two miles west to relieve some of the pressure. General Gill began to show concern about the enemy's true intentions, and he ordered the 1st Battalion, 126th Infantry, to the area. Lieutenant Colonel Cladie A. Bailey's men were to push the enemy back to the Drindaria River. They were also to relieve the Nyaparake Force with Company G, 127th Infantry. Captain Bottcher's men were to go into reserve.

Initially, the advance went well. Nyaparake Force was relieved by Company G on May 31st. Colonel Bailey's troops pushed beyond the position manned by Company G and succeeded in reaching the village of Yakamul, where resistance stiffened. Elements of both the *78th* and *80th Infantry Regiments* had been identified as opposing the advance. Clearly one infantry battalion could not handle the job assigned to Colonel Bailey's battalion. To make matters worse, artillery units of the *26th Field Artillery Regiment, 20th Infantry Division,* supported the Japanese defenders. When attempting to continue the advance on the first of June, the 1st Battalion, 126th Infantry found the going extremely difficult, and progress was limited to a mere 400 yards. The strength of the enemy opposition convinced General Martin that Colonel Bailey's battalion was overmatched, and he directed it to withdraw to the village of Yakamul, which was to be developed into a defensive base. Orders were still issued on the assumption that the enemy action was covering a major withdrawal of their forces westward. The 1st Battalion, 126th Infantry, was still under orders to develop the enemy situation. The enemy followed the Americans to Yakamul where they attacked on the night of June 1st, doing little damage.

The following morning the battalion was divided into two large patrols. The first, consisting of Company A, Battalion Headquarters Company, and part of Company D, was to remain to defend Yakamul. The rest of the battalion, Companies B, C and the remainder of Company D, were to patrol under Colonel Bailey's command. Shortly after Colonel Bailey's patrol moved south, the Japanese attacked the Yakamul base. The defense force, commanded by Captain Gile A. Herrick of Company A, easily beat off the small attacks. It was not until the following day, June 3rd, that it was realized that the attacks had been designed to encircle Yakamul. Captain Herrick's force was now surrounded on three sides, with the sea to its back. Late on June 4th a company of Japanese infantry attacked the Yakamul perimeter, after hours of artillery and machine gun preparation. The attack was designed to split Captain Herrick's forces. A small creek ran between Company A and the rest of the base force. The Japanese, using this creek, infiltrated between the two American forces and separated them with rifle and machine gun fire. Seeing the intent of the enemy, Captain Herrick ordered Company A across the creek into the main position. Because of the heavy and accurate enemy fire the withdrawal was a slow process. The Japanese continued to increase the pressure on Company A and just before dark overran some of the Company A positions. At this point it appears that some of the soldiers panicked, abandoning radios, weapons and between twenty and thirty of their wounded. Several of the wounded managed, under cover of darkness, to return to American lines, but at least eight men were counted as missing the following day.

Captain Herrick, using every available man including walking wounded, defended the main position against the continuing enemy attack. He managed to get word of his plight to General Martin, who immediately ordered Colonel Bailey's force to return to Yakamul. Radio difficulties prevented the message from getting through until after the enemy had over-run Company A. As soon as he received General Martin's message, near midnight, Colonel Bailey started back to Yaka-mul, only to run into a Japanese trailblock. Rather than add to the delay by fighting his way through the trailblock, Colonel Bailey and his force headed off into the jungle and detoured around the ambush. They managed to reach a position held by Company G, 127th Infantry, about two miles from Yakamul after struggling for twelve hours through the jungle. Reporting to General Martin before proceeding on to the relief of Yakamul, Colonel Bailey was told by the General to rest and feed his force, and then return to the main American perimeter. Captain Herrick's men would be evacuated by sea.

Small boats were sent to Yakamul on June 5th to embark Herrick Force. The Japanese, sensing victory, were still pressing hard. Captain Herrick had withdrawn his force to a defensive position along the beach. Rather than risk losing more men to enemy fire, Captain Herrick had all heavy equipment destroyed rather than carried to the beach. This left his men free to run for their lives when the boats arrived. Leaving only enough radios and machine guns to defend themselves and contact the boats, Herrick Force stood off the Japanese. The sudden American run for the boats apparently caught the Japanese by surprise, and their fire was neither heavy nor accurate as the Americans raced past them to the sea. Covered by rocket and machine gun fire from the boats the men of Herrick Force made good their escape, losing only one wounded man in the process. By nightfall the men of Herrick Force had rejoined the 1st Battalion, 126th Infantry. They had lost 18 men killed, 75 wounded and 8 missing. Japanese losses were estimated at about one hundred in killed and wounded.

While Herrick Force had been fighting for its life on the coast, the 127th Infantry had been busy inland. Enemy patrols had been seen coming and going with alarming frequency. Occa-sional ambushes made the trails unsafe for supply and commu-nication. A strong Japanese position was believed to have been established west of the Driniumor River, within the American outer defense perimeter. The 1st Battalion, 127th Infantry was ordered to drive the Japanese east of the river. After four days of attempting to outflank an enemy they could neither see nor hear, and after pressure from Colonel Howe, the battalion made a frontal attack only to find the enemy gone.

All this enemy activity along the eastern perimeter of the Persecution Task Force made the higher commanders reconsider their evaluation of Japanese intentions. Two infantry battalions were outposted along the Driniumor River, and both had been reporting strong enemy activity. Tentative plans were made for secondary defensive positions, in the event of a full scale enemy attack. Information coming in from patrols, prisoners and radio intercepts indicated that the enemy was present in strength. While the Southwest Pacific Headquarters Central Intelligence Bureau, commanded by Lieutenant Colonel Joe R. Sherr, listened in on the enemy radio transmissions, there was little they could say with certainty on Japanese intentions. A change in the enemy code had hindered operations, and not until late May, when a copy of the new code had been captured at Aitape, had they begun to read the enemy's mail with understanding once again. During early June there was insufficient data available for them to make any supportable conclusions as to the enemy's intentions.

The Japanese did not make things any easier for the allied intelligence evaluators. Almost as soon as the American commanders began to think that the enemy was preparing to attack at Aitape, the enemy disappeared. Instead of aggressively attacking the American defensive positions along the Driniumor River line they stayed on the east bank, actively preventing the American patrols from crossing and obtaining information. This counterreconnaissance screen proved highly effective, and very few patrols succeeded in crossing and returning safely. Even a landing from sea far east along the coast was repulsed even before all of the patrol could get ashore. Clearly, the Japanese were hiding something.

While the patrols were unsuccessful supporting operations were coming along much better. Fear of Japanese ambushes had caused the inland infantry battalion to establish a dropping

Troops at Aitape wait for a tank to knock out a Japanese pillbox.

ground for airborne resupply by clearing a patch of jungle. Miles of telephone lines were laid between units to secure communications, especially after suspicion arose that the enemy was tapping the American phone communications. Air support and liaison from American and Australian aircraft was improved, with the Australians dropping more than fifty tons of bombs along the eastern perimeter alone. The identification of the *20th* and *41st Infantry Divisions* east of Aitape had given the Air Forces a lucrative target, although an elusive one. It had also given Sixth Army Headquarter much to think about.

Similar thinking was going on at General MacArthur's headquarters. In the past the intercepts of enemy communications, known as Ultra, had proved reliable. Despite the fact that poor evaluation of some of those intercepts had caused problems at Biak, General MacArthur had come to rely on them. Concerned that Ultra was at least for the moment receiving mixed information from the intercepts, he nevertheless was anxious for the security of his main base and new forward headquarters, just established at Hollandia. General MacArthur inquired of General Krueger and General Gill on June 17th at to whether they felt the need for additional troops to defend the Driniumor River line. General Krueger, already thinking along the same lines, quickly agreed to more troops for Persecution Task Force. Advising General Krueger that there were two available divisions, the 43rd Infantry in New Zealand undergoing recuperation after its Northern Solomons campaign and the 31st Infantry

Division which was still undergoing amphibious training in eastern New Guinea, General Krueger selected the 43rd Infantry Division, although its arrival would take a month. In the meantime General Krueger moved forward the 112th Cavalry Regimental Combat Team as an temporary reserve in the event the enemy attacked before the 43rd Infantry Division could arrive.

Practically within hours of these decisions additional information began to come from the newly translated Ultra intercepts. The information, confirmed by patrol reports, indicated that major Japanese units were east of the Driniumor River and that they were preparing to attack the American defense perimeter. Both the *20th* and *41st Infantry Divisions* had been identified by Ultra and confirmed by patrol reports. This meant that the bulk of the enemy forces in eastern New Guinea were on their way to Hollandia.

The enemy which had been bypassed by the landings at Hollandia and which had been the principal Japanese force defending eastern New Guinea was the *18th Army*. The Imperial Japanese Army organization had no equivalent of the United States Army corps. The next higher organization above division level was the army, which controlled two or more divisions, depending on its mission. The *18th Army* was the highest ground force command in the Hollandia area. It commanded three divisions, the *20th, 41st* and *51st Infantry Divisions*. It had fought the Allied forces pushing west for months, holding the Australians at Wewak for some time before the Hollandia landings. Those landings had disrupted the Japanese plans which had called for a prolonged defense of eastern New Guinea until the "decisive battle" had decided the war's outcome. Those plans were nullified by General MacArthur's landings at Hollandia. The *18th Army* was now cut off from its supports and the entire defensive line had to be moved back to Geelvink Bay. This left the *18th Army* stranded. *Imperial General Headquarters* in Tokyo concentrated its efforts on reinforcing the newly established main line of defense, Geelvink Bay, and ignored the plight of the *18th Army*. They ordered them to move to western New Guinea, and then left them to their own resources while making attempts to restructure the new defense line.

This was unacceptable to both the commander of the *18th Army* and his immediate superior at *Second Area Army* headquarters. Lieutenant General Korechika Anami commanded the *Second Area Army* and saw no need to waste three of his most experienced divisions by letting them stagnate in the jungles of New Guinea. His responsibilities to hold the new defense line as ordered from Tokyo could only be helped if the *18th Army* took some positive action against the Allied drive into Geelvink Bay. His interest in the fate of the surrounded army was in many ways echoed by its commander, Lieutenant General Hatazo Adachi. General Adachi saw no purpose to letting his devoted army starve in the miserable jungles of New Guinea without some purpose. He felt that his soldiers could make a notable contribution to their nation's war effort even in the difficult circumstances they found themselves in by May of 1944. General Adachi was steeped in the Japanese military traditions, and that tradition did not have a place for withering on the vine while the war went on without him. The son of an army officer, with two brothers also in the army, and a graduate of the Japan Military Academy, class of 1909, he had already had extensive combat experience in Manchuria and China. The sixty-one year old general was not about to sit idly by in the jungles of New Guinea while the Americans marched to Japan.

General Adachi was going to attack and destroy the American force around Hollandia. His superiors did not specifically order him to do so. This dichotomy was what led to confusion in the American intelligence community. While many signs led to the belief that an attack was coming, there were equally strong other signs that the *18th Army* would bypass Hollandia and move to defend the western end of New Guinea. Both *Imperial General Headquarters* in Tokyo and to some extent *2nd Area Army* in New Guinea believed that the 18th Army was going to avoid combat while moving west. While General Korechika knew that General Adachi wanted to attack, he had no current information of General Adachi's plans. The loss of Biak cut communications between the *18th Army* and all of its higher commands, so that while they acted in the belief that General Adachi was moving westwards as originally ordered, he had no such intention.

General Krueger decided by the middle of June that he could not afford to be unprepared. When General MacArthur, also concerned about the pending situation at Aitape, offered reinforcements, General Krueger accepted. The first of these to arrive would be the 112th Cavalry Regimental Combat Team. The 112th Cavalry was not horse mounted. Like the 1st Cavalry Division which had seized the Admiralty Islands the previous year, the 112th Cavalry was actually a small infantry regiment. It was a Texas National Guard regiment which had been federalized in 1940. Filled up with draftees from all over the nation, it had been hurriedly shipped to New Caledonia in July 1942 when fears for that island's safety were still fresh. Jungle training began on New Caledonia and lasted until the regiment, which had only two battalions instead of the normal regiment's three, landed unopposed on Woodlark Island in the Solomons in July of 1943. By that time the regiment had been enlarged into a regimental combat team with the addition of the 148th Field Artillery Battalion and engineer and medical attachments. Colonel Alexander M. Miller, III commanded the regiment while Brigadier General Julian Cunningham led the combat team. After serious combat on New Britain the combat team had been resting at Finschafen before getting the call to Aitape.

Although the Japanese had established an effective screen to prevent American patrols from learning of their dispositions, there were occasional successes by the Americans. In one such case, documents were captured which clearly showed that once the Japanese had finished their preparations there would be an all out attack on Aitape. The Japanese were in the process of pre-attack reconnaissance. When they were finished they would attack.

This information was passed back from General Martin through General Gill to General Krueger. Along with this data went General Gill's request for additional air and artillery support. General Krueger was entirely receptive, and the planned move west of Number 71 Wing, Royal Australian Air Force, was halted and they were assigned to provide air support to Persecution Task Force. General Krueger also reconsidered his decision regarding the 31st Infantry Division, which he had earlier wanted to keep in reserve, and instead ordered one of its regiments, the 124th Infantry, forward to Aitape. The 43rd Infantry Division, alerted earlier, was now ordered forward as well. With these new reserves on the way to Aitape, the 112th Cavalry Regiment, less its 148th Field Artillery Battalion, was ordered into the Driniumor River Defense Line. This now placed the entire 32nd Infantry Division, the 112th Cavalry Regiment, and parts of the 31st and 43rd Infantry Divisions in the defense force covering Aitape. American military doctrine of this period required that a corps command be established to coordinate such a large force. Accordingly General Krueger ordered the XI Corps forward, under the command of Major General Charles P. Hall, to take command of the forces around Aitape.

General Charles P. Hall was a native of Mississippi, and a graduate of the United States Military Academy, class of 1911. Commissioned into the infantry, he first served along the Mexican Border, then sailed for France with one of the first American divisions to fight on the Western Front. He saw combat in nearly all the major and several minor campaigns in that war, earning several decorations for bravery including the Distinguished Service Cross, three Silver Stars and the Purple Heart. After the war he attended the Infantry School, the Command and General Staff College and finally the Army War College. He served a two year tour of duty in the Philippines after which he returned to the Infantry School as an administrator. With America's entry into World War II, he commanded an infantry regiment, was an assistant division commander and then organized and trained the 93rd Infantry Division before being promoted to command the XI Corps in October of 1942. The command at Aitape was his and his corps' first combat assignment of the war.

The day after General Hall took command he received disturbing news from Sixth Army Intelligence officers. According to their best information, the Japanese attack would come on June 29th. General Hall would be in command little more than a day before he had to face a major enemy attack. He quickly reorganized his new command. Leaving a minimum of troops in the west, where no attack threatened, he moved most of his engineer troops there as an emergency reserve should the enemy suddenly appear. The bulk of his combat troops were moved to the threatened eastern sector. The 32nd Infantry Division, with its 127th and 128th Infantry Regiments, awaited the arrival of the 112th Cavalry Regiment on the Driniumor River Line. The division's third regiment was left as a skeleton holding force along the western defense sector. General Gill approached General Hall, whom he had not met before, and suggested that since his division had held the line for the last month or more, he allow his staff officers to brief the staff of XI Corps. General Hall readily agreed, and had General Gill brief him as well. General Martin retained command of the forward line of defense, the Driniumor River line, while General Gill retained command of the 32nd Infantry Division, reporting for tactical direction to General Hall. Having made their dispositions, the Americans waited for the Japanese to attack.

The attack didn't come. Ultra had intercepted a message from Lieutenant General Nakai Matsutaro, commanding the *20th Infantry Division*, to General Adachi asking for a preliminary attack to dislocate the American defenses prior to the main attack. However, the *41st Infantry Division* was not yet in position to launch an attack, so the planned June 29th attack never materialized. The Japanese, who despite legends to the contrary, had as much trouble with the jungle as the Americans, couldn't move very fast under the primitive conditions of New Guinea. They could not keep to their own schedules, and so the Americans would be granted a few more days in which to strengthen their defenses.

General Krueger now decided, with the failure of the expected enemy attack to occur, to change his plans. He ordered General Hall to conduct an active defense. He wanted the Japanese kept as far from the airfields as possible. So, like General Matsutaro, he ordered a pre-emptive move by XI Corps. Patrols were to actively pursue the enemy, and to fight him whenever found. Further, General Krueger ordered General Hall to defend the Driniumor River Line as if it were the main defensive position, not as originally intended as an outpost line of defense.

The patrols went out as ordered. Nearly all were met by a fierce Japanese counterreconnaissance screen. Few patrols got very far, and little in the way of important information was brought back. The Americans still could not pinpoint the location of either the *20th* or *41st Infantry Divisions*. The *51st Infantry Division* was still assumed to be fighting a rearguard action against the Australians at Wewak. The lack of precise information caused additional concern at Sixth Army Headquarters. General Krueger, now impatient at the enemy's delay, ordered General Hall to push out strong patrols to locate and engage the main enemy forces. Accordingly, General Hall passed on the orders to Brigadier General Clarence A. Martin, still commanding Persecution Covering Force defending the Driniumor River line. General Hall's plan, to land two battalions of the newly arriving 124th Infantry behind the enemy's main line of resistance, was postponed to comply with General Krueger's directive. Neither General Hall nor General Martin felt that the push out east from the Driniumor River would be successful.

General Hall determined to hold the 124th Infantry in reserve in case his plan to use them in an amphibious landing behind Japanese lines could later be implemented. Therefore, he drew his combat patrols from the Persecution Covering Force. General Martin had five battalions assigned to his command. He ordered a two pronged attack. The 1st Battalion, 128th Infantry, would advance along the coast while the 2nd Squadron of the 112th Cavalry would advance inland. Each would move to the Harech River, where they would establish contact with each other and patrol aggressively. During the advance to the Harech River minor Japanese resistance was to be speedily overcome. The battalions left along the Driniumor River line would send out patrols to mop up bypassed enemy resistance.

The 1st Battalion, 128th Infantry, moved out early on July 10th. Led by Company B, the initial advance was uneventful and rapid. The battalion advanced some three miles in three hours before they ran into the first opposition. A company of Japanese infantry was dug in defending a position along the battalion's route. After an infantry attack failed to dislodge the Japanese, American artillery fire was called down on the enemy position. That fire scattered the enemy force. Company B continued its advance, only to be stopped by another enemy force. This time several artillery barrages were required to dislodge the enemy. Nevertheless, before darkness the 1st Battalion had reached a good defensive position less than a mile from Yakamul, scene of previous bitter fighting. The battalion dug in for the night.

The southern pincer was the 2nd Squadron, 112th Cavalry. This unit had only been at Aitape since June 28th. Arriving at the beaches, it had then spent two days marching in rain and mud to the Driniumor River. Here it relieved the 3rd Battalion, 127th Infantry, and proceeded to dig defensive positions. Still unaccustomed to the heat, mud and insects which prevail in New Guinea, the squadron pushed out patrols. Ambushes were frequent and the first combat casualty was an officer leading a patrol east of the Driniumor which was ambushed. Now, on July 10th, the 2nd Squadron, 112th Cavalry, was ordered to move to the Harech River. Unlike the 1st Battalion, 128th Infantry, the 2nd Squadron had to await the arrival of its sister 1st Squadron on the Driniumor River Line to take over its position's before it could advance. As a result, it was nearly midday before the American cavalrymen advanced across the Driniumor.

The squadron crossed the river and began the tortuous task of cutting a path through the primitive jungle. There was no sunlight coming through the thick jungle canopy and each step had to be laboriously hacked out by man and machete. A platoon of Troop G provided flank security, and had to hack their own way through the jungle. The strain of the unknown combined with the climate took a heavy toll of the Americans, as it had of the Japanese in their struggle from Wewak to Aitape. By nightfall, after an afternoon's hacking through the jungle, the squadron had advanced only one mile beyond the Driniumor River. Because they avoided the use of native trails, the cavalrymen had also avoided running into the enemy. With their last strength, the cavalrymen dug their night defensive positions.

From XI Corps headquarters came orders to push on the next day, July 11th. These orders were received by the 1st Battalion, 128th Infantry, but not by the 2nd Squadron, 112th Cavalry which had lost all communications with the main line of defense. Back along the Driniumor the attacking battalions had been replaced by other units. While the 1st Squadron had replaced the 2nd in the south, the 2nd Battalion, 128th Infantry had moved into the vacated positions of its sister 1st Battalion. As night fell on July 10th along the Driniumor River line the American defenses were held from north to south by the 2nd Battalion, 128th Infantry; the 3rd Battalion, 127th Infantry; and the 1st Squadron, 112th Cavalry. Along the north flank of the line the 1st Battalion, 128th Infantry was some three miles ahead of the main line, while in the south the 2nd Squadron, 112th Cavalry was about one mile in front of the line. The infantrymen had encountered enemy opposition and so the Japanese knew they were there, but the cavalrymen had not run into the enemy and their presence was not known to the Japanese. Also along the eastern bank of the Driniumor River were the *20th* and *41st Infantry Divisions*, reinforced with a part of the *51st Infantry Division*.

By nightfall on the 10th of July most Japanese units were finally in position for the long planned attack. Facing the 2nd Battalion, 128th Infantry was the *237th Infantry Regiment, 41st Infantry Division* under Colonel Masahiko Nara. He had in support the *1st Mountain Artillery Battalion*. The *78th* and *80th Infantry Regiments* of the *20th Infantry Division* faced the southern part of the 2nd Battalion, 128th Infantry and the 3rd Battalion, 127th Infantry. These Japanese units were supported by the *26th Field Artillery Regiment*. The Japanese had overcome tremendous hardship to get these units into position. There were many gaps, especially in the areas of supply and intelligence. For example, the Japanese did not know that the 112th Cavalry was in the line, although they expected to meet the 32nd Infantry Division.

The Americans were not completely unaware of what lay in front of them. Patrols had been partially successful, particularly those from the 3rd Battalion, 127th Infantry. On June 27th Sergeant Edward Madcliff and a patrol from this battalion had ambushed a supply party for an enemy artillery unit. This group, led by a Japanese captain, had maps and documents which clearly pointed to an attack, and even gave some details. Now, a few days before the attack, Lieutenant Colonel Edward

Block, commanding the battalion, consulted with Captain Leonard Lowry, commanding Company I. Together, they asked Sergeant Madcliff to take a patrol east of the Driniumor to get additional information on Japanese intentions. The sergeant and his squad remained on the east side for two days, observed and reported numerous parties of Japanese. Reporting that at least two full companies of Japanese infantry were in position opposite the 3rd Battalion, Sergeant Madcliff allowed at least his own battalion to be better prepared for what was coming.

Lieutenant Colonel Bloch was preoccupied with his own front, and did not pass on Sergeant Madcliff's findings to higher headquarters. Not that it made a difference, since the Japanese attack was expected at all levels, and could not be prevented. Patrols of the 2nd Battalion, 128th Infantry to the north of Colonel Bloch reported only one contact in the days before July 10th. This was because the Japanese in this area had more trouble than their comrades in getting into position for the attack. In fact, the *237th Infantry Regiment* did not move into attack positions until the night of July 10th. In the south a patrol from Troop A of the 112th Cavalry ambushed a well armed enemy patrol and dispersed it. The report of this action was apparently the only one to reach higher headquarters before the attack.

Although the front line combat troops knew by now that an attack was only hours away, this information had not filtered upward. This was due to a number of factors. Most of the patrol reports had not been forwarded. The signals coming in from the Japanese via Ultra were still confusing. And the Japanese were late by their own timetable, creating doubt as to their real intentions. But they were coming, some 20,000 of them. The *18th Army* had finally arrived. It was in position. It would attack the Driniumor River line during the night of July 10th, 1944.

CHAPTER XI

Logs in the River

The Japanese plan of attack was to break the Driniumor River defense line, then advance quickly to the main line of resistance around the Tadji Airfield complex, from which the American and Australian aircraft were supporting the far flung operations of the Sixth Army and the Australian ground forces. After forcing the Americans off the Driniumor River the Japanese planned to use the village of Chinapelli to reorganize before conducting their main attack on the Tadji airstrips. Assaulting forces consisted of the *237th Infantry, 80th Infantry* and *78th Infantry Regiments* supported by the *8th Independent Engineers, 41st Mountain Artillery* and *26th Field Artillery Regiments*. All of these units came from the *20th* and *41st Infantry Divisions* except for the engineers which were a unit attached directly to the *18th Army*. The *66th Infantry Regiment* of the *51st Infantry Division* was to be held in reserve. The rest of the Japanese forces, chiefly the remainder of the *51st Infantry Division*, had been left behind near Wewak to delay the oncoming Australian infantry.

The Japanese attack began at midnight, July 10/11. Despite many problems, some of which had not been resolved by H-Hour, the Japanese came. First to attack, perhaps five minutes ahead of schedule, was the *1st Battalion, 78th Infantry*. This force came screaming out of the jungle darkness at Company G, 128th Infantry. The Japanese had done a thorough job of reconnaissance, and groups quickly headed for the company and battalion command posts. However, there were serious gaps in the information available to the Japanese. They did not know, as we have seen, that the 112th Cavalry was on the line, nor did they know about some recently arrived reinforcements that had come up only that day. Another gap was discovered almost immediately when the first Japanese assault troops stumbled into previously unreported barbed wire, strung by Company G just hours before the attack.

Despite these unpleasant surprises, the *78th Infantry* continued its attack. Losses from American mortar and machine gun fire were heavy, but the most serious losses resulted from American artillery fire. The moment the attack was reported, American artillery opened fire on pre-registered routes of approach. Both the 120th and 129th Field Artillery Battalions fired all batteries as rapidly as possible. These artillery concentrations caught the Japanese of the *78th Infantry Regiment* concentrated in attack groups, and caused heavy casualties in that regiment. The *1st Battalion, 78th Infantry*, for example, was reduced from some 400 men to about 30 soldiers in the opening minutes of the attack. With the effective support they were getting from their artillery, the men of Company G were holding their positions.

Next to be hit was Company E, 128th Infantry. Troops of the *80th Infantry* attacked after midnight, only to be repulsed. However, after about an hour's lull, troops of the *237th Infantry* renewed the attack. This time the Japanese were successful and the company command post was overrun along with most of Company E's positions. Other defense positions were surrounded. The company commander, Captain Thomas Bell, lost contact with much of his command. Like Captain Ted Florey's Company G, however, the men of company E were holding their ground, although surrounded. The sight of hundreds of Japanese soldiers screaming and yelling, waving their arms and shooting everywhere was briefly unnerving. But the 32nd Infantry Division was now a veteran outfit, and they quickly settled down to the business of repelling the enemy's attack.

There were surprises for the Japanese in this area as well. The commanders of the troops attacking the 2nd Battalion, 128th Infantry, were shocked by the volume of fire returned by the Americans. Their scouting reports had missed more than the 112th Cavalry and the barbed wire. They had missed the well sited and ample supply of American automatic weapons and mortars within the American perimeters. And of course they had no way of knowing the strength of the American artillery. After Major Moritoshi Kawahigashi's *1st Battalion, 78th Infantry,* had been decimated Major Shigemiche Yamashita brought his *1st Battalion, 237th Infantry* into the same fire. Like most Japanese units, "they were thinking more about breaking into the American positions to seize rations then they were about the possibility of being killed." Yet the shock of the American response was more than the most pessimistic Japanese had prepared against. American machine guns glowed red hot from the fire they continued to pour into Japanese ranks, while those Japanese who had crossed the Driniumor safely found themselves entangled in the barbed wire, helpless targets for American guns. One soldier in Company E, a Browning Automatic Rifleman, fired twenty-six magazines of ammunition in less than fifteen minutes. By the end of that time his weapon was so hot that it would only fire single shots, which he continued to do throughout the attack.

Major Masao Koike and his men of the *3rd Battalion, 78th Infantry* watched this spectacle in horror. Their comrades were being cut to pieces while they watched hidden on the east bank. Then came the time for this unit to cross. Their orders called for them to cross just south of the *1st Battalion,* which they did. They, too, were savaged by the American artillery and automatic weapons fire, but fortune had smiled on this battalion, for it passed through gaps in the American line and reached the west bank of the Driniumor relatively intact. It seems that the attack of the *1st Battalion* served as a diversion for the *3rd Battalion's* attack. The rest of the *78th Infantry Regiment,* less its *1st Battalion* still battering itself to destruction against the 128th Infantry, crossed intact to the location found by the *3rd Battalion.*

The *78th Infantry* had attacked at the juncture of Companies G and E, 128th Infantry. After this attack was well underway, the *1st Battalion, 237th Infantry,* came out of the jungle to attack Company E's left flank where it joined with Company F, holding positions along the coast. Supported by their own artillery fire, the *1st Battalion* attacked an already hard pressed Company E. Flares lit up a frightening scene. Mortars, artillery of both sides, machine guns, grenades and rifle fire tore apart the jungle and the men within it. Captain Bell now had more than his command could handle. Attacked by two Japanese battalions, one on each flank, Company E still resisted stubbornly. The Japanese units continued to suffer tremendous losses. When the *4th Company, 237th Infantry Regiment*, tried to cross the river where a small island called "Kawanakajima" divided it into two, they were literally wiped out before any of them set foot on the west bank. Major Yamashita, commanding the *1st Battalion, 237th Infantry*, led the remainder of his command to the north, where they also crossed between two American companies, E and F. A second Japanese force had now successfully crossed the Driniumor, albeit with heavy losses.

Assailed on all sides by aggressive Japanese troops, Company E now began to find itself completely surrounded, ammunition running low, and the Japanese too close for effective artillery support. At about 0200 in the morning the company command post was overrun, and many of the fighting positions surrounded or eliminated. Control broke down with the loss of the command post. Although individuals continued fighting until ammunition was exhausted, the company began to withdraw. The command post, the 1st platoon together with the weapons platoon united and withdrew northwest, towards the sea. Some men of the 2nd and 3rd platoons joined Company F to the north. Supporting heavy weapons men from Company H did likewise. Others of Company E joined Company G to the south, while several others straggled back to the American rear. After battle estimates listed ten men killed and twenty wounded in Company E as a result of this action. Post war estimates put the Company as outnumbered ten to one, but it nevertheless held its position until out of ammunition.

At about the time Company E was overrun, Company F reported to General Martin that it had lost contact with Company E. To the south, Company G refused its left flank to protect that area from the Japanese who had defeated Company E. A half mile gap now existed in the Driniumor River line, and the Japanese had occupied that area in force. The Japanese continued to push units across the river, to reinforce the assault elements. The first phase of the Japanese plan had succeeded.

The American Driniumor River line had been breached. However, the cost had been tremendous. No less than 800 Japanese troops had died in the early hours of July 11th. Further, the attack had seriously disorganized the attacking units, so that they were unable to immediately follow up their success. It was to prove an expensive victory for the Japanese.

While the attack was in progress the other American units defending the Driniumor River line could see and hear sounds and sights of battle, but except for skirmishing along the front of Company F, 128th Infantry, there were no other attacks that night. With dawn the next steps were up to the American commanders.

The first level of command in the American hierarchy which needed to make decisions was the Force Commander, General Martin at Persecution Covering Force headquarters. Brigadier General Clarence Ames Martin was another native of Virginia and, like his commander General Gill, was a graduate of Virginia Military Institute, class of 1917. Commissioned into the U.S. Army as a lieutenant of infantry, he saw combat late in 1918 in France. After serving with the occupation forces, he returned to the United States where he attended the Infantry School at Fort Benning, Georgia. He later served as a Professor of Military Science at Tennessee Military Institute. Sent to the Philippines, he served with the 26th Philippine Infantry Regiment, known as the Philippine Scouts. After several years there, he returned to Virginia where he both served with infantry units and as a Professor of Military Science at Virginia Military Institute. He attended the Command and General Staff School and the Army War College. With the federalization of the National Guard in 1940, he served with the Tennessee National Guard's 30th Infantry Division until assigned to General Eichelberger's I Corps in 1942. When I Corps took over the failing Papuan campaign, General Eichelberger had Colonel Martin replace one of the regimental commanders of the 32nd Infantry Division where he was to earn a Distinguished Service Cross. At the end of the Papuan campaign, he was promoted Brigadier General and assistant division commander of the 32nd Infantry Division. General Gill had assigned him the responsibilities of the Driniumor River covering force, officially called the Persecution

Covering Force, upon arrival at Aitape. General Gill considered General Martin "very capable" and felt he was performing "magnificently." Later, he would be promoted to major general and command the 31st Infantry Division during the liberation of the Philippines.

In mid-July, however, General Martin had some serious problems. As the commander of Persecution Covering Force, he knew his command was under a major enemy attack. He also knew that a breach had been driven into his lines. He had no reserves available to seal off that breach nor to counterattack. His information was, at dawn of July 11th, scanty. He did not know the size of the gap in his lines, did not know what had happened to Company E, nor how many Japanese had managed to cross the Driniumor River. General Martin requested and received permission from General Hall at XI Corps to withdraw the two advanced units of his command, the 1st Battalion, 128th Infantry and the 2nd Squadron, 112th Cavalry. The infantry received its orders during darkness, and withdrew hurriedly. No Japanese were encountered and the battalion reached American lines at dawn. General Martin's orders to the 2nd Squadron were delayed by communication failures, and did not reach the cavalrymen until full daylight had arrived. Once received, however, the cavalrymen acted with dispatch, covering the mile that had taken several hours to advance over the previous day in one hour this day.

Once the 1st Battalion, 128th Infantry, had recovered from its night march back to its own lines, it was ordered by General Martin to counterattack along the banks of the Driniumor to restore Company E's former positions. The battalion advanced south along the bank of the river for perhaps half a mile without opposition. Then, as Captain George Royce's Company C was leading the advance, they were hit with heavy and accurate Japanese automatic weapons fire which forced them to cover. Repeated attempts to advance were met with this same intense fire. Casualties began to mount alarmingly. Then, after some hours of this type of battle, the Japanese attacked the company's line of communications. In danger of being surrounded, Captain Royce asked for and received permission to withdraw.

Even withdrawal was difficult along the Driniumor. Having

Close view of a captured Japanese light machine gun used extensively throughout the New Guinea campaign. (National Archives)

received permission to withdraw, Captain Royce found that it was easier said than done. The two leading platoons of Company C were literally trapped under a hail of automatic weapons fire. There were numerous wounded men who could not move under their own power. Leaving these men behind would mean their certain death. Staff Sergeant Gerald L. Endl, who commanded the lead platoon, would not leave his men behind. Already conspicuous by his many attempts to get the attack moving, he now devoted his attention to getting his men safely back to American lines. Facing a reported six light and two heavy machine guns, Sergeant Endl attacked alone in order to draw attention to himself while others in his platoon rescued seven wounded men lying in the line of fire. Using a hand held machine gun, he kept the Japanese busy for a critical ten minutes while all seven wounded Americans were pulled to safety. Then, while withdrawing to his platoon, he discovered another four men lying wounded in the open. Sergeant Endl made four trips through the same murderous enemy fire, each time bringing out a wounded man. As he made his last trip carrying a wounded man, a Japanese machine gunner found him and the heroic Sergeant died. He was awarded a posthumous Medal of Honor.

With the failure of the 1st Battalion to close the gap along the Driniumor River Line, proof of the strength of the Japanese, General Martin knew that holding along the river was now impossible. He decided that the entire force would withdraw to the next river to the west, known as the "X-Ray River." Here Persecution Covering force would establish a new defensive line to delay the enemy's attack. The 1st Battalion, 128th Infantry and the remnants of the 2nd Battalion, withdrew along the coast to the vicinity of the village of Tiver. Here, using the west bank of Koronal Creek, they established a new defensive position. Company F of the 2nd Battalion and many stragglers from that battalion were added to the defensive force. Under cover of allied aircraft attacking the Japanese, the battalion settled in for the next round of battle. The balance of the day was spent watching as Fifth Army Air Force planes sought out Japanese troops and supplies. The 3rd Bomb Group, under Lieutenant Colonel Richard Ellis, and the 465th Fighter Wing, under Lieutenant Colonel Charles MacDonald bombed and strafed suspected enemy positions. Despite their best efforts, these attacks did little damage, for the Japanese had expected them and dispersed or dug in their troops and supplies. The intervention of the *248th Flying Regiment*, flying out of bypassed Wewak, further dampened American air efforts. Although the Japanese effort to bomb American defensive positions failed, it did draw off enough American planes to reduce American attempts to destroy the bulk of the Japanese ground forces. At the cost of twelve fighters and ten bombers, the *248th Flying Regiment* wrecked itself at no cost to the Americans. About all the action produced was additional kills for the American air ace, Major Thomas McQuire.

While all this activity was going on in the north, the southern part of the Driniumor River line was quiet. In large part because the Japanese had failed to discover their presence, the cavalrymen of the 112th had remained unmolested. General Cunningham, commanding the combat team, received orders to withdraw to the X-Ray River at mid-afternoon, but the sounds of battle and a sense of general unease made him request an earlier departure, which General Martin approved. The 112th Cavalry moved out late in the morning, heading west for the next river line.

Although the 112th Cavalry had not been attacked, the sights and sounds of the battle to the north encouraged their rapid departure. Supplies and equipment which could not be easily carried were buried in empty foxholes or destroyed. By noon, both squadrons were ready to withdraw. The 2nd Squadron led the way. Native bearers were used to help speed the journey. As the 2nd Squadron withdrew torrential rains began as they had during the regiment's trip to the front days earlier. The rain, jungle, haste and presence of the enemy all contributed to making the return journey even worse than the trip to the front had been. Troop F, forming the rear guard, did not make it back to the X-Ray River before darkness, and rather than risk "friendly fire" from their comrades in the dark, spent the night huddled together in the jungle. The 2nd Squadron, by their own estimate, were in no position to fight on the morning of July 12th.

Brigadier General Julian Wallace Cunningham was a native of Pennsylvania, and had grown up in Washington, D.C. After graduating from George Washington University with a Bachelor of Arts degree in French in 1916, he was commissioned a second lieutenant of cavalry in the regular army. Lieutenant Cunningham was sent to various military schools during the First World War, after which he served as regimental adjutant of the 7th Cavalry, which did not get overseas during the war. During the interwar years he served with the Massachusetts National Guard before attending the Command and General Staff School. After serving for three years in the Philippines with the Philippine Scouts, he returned to the United States where he served with the Connecticut National Guard. In May of 1941, he took command of the 112th Cavalry Regiment at Fort Clark, Texas. Leading the regiment overseas, he was promoted to Brigadier General and commander of the 112th Cavalry Regimental Combat Team, which he led to Aitape in June of 1944. In addition to his own regiment, General Cunningham also commanded the 3rd Battalion, 127th Infantry, along the Driniumor.

When the 112th Cavalry was ordered to withdraw, so was the 3rd Battalion, 127th Infantry. Originally planned as an orderly withdrawal with each unit following the preceding one, the plan quickly fell apart under the miserable conditions of jungle, rain, and poor communications. The 3rd Battalion was unable to follow the 112th Cavalry back to the X-Ray River. They, too, suffered severely from the heavy downpour. Colonel Bloch managed to collect his headquarters and Companies K, M and L. This group, like the cavalry's Troop F, spent the night isolated in the jungle and reached their new positions after daylight. The balance of the battalion, together with Company G of the 128th Infantry, became separated and returned independently under the command of Captain Leonard Lowry, Commanding company I. This group was not lucky enough to escape without a battle. Captain Lowry, a Native American, led his group with distinction, and brought out his 500 men from some 10 different units safely. After two difficult nights in the jungle, fending off Japanese attacks, Lowry Force reached the X-Ray River at dawn on July 13th.

Daylight of July 12th was spent by all American units, excepting only Lowry Force, still struggling through the jungle, in reorganizing and preparing to defend the new line of defense. Patrols were sent to both establish contact with the enemy and determine what was happening in the nearly mile wide gap left by the dissolution of the 3rd Battalion, 127th Infantry. Little contact was made with the enemy. Some stragglers were encountered, but no major units of the attacking forces were discovered. General Krueger, still skeptical over the true nature of the enemy's intentions, ordered General Hall at XI Corps to restore the Driniumor River Line at once. General Martin was first ordered to attack, then relieved of command and assigned to a rear sector. General Gill felt that General Martin, who had been in combat for several months before Aitape, was tired. With the concern for the coming attack keeping him from getting much rest for several days before the enemy struck on July 10th, General Martin, who was described by General Gill as "delicate," had exhausted himself. General Hall agreed, and placed General Gill in command of Persecution Covering Force. General Hall also added the 124th Infantry Regiment, less one battalion, which he had previously held as a reserve force, to Persecution Covering Force. This regiment, part of the 31st Infantry Division, had landed at Aitape on July 5th.

The forces General Gill had for his counterattack were mixed. There were the 127th and 128th Infantry Regiments of his own 32nd Infantry Division. They were disorganized and tired from their recent experiences, but combat experienced. There was the 112th Cavalry Regiment, likewise exhausted by its retreat but otherwise unscathed. Finally, there was the 124th Infantry Regiment of the 31st Infantry Division, fresh but without combat experience.

General Gill's first step was to organize his command. He had been critical of General Hall's handling of the campaign before the enemy attacked. He felt that XI Corps, particularly General Hall's staff, had not taken the warnings he and General Martin had forwarded to them about the impending attack seriously. General Hall had relied on his staff, and advised General Krueger that no attack was imminent, which resulted in the dangerous decision to send large American forces into the heart of the coming assault forces. Now the battle rested with General Gill. He ordered the 112th Cavalry, with the 3rd Battalion, 127th Infantry still attached, to anchor the southern end of the line, and attack from there. The 1st Battalion, 128th Infantry, and the 1st and 3rd Battalions, 124th Infantry under the command of Brigadier General Alexander N. Stark, Jr., assistant division commander of the 43rd Infantry Division, would attack in the north and the center. The 2nd Battalion, 128th Infantry, was held in reserve. Four artillery battalions, the 120th, 129th, 149th and 181st would provide supporting fires for the coming attack.

General Gill originally scheduled the attack for the morning of the 12th, but the 124th Infantry Battalions could not get to the starting line by that time, and the other units of the force could use another day to rest and replenish themselves. So the attack was postponed until early morning, July 13th. The goals of the attack were for General Cunningham's reinforced cavalrymen to re-establish themselves in their old positions along the Driniumor while the 124th Infantry, under General Stark, moved along the coast to the Driniumor, then spread south until that huge gap was closed and contact restored with General Cunningham's forces.

First to move off was the 1st Battalion, 128th Infantry, before dawn on July 13th. Moving first under cover of full darkness, then in full daylight, the battalion advanced several thousand yards without opposition. As the leading platoons crossed a small stream about mid-morning, it was ambushed by Major Iwataro Hoshino's *Coastal Attack Force*. This unit, largely made up of artillery units supported by infantry, brought heavy fire on the leading American troops. The Americans brought up tank destroyers and began returning fire. However, the *Coastal Attack Force*'s fire was accurate enough to damage one tank destroyer and force the withdrawal of the others. Supporting landing craft at the water's edge were similarly forced off by this accurate fire.

The Americans then called for close supporting fires from the 129th Field Artillery Battalion, which succeeded in knocking out several Japanese weapons. The 1st Battalion, 128th, then moved behind a curtain of artillery fire, keeping the Japanese from setting up more delaying positions along the route. The continuing American advance forced the *Coastal Attack Force* to move south into the jungle for safety. By the evening of July 13th the 1st Battalion, 128th, had reached the mouth of the Driniumor River and settled in for the night. The battalion was unable to contact any other American unit, and spent the night in isolation. More than sixty dead Japanese had been counted in the advance, all from the ill-fated *Coastal Attack Force*.

Next to attack was the 3rd Battalion, 124th Infantry. Followed by the 1st Battalion, the 3rd almost immediately encountered opposition from the *1st Battalion, 237th Infantry*. As usual in this type of jungle fighting, the opening of the battle was an ambush of the leading elements of the American column. However, Company L, leading the attack, managed to drive off the Japanese and continue the advance. Continuing sniper and small arms fire harassed the Americans, but there was no opposition strong enough to delay the attack, during which the jungle confused the two novice battalions into losing contact with one another.

The 1st Battalion, 124th, reached the Driniumor before dark.

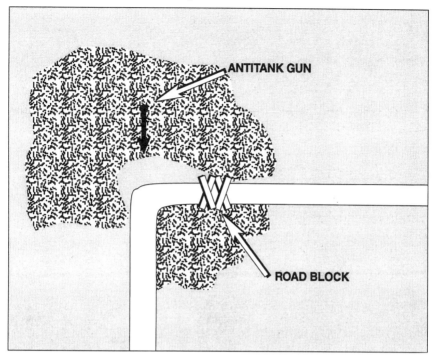

Typical Japanese road block, used throughout the Pacific. Lighter weapons were also used against infantry.

The 3rd Battalion failed to reach the river and spent the night in the jungle. The 1st Battalion, once it reached the river, did manage to establish contact with the 1st Battalion, 128th Infantry, also dug in on the Driniumor. All units, although not in contact with each other, were in radio communications with General Stark's headquarters. Each was in a defensive position preparing to repel any enemy attack.

In the south, the 112th Cavalry had also moved east at first light. A platoon from Troop B moved into the jungle from the X-Ray River and advanced towards the Driniumor. After about half a mile the platoon ran across about twenty enemy soldiers crossing a stream. A fight broke out between the 112th and the *20th Infantry Division's* leading elements. General Gill was later to feel that this was the lead of a force trying to encircle the remnants of the Persecution Covering Force while also reaching the American airfields at Tadji. The failure of the enemy to learn of the presence of the cavalrymen had stymied their plans. The enemy's opposition was dispersed by the artillery support of the cavalry. They too, reached the Driniumor by nightfall. Troops B, C, F and G dug in on the riverbank while Troops A and E were placed in reserve. Infiltrators harassed the cavalrymen all night, but no attack developed. The Japanese command was having its own problems. The advance of the 112th Cavalry had placed them between the bulk of the *20th Infantry Division* and the rest of General Adachi's forces. The *78th* and *80th Infantry Regiments* were now cut off from the *18th Army*. July 13th closed with four American battalions in position at the Driniumor River, one nearby, and the Japanese in force on both sides of the river. The large gap between the American forces had not been closed, leaving the Japanese an avenue for reinforcements and re-supply.

The Americans spent Bastille Day, 1944, consolidating their positions. The 1st Battalion, 128th Infantry, and the two 124th Infantry Battalions settled into defensive positions along the Driniumor and made physical contact with each other. Things to the rear were more difficult. The 2nd Battalion, 128th Infantry, was still resting at the village of Tiver after its mauling along the Driniumor. Here they were found by Colonel Nara and his *237th Infantry Regiment*. After darkness on the 12th he had probed the American defenses and overrun an outpost of Company F. In the late afternoon of July 13th he again attacked, this time against Company E which had suffered so severely at the Driniumor. This unit had lost none of its courage, however, and it drove off the attackers unaided. By the 14th of July, Colonel Nara, having conceded that he could not destroy the 2nd Battalion, 128th Infantry, withdrew in search of easier prey.

The 112th Cavalry, with the 3rd Battalion, 127th Infantry attached, tried to close the gap in the American line on the 14th. The 3rd Battalion, 127th, was to attack north along the river to make contact with the 124th Infantry, thereby closing the gap in the Driniumor River Line. Despite every effort by the 3rd Battalion, they could not reach the 124th Infantry. The gap, which was at first thought to be 1,500 yards wide, was more likely 2,500 yards wide at this time. The 112th Cavalry, ordered by General Cunningham to close the gap, ordered patrols out to lead the advance. In the early morning of the 14th a patrol from Troop F, crossing the Driniumor, was ambushed and withdrew covered by friendly machine gun fire. Artillery support was called in, but fell in error on the retreating cavalrymen, causing four casualties. Despite this type of difficulty, patrols stayed out in front on the American side of the Driniumor. There was much confusion among American units, with the 124th Infantry re-porting themselves in a position where the cavalrymen were waiting for them. To end a frustrating day for the cavalry, they were strafed by friendly Australian aircraft who mistook them for Japanese troops. All in all it was an unproductive day for the cavalrymen.

During this time General Adachi learned that the Americans had returned to the Driniumor and that his forces were split. The *78th* and *80th Infantry Regiments* were combined into one unit under Major General Sadahiko Miyake. These units, both suffering from severe casualties, were now known as the *Miyake Force. Miyake Force* and the *41st Infantry Division* were now ordered to destroy the Americans along the Driniumor while the *20th Infantry Division* attacked their rear areas. These attacks were to begin during the night of July 14/15.

As darkness approached on the 14th General Cunningham was ordered by General Hall to send a troop to close the gap. This reflected the still prevailing feeling at XI Corps that the enemy attack was only a diversion. To send one troop of cavalry against two reinforced Japanese infantry divisions has no other explanation. Fortunately, Troop E moved north along the Drini-umor early on the 15th, but General Adachi's attack failed to materialize. The Americans were unaware that strong enemy forces lurked nearby, preparing to attack and destroy them. Led by Private First Class Carlos A. Provencio, the men of E Troop moved around the enemy positions in the gap until it met with the 3rd Battalion, 124th Infantry. Here the cavalrymen were given food and then rested while their contact was reported. However, communications failed once again and General Cun-ningham spent the day in ignorance of the fate of Troop E. When late on the 15th the 3rd Battalion, 124th Infantry, was ordered to attack south and formally close the gap, the lateness of the day caused the postponement of the attack.

The night of the 15th was marked by bursts of anger among the top American commanders. General Cunningham was angry at the 124th Infantry, which continued to report itself at a position he knew to be false, because his own troops were there. General Gill was upset with General Cunningham's failure to close the gap in the Driniumor River line, largely because both were unaware that Troop E had in fact made contact with the 124th Infantry. General Gill also believed the reports of the 124th Infantry, which made it seem an easy task to move a few yards to close the gap. And finally, when he learned that Troop E had made contact with the 124th Infantry, General Cunningham was angry that the 124th Infantry had "kept" Troop E from returning to the 112th Cavalry on July 15th. Except for Troop E's contact with the 124th Infantry, finally known to most of the American commanders, it had been another frustrating day for Persecution Covering Force.

By late on the 15th, having been questioned by several higher commanders as to the accuracy of his reports on his position, Colonel Edward M. Starr, commanding the 124th Infantry, began to think that perhaps General Cunningham was correct, and it was this doubt which resulted in the order to the 124th Infantry to attack south to make contact with the 3rd Battalion, 127th Infantry. At dawn on July 16th the 3rd Battalion, 124th Infantry, led by Troop E of the 112th Cavalry, moved south. It almost immediately ran into Japanese opposition. General Adachi was determined to keep open his lines of communication and supply across the Driniumor. The *1st Battalion, 239th Infantry Regiment* had been moved into the gap with instructions to hold it open against all comers. Similarly, Colonel Nara's *237th Infantry* had returned from attacking the 2nd Battalion, 128th Infantry, and started back towards the Driniumor to assist in widening the gap for the *18th Army*. Troops E quickly became engaged with the *1st Battalion, 239th Infantry* while almost immediately the *3rd Battalion, 237th Infantry* attacked the flank of the 3rd Battalion, 124th Infantry. This attack split the American forces. Companies I and K faced the attack of the *237th Infantry* while Troop E, Companies L and M moved south against the *239th Infantry*. After an all day fight, these units reached General Cunningham's lines. Some forty Japanese were reported killed along the way, but the dangerous gap in the Driniumor River line had basically been closed. The 3rd Battalion, 124th Infantry spent the next two days closing the gap in fact and fighting off repeated Japanese efforts to re-open it. It was not until July 18th that the gap would remain closed and the *239th* and *237th Infantry Regiments* were forced to withdraw. Even that would require more American troops.

Incredibly, the Japanese had still not discovered the presence of the 112th Cavalry. The *20th Infantry Division* continued to report to General Adachi that the American lines along the Driniumor were in disarray, and that the Americans were "fleeing" everywhere. Only when the 124th Infantry closed the crucial gap did it become clear to General Adachi that perhaps the Americans were not as defeated as earlier reported. This led to his re-grouping of his forces to re-open the Driniumor gap. General Hall, on the other hand, now understood that strong enemy forces were inside his lines. Despite continuing pressure from General Krueger to counterattack past the Driniumor River, he wanted to first clear his lines of supply and communication. As a first step towards clearing the west bank of the Driniumor, General Hall gave General Gill additional troops. The 1st and 2nd Battalions, 127th Infantry, were released from the main line of resistance protecting the Tadji airfields and assigned to General Gill at Persecution Covering Force. General Hall left the 126th Infantry Regiment and the 3rd Battalion, 128th Infantry to defend the airfields. General Gill, who had been asking for more troops since before the attack began, immediately put them to work. The reinforcements were assigned to sweep the west bank of the Driniumor to clear it of all enemy troops.

Between the 16th and 18th of July, the 2nd Battalion, 127th Infantry, conducted a series of relatively small actions which pushed the remnants of the *237th Infantry* towards the Driniumor. While this action eliminated much of the danger to the American rear, it did increase the difficulties of the 124th Infantry in trying to close the gap by causing additional pressure to keep open the Japanese lines of communication. By the end of July 18th the area immediately behind the Driniumor on the north was quiet. The northern sector, held by the 124th Infantry, remained quiet for several days afterwards, allowing the latest arrival to take a place in the front line. The first arrival from the 43rd Infantry Division, the 2nd Battalion, 169th Infantry, arrived on July 21st and joined the 124th on the defense lines.

While the northern part of the line was clearing its area, the southern part was trying to do the same, but with much less success. General Cunningham had requested of General Gill that an additional infantry battalion be assigned to his Combat Team. This request was rejected, largely because higher headquarters still had plans to use troops in reserve elsewhere. The 112th Cavalry was established on the river, with its open south flank protected by Troop A. Troops B and C were in position facing east, to secure the flank from attack from the south or rear. The 2nd Squadron continued the line along the Driniumor with Troops F and G holding the line and Troop E in reserve. Troop G tied in its defenses with the 3rd Battalion, 127th Infantry, next in line. In the several days since the cavalrymen had returned to the Driniumor River line they had fought a war of search and ambush with the Japanese. General Cunningham, concerned with all this activity, feared that the open south flank of his command invited an attack. General Adachi agreed, and on July 18th the attack came.

Two regiments of the *20th Infantry Division* had crossed the Driniumor in the original attack. These troops had continually missed the presence of the American cavalrymen. Now they had discovered them and had to eliminate them to open their own lines of communication. The destruction of the 112th Cavalry would also turn the flank of the entire American line along the Driniumor. In order to do this the two regiments, now known as the *Miyake Force*, planned to turn the 112th Cavalry's flank and destroy the regiment. The attack came on the night of July 18th.

Supported by elements of the *66th Infantry Regiment, 51st Infantry Division*, the attack struck Troop A first. Corporal Charles C. Brabham was just preparing for another night in the jungle, while some of his fellow soldiers were bathing in the Driniumor River when the *Miyake Force* came charging out of the jungle firing automatic weapons. The opening attacks caught many of the Americans out of position, and despite efforts of those like Private First Class Walter Stocks who manned a machine gun with one hand while aiding a wounded man with the other, Troop A was overrun and forced out of position. In the dark and rainy night, confusion reigned. Elements of Troop B were withdrawn to conform to Troop A's withdrawal. By dawn some two hundred yards had been ceded to the Japanese.

General Cunningham's first reaction was to re-organize Troop A and then prepare to recapture the lost ground. The General took one platoon from Troop E, then in reserve, and another platoon from the 3rd Battalion, 127th Infantry, combined them with the antitank platoon of Headquarters Troop, 112th Cavalry and at dawn sent them against the Japanese. The attack found the enemy gone. The ground was quickly retaken, but patrols sent out beyond the original perimeter found that the enemy remained there in strength. *Miyake Force* had withdrawn to reorganize for a renewed attack on the Americans. The advance American patrols, after discovering the enemy, withdrew under heavy fire and called for artillery fire. There was a delay in relaying this request and heavy Japanese fire continued to pour into the Americans. Second Lieutenant Dale E. Christensen, leaving his men under cover, advanced towards the source of the fire to spot and eliminate the worst of it. His rifle was shot out of his hands, but he continued to advance. Crawling on until he could see the enemy machine gun positions, he used hand grenades to destroy the most troublesome one, killing its crew and disabling the weapon. lieutenant Christensen then returned to his men and led them forward, reducing the rest of the enemy positions. The remaining Japanese, dazed by the now arriving artillery and Lieutenant Christensen's attack, fled into the jungle. The heroic Iowa Lieutenant was credited with personally destroying four enemy mortars and ten machine guns during this attack. Regrettably, when he tried to repeat this performance on August 4th, under similar circumstances in the same area, he was killed in action. For both of these actions, Lieutenant Christensen was awarded a posthumous Medal of Honor.

Lieutenant Christensen's valor had gained a day of respite for the cavalrymen. But the next day the Japanese again attacked in force. This attack was broken up by artillery fire, after which the 1st Squadron sent Troop A into the jungle after the Japanese. The troop successfully pinned down about a company of the *Miyake Force* some 600 yards deep into the jungle. Colonel Miller, commanding the 112th Cavalry, personally counted 129 enemy dead, while reporting that the cavalry had lost six dead and twenty-nine wounded. Additional casualties resulted from enemy stragglers attacking litter parties carrying wounded behind the front lines.

The Americans spent July 20th regrouping. So did the Japanese. *Miyake Force*, severely reduced in strength, was reinforced by the *79th Infantry Regiment*, some 700 men strong and accompanied by a sixty man mountain artillery company with one artillery piece. In addition, General Adachi had dispatched the *66th Infantry Regiment* to attack the north flank of the Americans when *Miyake Force* resumed operations. However, severe conditions within *Miyake Force* caused the *66th Infantry* to be used mainly as porters to supply the main attack force. Across the front line, Troop C replaced Troop A on the exposed flank of the 112th Cavalry. Supplies were airdropped and casualties evacuated. Troop C spent the evening of the 20th in apprehension as they listened to the enemy bringing up reinforcements and putting together the artillery piece. The final Japanese reinforcement, *Headquarters, 20th Infantry Division*, under the command of Major General Masutaro Nakai, arrived to coordinate the attack, which was scheduled for the afternoon of July 21st.

Confusion reigned as the attack was about to begin. The Japanese of the *79th Infantry Regiment* believed that the Americans were out of their original positions. Many of the attacking Japanese wore captured American uniforms, taken from overrun supply depots. This added to the confusion of identifying friend from foe. Communications, as usual for both sides, were inadequate. An American liaison plane informed the 112th Cavalry that there were some American troops in front of their lines, adding to the false impression that Japanese wearing American uniforms would cause among the cavalrymen. General Gill would later remark "One of our major difficulties was to keep our communications working effectively during the seesaw of the battle." Clearly, on July 21st neither American nor Japanese communications were effective.

The Japanese opened their attacks as scheduled in the late afternoon of July 21st. Shortly before seven o'clock the lone artillery piece the Japanese had managed to get into position opened fire on the positions held by Troop C. Firing out of the jungle at about 300 yards range, pointblank for artillery, the Japanese scored quickly. Early in the shelling the commander of the 1st Squadron, the Troop C commander and the artillery liaison officer were all wounded with one enemy shell. This left the American defense of the right flank temporarily without leadership. Even before their shelling stopped, the Japanese infantry attacked. Confusion reigned once again. The Americans were overcautious about opening fire, fearing to hit what they thought might be friendly troops. One cavalryman said later "Unless you looked them in the face you didn't know whether they were enemy or not." The Japanese did not know the exact location of the American positions nor the strength of the unit they were attacking. The fighting immediately became a confused melee of soldiers trying to stay alive.

Troop C, its positions easily infiltrated by Japanese dressed in American clothing, was quickly surrounded. The loss of the artillery officer and the usual communications difficulties delayed supporting fires for nearly an hour, during which Troop C was pushed back and separated from the rest of the regiment. For a short period there were Americans surrounded by Japanese, who were in turn surrounded by Americans. This confused situation eventually clarified in favor of the Japanese when additional units of the 79th Infantry joined in the attack, finally separating Troop C and freeing its comrades who had been caught between American fires. For the Americans, the late arrival of the artillery support brought an end to the ferocity of the Japanese assault, but Troop C remained surrounded and cut off from the rest of the 112th Cavalry.

General Cunningham reacted quickly to the isolation of Troop C. Troop B was ordered to establish contact with the surrounded cavalrymen. Aided by two platoons from Company I, 127th Infantry, Troop B tried several times to reach their trapped comrades, each time only to be pushed back. Fighting continued throughout the night, during which one platoon of Company I managed to join Troop C, only to become a part of the surrounded garrison. The other Company I platoon was cut off from friendly forces and was unable to advance or withdraw to a friendly perimeter. An enemy machine gun position, protected by rifle and automatic weapons fire, blocked the only withdrawal route. Private Donald R. Lobaugh volunteered to take out the enemy position. Crawling across thirty yards of clear space directly in front of the machine gun, he sent one grenade at the position, but missed. He then rose to his feet and charged with his weapon blazing. Despite repeated wounds he continued his attack until he killed the enemy troops manning the position, but was himself killed in the attack. His platoon destroyed the remaining enemy positions and withdrew safely to American lines. Private Lobaugh was awarded a posthumous Medal of Honor.

Troop C and the Company I infantrymen now with them created a circular perimeter to spend the night. Outnumbered five to one, only the disorganization of the enemy and the darkness prevented them from being overrun. Troop E was alerted at dawn to try and reach the surrounded Americans. Attacking with sixty men, Troop E was hit hard with enemy fire and booby trapped explosives. The attack quickly halted, and General Cunningham permitted Troop E to withdraw. The balance of the day was spent in varying attempts to contact Troop C. Each of these was repulsed by strong Japanese trail-blocks, resulting in additional American casualties. Neither Troop B nor Company I had any success in approaching the surrounded Americans. Meanwhile, Troop C could do little to help. Surrounded and under heavy enemy fire from automatic weapons and snipers firing from trees, movement was suicidal. The mindset of the Americans within that fiery perimeter became fatalist. They understood their situation, knew that the only force which could relieve them was itself under heavy attack, and knew that the enemy was determined to destroy them. They prepared to fight to the death.

Communication problems continued to plague American efforts to restore the situation. Troop C had now been out of touch with any other American units for two days and nobody outside their perimeter could be sure that they still existed. An American pilot, flying over the last reported position of Troop C, reported that he thought he had found them some seven hundred yards from their former position. Patrols sent to the reported area found only Japanese, whom they attacked and destroyed. Later this same pilot, again trying to find Troop C, did locate and report their correct position. Now, at least, General Cunningham knew where they were and that at least some survivors were still fighting. Rescue, however, remained a serious problem.

General Cunningham now organized a strong relief force. Troops A and B, with Troop E in support, would attack south along the Driniumor. At the same time, the 2nd Battalion, 127th Infantry, would attack from the west. Both would direct their attacks towards the area in which Troop C had been detected by the pilot. These attacks started late on the afternoon of the 23rd. The infantrymen of the 127th found that the Japanese had largely withdrawn from the area into which they were advancing. The cavalrymen, however, were bitterly opposed. The leading platoons of Troop A, under Second Lieutenant George W. G. Boyce, Jr., were forced to halt and establish a line of defense only a few hundred yards from Troop C. Ordered to resume the attack, Lieutenant Boyce led his men forward once again, only to be slammed to the ground by heavy enemy rifle and mortar fire. He discovered a shallow depression that extended from his platoon position towards Troop C. Leading his men into this depression, he continued the advance. Now the Japanese were on the high ground, firing down into his men and using grenades. One of these grenades fell among Lieutenant Boyce and several of his men. The New York lieutenant threw himself on the enemy missile to save the lives of the soldiers he commanded. He was awarded a posthumous Medal of Honor.

Lieutenant Boyce's death ended the advance for the day. It had become clear that the 2nd Battalion, 127th Infantry had the best chance of relieving the trapped cavalrymen, and that the chance of instances of friendly fire existed if both units continued to advance. While the cavalrymen waited, the infantrymen relieved Troop C and the men of Company I who had suffered with them. But the Japanese did not fade back into the jungle. The kept the reinforced perimeter under siege, preventing Troop C from leaving for another day. Additional forces trying to reach the 2nd Battalion were also kept away. Both Companies B and E, 127th Infantry, sent to join the 2nd Battalion, were stopped by Japanese defenses. These delays angered General Gill, who believed that only one Japanese regiment opposed General Cunningham's forces. General Cunningham, the focus of General Gill's anger, argued that there were two Japanese infantry regiments attacking his force. Actually, Japanese records show that both were wrong. The remnants of the entire *20th Infantry Division*, plus the *66th Infantry Regiment* of the *51st Infantry Division*, were in the area, more than 2,000 trained and experienced combat troops.

Success finally crowned the American's persistent efforts on July 25th. Both Companies B and E, 127th Infantry, broke into the 2nd Battalion's perimeter and permitted the relief of the long-suffering Troop C, which now withdrew. Some thirty cavalrymen had become casualties during the four day siege. General Cunningham now ordered the remaining troops of the 112th to clear the area west of the Driniumor of the enemy. The next three days were a confusing mixture of attack and counterattack. American and Japanese units attacked each other, often not knowing who they were attacking. In one instance, for example, both sides chose to attack Hill 56, each thinking the other side defended it in strength. Often only physical contact made each side aware of the other's presence. The thick New Guinea jungle continued to influence all events. Both sides became increasingly frustrated, especially the commanders.

Most frustrated of all was General Adachi. He had failed to breach decisively the American defense of the Driniumor. His *20th Infantry Division* was down to a shadow of its former self, capable of only defensive action. Despite his frustration, he remained determined to continue the attack. The *66th Infantry Regiment* and the entire *41st Infantry Division* were now brought south to turn the American flank. The planned attack of the *41st Infantry Division* along the coast was postponed. Large Japanese forces were infiltrated across the Driniumor and sent into the American rear to establish blocking positions for when the

Americans retreated, and to attack them from the rear. General Cunningham became aware of some of these dispositions from patrol reports. He reacted quickly. The 1st Battalion, 127th Infantry, was pulled out of the line and sent to the rear to establish defensive positions protecting the American's rear. The 2nd Battalion, 127th Infantry, assumed responsibility for the sector of the 1st Battalion on the Driniumor River line. General Cunningham also alerted all his units to expect an attack on the night of July 26th.

No attack occurred that night or the next day. The Japanese, as usual, were having logistical trouble. Troops and supplies took considerable extra time to move in the jungle conditions of New Guinea. Troop E and Company A, 127th Infantry, found and cleared a Japanese trailblock on the 27th. Dead Japanese were identified as being from the *66th Infantry Regiment*, justifying General Cunningham's fears of a new attack from multiple directions. Nonetheless, no attack materialized.

In the absence of the expected attack, General Cunningham ordered the 2nd Battalion, 127th Infantry, to attack and push the Japanese forces out of position, disrupting any attack plans they might have. This attack was accomplished easily, and no sooner had the infantrymen established a new defensive position then they were ordered to clear their own rear areas. Here Japanese units had infiltrated and established trailblocks. The 1st Battalion, 127th Infantry and the 1st Squadron, 112th Cavalry were also drawn into the effort to clear the American rear of enemy troops. This took the Americans all day, and involved some bitter local fighting.

General Hall, at XI Corps, now decided that the enemy had finished with his attack. He wanted them pushed away from the Driniumor River, so as to prevent continued harassing attacks on his forces. Occupied with preparing a four battalion attack along the coast, he paid less attention to the action on his inland flank. This now reduced the pressure on Generals Gill and Cunningham, allowing them time to prepare for the difficult problem of finally clearing their areas of the enemy. General Hall had also decided that the newly arriving troops of the 43rd Infantry Division would be used in his coastal attack, so that he had no need to withdraw units already attached to General Cunningham.

General Cunningham was still apprehensive about another enemy attack. In order to prepare for that eventuality, he restructured his forces once again. On July 28th, as organized resistance on Biak was declared to be at an end, General Cunningham formed basically a circle perimeter. The 3rd Battalion, 127th Infantry and the 2nd Squadron, 112th Cavalry, defended the line of the Driniumor, tieing into the 128th Infantry in the north. The 1st Squadron, 112th Cavalry established a line from the Driniumor east, protecting the vulnerable exposed flank. The 2nd Battalion, 127th joined this line and faced west, towards the rear, in effect closing off a huge section of jungle area just west of the Driniumor River. Like the cavalrymen of the 19th century, the Americans circled up and waited.

They didn't have to wait long. The following day, July 29th, each of the units in the perimeter except those along the river bank, was to advance and enlarge the secured area. This began with the 1st Squadron and 2nd Battalion advancing south and west. The Japanese were nowhere in evidence. Only the jungle delayed the advance. Not until mid-morning did the infantrymen of Company E encounter a strong enemy position. Their attack failed, leaving seven dead and nine wounded within their ranks. Artillery fire was called down and did some damage, but not enough to eliminate the enemy position. A renewed attempt to destroy this position took all day, at the end of which a Japanese counterattack caused the battalion to go on the defensive, preventing continuation of the attack. After losing eleven killed, thirty-nine wounded and nine missing, both American units were withdrawn. The next two days were used for rest and reorganization. General Cunningham's units had been in the jungle fighting for three weeks, and they were tired. They had suffered some one thousand casualties. While keeping patrols active to prevent surprises, adjustments were made within the units to compensate for the 106 killed, 386 wounded, 18 missing and 426 evacuated sick. During this reorganization, Company C, 127th Infantry, was driven in from an outpost position to the main perimeter after being briefly surrounded on July 30th. No other serious action took place during this time. As part of the reorganization, the 2nd and 3rd Battalions, 127th infantry, exchanged places in the lines to enable the 2nd Battalion to get some rest. There was no relief available for the cavalrymen, so they had to carry on without it.

The attack that General Cunningham had been expecting was still in the staging phase. The Japanese had suffered severely in the past few weeks, and they also needed rest and reorganization in order to continue as ordered by General Adachi. The *41st Infantry Division*, less the *1st Battalion, 239th Infantry* which was left behind to keep the 128th Infantry busy, was moving south to join with the remnants of the *20th Infantry Division* and the *66th Infantry Regiment* in the planned attack. Final orders for the attack were issued by General Adachi on July 28th, which set the attack date for July 30th. However, once again the jungle intervened, and the *239th Infantry* became lost in the jungle and delayed in its arrival. The attack was again postponed.

General Adachi now set his attack to begin on August 1st. General Cunningham, now having finished his rest and reorganization plans, ordered a renewal of the clearing operations for August 1st. Each planned to attack the other at the same time. Some 4,000 Japanese combat troops would face the tired but prepared 112th Cavalry and 127th Infantry.

General Hall did not wait for General Adachi. He had spent the last few days preparing his own attack along the coast. He ordered the 124th Infantry Regiment, reinforced by the 2nd Battalion, 169th Infantry, to attack the Japanese defensive positions inland along the Driniumor. This attack was to start on July 31st with three battalions attacking and the fourth in reserve. They were instructed to attack east to the next river, the Niumen, clearing all the area in between the two rivers of the enemy. Commanding the attack was Colonel Edward M. Starr, the commanding officer of the 124th Infantry. In overall charge of the operation was Brigadier General Alexander Newton Stark, Jr., the assistant Division Commander of the now arriving 43rd Infantry Division. General Stark, son of a career army doctor and graduate of Mercerburg Academy, Pennsylvania, class of 1917, had served in World War I where he was awarded the Distinguished Service Cross. After a brief hiatus in civilian life, he returned to the Army and made it his career, which after the usual assignments and schools, had posted him to the 43rd Infantry Division, a National Guard unit drawn originally from the states of Maine, Vermont, Connecticut and Rhode Island, as the assistant division commander. The division had seen severe combat on Guadalcanal and in the Northern Solomons before its arrival in New Guinea.

Together with Colonel Starr, the attack force was distributed for the attack. The 2nd Battalion, 124th, under the command of Lieutenant Colonel Robert M. Fowler, would move along the coast. Next inland would be Lieutenant Colonel George D. Williams' 1st Battalion, acting as the right flank unit. Major William F. Lewis' 2nd Battalion, 169th Infantry, would follow the 3rd Battalion, 124th and act as a reserve. The 128th Infantry would assume responsibility for the Driniumor River line in this area once the attacking force, named "Ted Force" after Colonel Starr, advanced.

The 149th Field Artillery Battalion reinforced with the cannon company of the 124th Infantry Regiment would support the attack. The 129th Field Artillery Battalion was also on call. Opposing "Ted Force" was the *1st Battalion, 239th Infantry Regiment*, left behind by General Adachi when he moved the *41st Infantry Division* south to crush General Cunningham's forces. This unit faced Colonel Fowler's 2nd Battalion, which was the only one to encounter serious opposition when the Americans advanced towards the Niumen River. Despite the best efforts of the Japanese, who in this instance were heavily outnumbered, "Ted Force" reached their objectives by the morning of August 1st. The reinforced 124th Infantry spent the next few days clearing their area of stray Japanese and preparing for their next attack. General Adachi's right flank had been turned.

At the same time that "Ted Force" achieved its objective, General Adachi's attack in the south finally materialized. While waiting, Lieutenant Colonel Clyde S. Grant had prepared his 1st Squadron defenses as best he could in the thick jungle. Once again Troop C anchored the left of the defensive line, with Troop A next between Troop C and B. The outpost line of defense heard the Japanese coming early on August 1st. Major Hidea Imamura was leading his *1st Battalion, 238th Infantry* against the

1st Squadron. The *3rd Battalion, 78th Infantry*, was moving in support of Major Imamura's attack. Captain Keiji Karai's *4th Company* would lead the attack.

The Japanese attacked in a frenzy, and even the strong American defenses could not keep some of them from penetrating the perimeter. Nevertheless, the Americans held their positions. Troop C, once again in the forefront of the battle, held and wiped out the leading Japanese assault wave. Captain Karai's *4th Company* was decimated and the survivors driven off into the jungle. While killing five troopers and wounding six more of Troop C, 150 Japanese soldiers had been killed and countless others wounded. No breach had been made in the American lines. The *1st Battalion, 238th Infantry* ceased to exist.

The Japanese continued to attack throughout the balance of the day and into the night, but their efforts were now more in the way of harassing attacks than a full scale assault. American casualties continued to mount from these attacks and from friendly fire, so mixed were the opposing forces. Casualties from disease also became acute, causing concern at General Cunningham's headquarters that the 112th Cavalry was approaching the point of exhaustion. Despite this concern, there was still no American unit available to relieve the cavalrymen, so they stayed in the line.

The Japanese did not give up following the debacle on the 1st of August. They returned again on the 2nd, this time directing their efforts against the 1st Battalion, 127th Infantry. The remnants of the *80th* and *78th Infantry Regiments*, less than two hundred men now, attacked as ordered. Using what was left of their artillery, the Japanese charged the lines of Company B, 127th Infantry, only to be cut down in waves by the American artillery support, combined with mortar and small arms fire. This attack was a complete failure. While that attack was faltering, another force of Japanese from the *41st Infantry Division* attacked the adjoining 1st Squadron. This force of about 250 Japanese were dealt the same punishing fire which had met the previous attack, and the enemy troops were quickly wiped out. Sporadic attacks continued into the morning hours of August 3rd, but the Japanese had finished attacking entrenched American infantry. As a final assurance that the Japanese had no chance to accomplish their mission, the 1st Battalion, 169th Infantry from the 43rd Infantry Division, arrived to add its strength to the defending force's positions.

The final Japanese attack along the Driniumor occurred on August 4th. By this time General Adachi had learned of Ted Force and further that those Americans were coming south behind him. He had to leave now or face complete annihilation of the remainder of the *18th Army*. He knew he could never attack the Aitape airfields, despite the heroic exertions of his soldiers. Supplies were exhausted so that even if the enemy were not on his rear, he could not sustain another major attack. General Adachi ordered the remnants of his *41st Infantry Division* to keep the Americans busy along the Driniumor while he and the rest of the survivors of the *18th Army* withdrew into the jungle. Some 200 Japanese obediently attacked the 1st Squadron, 112th Cavalry at dawn on August 4th. Attacking with a fatalism borne of hunger, disease and failure, the Japanese were massacred. Before lunch on August 4th 185 Japanese lay dead in front of the cavalrymen's lines. A cavalryman bringing up supplies remarked that the dead Japanese soldiers lay like logs in the river.

CHAPTER XII

Sansapor and
Morotai—Finishing the Job

The conquest of Noemfoor gave the Sixth Army another airfield closer to the Philippines. The airfields on Noemfoor and Biak could also put Fifth and Thirteenth Army Air Force aircraft within range of the rest of New Guinea. It could not, however, put those aircraft within range of any of the Philippine Islands. It had long been planned at General MacArthur's headquarters that an air and naval base would have to be seized at the tip of western New Guinea to provide air and naval support for the next step past New Guinea. Targeted for this attack were the Japanese bases at Sorong and Waigo Island, just offshore at Sorong. There were several reasons for the choice of these two areas. Sorong had the inevitable airfields and attendant installations. Waigeo Island would also be ideal both for additional air bases and additional accommodations for naval forces. Additionally, Sorong was only 30 miles from a major oil field, located at Klamano. This former Dutch oil producing field had been bombed into disuse by the Allies, but Allied planners had stockpiled oil equipment in California for a quick restoration of oil production.

Rapidly changing events in the Pacific War soon altered all these plans, however. The capture of Biak and Noemfoor made the airfields at Sorong unnecessary. The needed naval installations could be established elsewhere, where opposition would be less than that expected at Sorong. The question of the need for oil was settled in Washington. Headquarters, Army Service Forces and the Army-Navy Petroleum Board determined by late July, 1944, that the progress of the war would remove any necessity of obtaining oil from Klamano. With these new decisions, by the time Noemfoor had been secured new plans were being drawn at Southwest Pacific Headquarters. General MacArthur's planners began to expedite plans which had been scheduled for later in the year.

The U.S. Submarine S-47, commanded by Lieutenant Lloyd V. Young, had been on its way to Waigeo to land a scouting party of Alamo Scouts, Fifth Army Air Force terrain experts, naval experts and Intelligence Bureau agents. When the decision was made to abandon Waigeo and Sorong, new locations had been tentatively selected at Sansapor and Mar, two villages some 55 miles northeast of Sorong. The S-47's scouting party was diverted to these new locations. After a week ashore inspecting the entire area, and a successful extraction by the submarine, they reported that the area was suitable for airfields and naval facilities. This favorable report prompted General MacArthur to order the Sixth Army to seize the Sansapor-Mar area beginning July 30th.

This rush of planning and execution caught the Seventh Fleet by surprise. When General MacArthur's headquarters directed Admiral Fechteler to prepare for the Sansapor-Mar operation, using the code name "Globetrotter," the Admiral had to hurry back from Noemfoor to Hollandia to find out what the code name meant. Nevertheless, as in the previous rushed operations, the navy was able to scrape up enough forces to transport a reinforced 6th Infantry Division to Sansapor as directed. General Krueger had selected the now experienced 6th Infantry Division as his assault force for Sansapor. General Krueger called a planning conference for July 8th, at which it was decided that enemy opposition could be expected to be light, and because of that expectation, no bombardment would be conducted in order to maintain the element of surprise as long as possible. Both Major General Ennis C. Whitehead, commanding the Fifth Army Air Force, and Admiral Fechteler agreed with General Krueger.

The planning conference of July 6th settled all matters except

Shadowy figures of men of the 6th Infantry Division move through the surf and onto the beach at Sansapor. (National Archives)

the ones concerning airfield construction. Information was lacking as to what types of fields would be needed, and where they should be located. This information was necessary if the right type of aviation engineer units were to be assigned to the task force for Sansapor, soon to be known as Typhoon Task Force. Another scouting party, traveling this time by PT boat, departed Noemfoor and spent three days acquiring the necessary terrain information. The absence of the enemy, and the open reception given the scouts by the native population encouraged the planners that the operation would go smoothly.

For once, the planners had everything right, including the lack of enemy opposition to be expected. The landings went very much like a training exercise. Colonel Forbie H. Privett's 1st Infantry Regiment landed precisely on time at Mar on the morning of July 30th. Moving inland without a shot fired or an enemy in evidence, it was not until more than an hour after the landing that the 2nd Battalion found and killed three Japanese soldiers. As had happened on previous operations, terrain and

Work party takes a break and listens to a portable Victrola on the beach at Sansapor. (National Archives)

jungle conditions hampered the operation more than the enemy. The 1st Field Artillery Battalion was quickly ashore and ready to fire, but no targets presented themselves. The engineers were also quickly put ashore and under the direction of Brigadier General Earl W. Barnes, who brought an advance headquarters of the Thirteenth Army Air Force ashore, they selected sites to begin airfield construction. The 836th Engineer Aviation Battalion was working before lunch.

While the 1st Infantry had gone ashore at Mar, the 6th Cavalry

Reconnaissance Troop, reinforced with soldiers from the 63rd Infantry Regiment, had seized the offshore islands of Middelburg and Amsterdam without opposition. Here occurred the only American fatality of the day, a soldier killed by the accidental discharge of a friendly weapon. The beachhead was secure, engineers at work, and opposition nonexistent. It had been a very good day for the 6th Infantry Division, especially after their days at Lone Tree Hill.

The next day, July 31st, was equally good. The 3rd Battalion, 1st Infantry, moved by sea to Sansapor. As at Mar the day before, the Japanese were nowhere to be found. The 3rd Battalion went ashore after the briefest of bombardments from one U.S. destroyer and established a beachhead without difficulty. There were no casualties.

The enemy was staying away from Sansapor. Responsible for the security of the beachhead, the 6th Infantry sought them out. Patrols went out constantly to see where the enemy was, and find out his intentions. Occasional captures of sick and wounded Japanese took place, as when on August 3rd a Japanese hospital was captured, putting 92 sick and wounded Japanese troops into American prisoner of war enclosures.

Contrary to the impression they gave the Americans, the Japanese were not idle. The *Headquarters, 2nd Army* and the *35th Japanese Infantry Division* had been bypassed at Manokwari by the landing at Sansapor-Mar. They now served no useful purpose at Manokwari, and so both units began to move west to Sorong. A provisional combat unit was organized from the numerous service personnel among the Japanese forces, and this newly created *1st Independent Brigade* joined in the movement to the Sorong area. None of these units intended to attack the 6th Infantry Division, as their supplies were nearly gone, and they were forced to live off the land. In fact, the dispositions of the three largest enemy units, *Headquarters, 2nd Army, 35th Infantry Division*, and *1st Independent Brigade*, were determined by the availability of natural food sources rather than strategic or tactical considerations. So effective was the American sea and air blockade that the enemy had received no supplies in several months.

Nevertheless, the attempts by the Japanese to reorganize and

Army engineers used metal links to create airstrips in jungle conditions, in this case near Buna early in the campaign.

relocate their forces led to occasional clashes between patrols of the 6th Infantry Division and the moving Japanese. During these clashes which lasted throughout August and well into September, 385 Japanese were reported killed and an additional 215 were captured. American losses, all within the 6th Infantry Division, were 14 killed, 35 wounded and 9 non-battle injuries. Nine men also died from scrub typhus, the same disease which had struck down so many of the engineers on Owi Island. Airfield construction was proceeding according to plan and the airfield at Mar was operational by September 2nd. Together with the fighter strip constructed on Middleburg Island the Allied air forces conducted from these fields bomber and fighter sweeps throughout the area. The Japanese in western New Guinea remained dormant for the duration of the war. The *2nd Army Headquarters*, the *35th Infantry Division* and *1st Independent Brigade*, along with many miscellaneous units were forced to wait out the war's end in the jungles of New Guinea.

For the Americans, it was time to move off New Guinea. Sansapor-Mar was the western end of New Guinea, but it was not the end of the campaign. For General MacArthur the next step was the island of Morotai. The selection of Morotai was once again decided by the range of the Southwest Pacific's air cover. From Sansapor the Allied air forces could still not reach the Philippines to support a direct assault there. The solution was to seize an intermediate position somewhere between New Guinea and the Philippines. There were two likely targets, the islands of Halmahera and Morotai. A review of intelligence reports indicated that there was a strong enemy garrison on the

Soldiers of the 6th Infantry Division move inland from the Sansapor beaches. (National Archives)

island of Halmahera, while Morotai was believed to be lightly held. Further, Halmahera was within easy range of enemy counterattacks by air and sea from the Philippines. Morotai became the next target by process of elimination. It was within range of American aircraft, believed lightly defended, and less likely to be the target of enemy attacks. Before the 6th Infantry Division had boarded ships for Sansapor, General MacArthur had officially selected Morotai as the next objective.

The island of Morotai has been compared to Noemfoor, except that it was considerably larger. Roughly oval shaped, the island is forty miles long north to south and about twenty-five miles wide. The island has numerous beaches, many fringed with reefs, again like Noemfoor. The island has inland peaks rising to more than 3,500 feet, and the interior terrain is extremely difficult for troops. Like all previous operations,

Morotai was covered with thick jungle growth. Indeed, its only saving grace from the point of view of the Americans was the lowland in its southwest corner called the Doroeba plain. Here airfields could be constructed. These fields could provide the air support needed to invade the Philippines.

The Japanese had not paid much attention to either Morotai or Halmahera until early in 1944, when it appeared that their outer line of defense was being breached. Then they had selected Halmahera as their main defensive position. Nine airfields were constructed there, and the *32nd Infantry Division* heavily reinforced with service units, was sent there to defend the island. On Morotai the Japanese constructed one airfield on the Doroeba plain which they soon abandoned. The only garrison force on Morotai was the *2nd Raiding Unit*, commanded by Major Takenobu Kawashima. Its officers were Japanese but most of its enlisted men were Formosans. The unit was divided into four companies. A plan existed for a counterattack from Halamera, should Morotai be invaded. However, by September the Japanese had no way to move forces by sea.

General Krueger assigned the 31st Infantry Division, reinforced by the 126th Infantry Regimental Combat Team of the 32nd Infantry Division, to seize Morotai. Major General Hall's XI Corps was charged with overall responsibility for the invasion. XI Corps would coordinate the assault and support forces designated for Morotai. Changing roles from Persecution Task Force at Aitape, XI Corps now became Tradewind Task Force. The 6th Infantry Division at Sansapor was designated as Tradewind Task Force Reserve.

Transportation was once again provided by Admiral Daniel E. Barbey's VII Amphibious Force. Because the 124th Infantry Regiment was still at Aitape, while the rest of the 31st Infantry Division was still at Maffin Bay, the units were boarded from those locations. The assault units carried out a quick rehearsal at Wakde on September 6th, then Tradewind Task Force sailed for Morotai. The assault was to begin on September 15th.

After a bombardment by aircraft and destroyers, the assault troops of the 31st Infantry Division's 155th and 167th Infantry Regiments were landed by landing craft on Red Beach. The 124th Infantry assault elements were less fortunate, and had to

General MacArthur surrounded by some of his troops on Morotai. The island was secure and this was another "photo opportunity." (U.S. Army)

wade ashore from the reef fringing White Beach to reach Morotai. There was no opposition, which was fortunate for the 124th Infantry who otherwise could have repeated the fate of the 2nd Marine Division at Tarawa when they were forced to wade ashore into intense enemy fire. Later both White and Red Beaches would be abandoned because reef and soil conditions were too difficult to continue to use them as landing beaches. The 4th Engineer Special Brigade, responsible for shore party and small craft operations, located a more suitable beach and moved all future operations to Blue Beach.

By the end of September 15th the beachhead had been established, the three infantry regiments had joined to form a solid defensive lines, and no serious opposition had been encountered. At a cost of seven men wounded, the 31st Infantry

Division had secured the beachhead and killed twelve Japanese and captured another.

For the next three weeks the Americans scoured the island with patrols, while the 126th Infantry landed on several offshore islands and secured them. Opposition came only in the form of patrol actions, with small groups of enemy troops being encountered and dispersed. By October 4th, when General Krueger declared the operation over, 30 Americans had been killed, 85 wounded and 1 missing against reported enemy casualties of 104 killed and 13 captured. To this must be added some 200 more enemy believed killed by PT boats who intercepted them coming from Halmahera. As on Owi Island earlier, several hundred men, mostly service troops, fell ill on Morotai from a combination of illnesses, chiefly malaria and dengue fever. Strict enforcement of the use of DDT kept another scrub typhus outbreak from occurring, and the 31st Infantry Division was completely unaffected by the disease problem.

The landings at Sansapor and Morotai were the end in New Guinea as far as the Americans were concerned, although Australian army, air and naval units would continue to be heavily engaged in New Guinea until the end of the war in 1945. Elements of the 93rd Infantry Division moved in to relieve the 6th Infantry Division at Sansapor early in 1945. General Sibert's move to command X Corps took effect and Brigadier General Charles E. Hurdis took command of the 6th Infantry Division. Soon all the American units would move on to the Philippines, the objective of the bloody campaign they had just completed.

MacArthur's Flyboy

One of General MacArthur's most important subordinate commanders was his Air Force commander. In the absence of strong naval support and without aircraft carriers to provide air support at his far flung battlefields, he needed to have dependable land based air support available to protect his ground troops, soften up the next target, and provide transport for much of his supplies and equipment. The Western New Guinea campaign, as we have seen, was in large part based upon the distances General MacArthur's air support could cover an operation from their latest bases.

General MacArthur's early experiences with the Air Corps were less than favorable. In the opening days of the war his Air Corps stationed in the Philippines was largely destroyed in the first few days and never replaced or reinforced. This dissatisfaction continued to the end of his Philippines adventure. When PT-41 left him off on an island still held by the American forces, he and his party were supposed to fly the rest of the way to Australia. So poor were the two planes sent to fetch him to Australia that he refused to allow his party, which included his wife and son, to fly in them, and demanded aircraft in more flyable condition be sent for him, which they were.

The experiences in the Philippines were aggravated by his relationship with his Air Force commander in the Philippines, Lieutenant General George H. Brett. General MacArthur was disappointed in General Brett's concept of how air power could be used to advance the army's infantry to its objectives. This difference of opinion was intensified by the problem between General Brett and General Richard K. Sutherland, MacArthur's Chief of Staff. By the time General MacArthur and his staff settled in Australia, the two men loathed each other. General MacArthur throughout the war chose to ignore his Chief Of Staff's problems in working with others. Although they rarely agreed on most matters, there was universal agreement among General MacArthur's top commanders that General Sutherland was egotistical, arbitrary and openly antagonistic to them. Yet because he was one of the "Bataan Gang," offi-

cers who had served General MacArthur faithfully during the dark days in the Philippines, he stood by him. Even General Sutherland's flagrant diobedience of General MacArthur's own direct orders to him when he brought his Australian mistress to New Guinea with him failed to cause his removal, although the relationship between the two did noticeably cool after that.

Given the status of the MacArthur-Sutherland relationship, it was General Brett who had to go. His replacement was General George Churchill Kenney. General Kenney was another one of those officers with unusual military backgrounds who seemed to gravitate to the Southwest Pacific Theater of Operations. Born in Yarmouth, Nova Scotia, while his parents were visiting there from Brookline, Massachusetts, he showed no early interest in the military. He attended the Massachusetts Institute Of Technology, graduating in 1911 as an engineer. He worked as an engineer on railroad location and had his own construction business. His passion was in flying, however, and he enlisted in the Army in 1917 to learn to fly. Returning to M.I.T. as an aviation cadet, private first class, he took his ground schooling. He distinguished himself in the First World War, rising to command the 91st Squadron, flying 150 missions and shooting down two enemy aircraft before working on special missions for General Billy Mitchell. His decorations included the Distinguished Service Cross and Silver Star. After the war he added to his engineering background by attending the Air Service Engineering School. Assigned to the Air Service Engineering Division he began to make a name for himself by coming up with innovations for Army aircraft. All aircraft in the First World War had had their machine guns mounted on their cowlings, firing through the propeller. Captain Kenney introduced the concept of having machine guns installed on the wings, reducing the risk inherent in shooting weapons through one's own propeller. He also upgraded the weapons carried by U.S. aircraft from thirty caliber to fifty caliber, a more damaging size bullet to enemy aircraft. Other innovations credited to Captain Kenney were oxygen apparatus which responded to the demands of the pilot, installing protective armor on aircraft, leak-proof gasoline tanks and supercharging all planes expected to operate at high altitudes.

In 1927 Captain Kenney was a rising star, and so he was sent to the Command and General Staff School at Fort Leavenworth, Kansas. While attending schools, which included the Air Corps' Tactical School at Langley Field, he developed the idea of what he called "attack aviation," using aircraft at low levels to attack enemy troops and positions in support of friendly troops. Promoted to Major, he next spent two years on the staff of the Air Corps Chief of Staff, served as an instructor at the Army's Infantry School at Fort Benning, and then was promoted to Colonel and given command of the 97th Observation Squadron. At about this time the Air Corps received a new chief, General Henry H. (Hap) Arnold. General Arnold noticed Colonel Kenney's enthusiasm and began a tradition of using him for difficult

situations. One such situation developed when pilots on the west coast reported ongoing difficulties flying the P-38 fighter plane and the A-29 Lockheed Hudson bomber. Kenney, now a major general, solved that problem by taking each plane up in the air in front of the pilots, and showing them exactly how to handle each aircraft. There were no more complaints about either plane.

General Kenney's most difficult job came when he was ordered to the Southwest Pacific Theater as the new Air Corps commander. He knew of the problems that had preceded his arrival. He knew that General Sutherland could be a problem, knew that many of General MacArthur's problems with the Air Corps were indeed originating within his new command. Generals MacArthur and Kenney met for the first time in June of 1942. General MacArthur delivered a lecture for some ninety minutes, a not unusual event, while General Kenney listened quietly. The lecture was severely critical of General Kenney's new command. Finally, after being patient for nearly two hours, General Kenney interrupted his new commander and explained that he intended to run the air operations. Should General MacArthur ever have any doubts as to his personal loyalty to him, all he need do was ask, but that would be unnecessary because General Kenney stated that the moment he felt any doubt he would request reassignment. General MacArthur had heard something similar from Admiral William H. (Bull) Halsey earlier, and Admiral Halsey had proved a successful and loyal subordinate. General MacArthur turned to General Kenney and announced that he thought they would get along just fine. And that is exactly what happened.

General Kenney refused to deal with General Sutherland, and took up his Air Corps matters up with General MacArthur personally. He established his own headquarters near wherever General MacArthur's headquarters happened to be, for easier access. He sent home dozens of officers left to him by General Brett who did not measure up to his own standards, and brought in a few of his own. One such Kenney man was Brigadier General Ennis C. Whitehead, an old acquaintance of General Kenney's who ran the day to day operations of the Fifth Army Air Corps, General Kenney's official command until June 1944. In constant communication with Whitehead, Kenney left the details in his subordinate's hands while he kept the Air Corps presence at Headquarters, Southwest Pacific Area.

General Kenney had many problems to resolve. The Fifth Army Air Force was at the end of a long supply line, most of which was on its way to Europe. Kenney became adept at begging, borrowing and sometimes stealing what he needed to get his job done. As equipment was improved, another facet that Kenney continued to excel at, and tactics were improved, the Air Corps became MacArthur's "flying artillery." Kenney's innovations allowed Whitehead's flyers to catch enemy fighters lined up at their airfields, much as had happened to General Brett's planes in the Philippines, when they believed that the American planes had insufficient range to reach them. Kenney solved that problem by adding long range fuel drop tanks to his aircraft.

General Kenney also got a chance to put into practice his "attack tactics" and much of the flying done by the Fifth Army Air Force, especially in New Guinea, was low level direct bombing and strafing of enemy targets. By June of 1944 Kenney was again promoted to command what was now called the Southwest Pacific Allied Air Forces, which included the Fifth and Thirteenth U.S. Army Air Forces, the Royal Australian Air Force units in the Southwest Pacific, and some Dutch air units. Kenney served in that capacity, still at MacArthur's side protecting his Air Corp units, till the end of the war.

After the war General Kenney served briefly as an American Military representative to the United Nations, commander of the Strategic Air Force, and then moved into the newly established U.S. Air Force. His last post before retirement in 1951 was as commandant of the Air University, Maxwell Air Force Base, Alabama.

CHAPTER XIII

On to Manila

Yet even while the 6th Infantry Division was moving on Sansapor, and before the 31st Infantry Division boarded enroute for Morotai, the 124th Infantry Regiment of that division had unfinished business at Aitape. General Adachi had known for some days that the attacks of August 1st would be his last chance to penetrate the American defense lines. Those attacks had failed and his forces were decimated. Supplies were non-existent. A strong enemy force was now attempting to turn his northern flank. Initially, due to poor communications, General Adachi believed that the American force on his flank was only of battalion strength. He ordered the remnants of the *237th Infantry Regiment* to hold open his crossing site at Niumen Creek, to his rear. Then he ordered the *66th Infantry Regiment* to form a rear guard to protect the bulk of the *18th Army* while it retreated. The retreat was scheduled to begin August 5th.

General Adachi became aware of the size of Ted Force on August 3rd, and promptly ordered his retreat to begin at once. The *20th Infantry Division* was to retreat beginning the same day, August 3rd, and the *41st Infantry Division* no later than the 5th. The survivors of the *8th Independent Engineer Regiment* were to assist the *237th Infantry Regiment* survivors in holding open the crossing site at Niumen creek. This combined force took position on a ridge directly in the path of Ted Force and defended it when attacked by Colonel Williams' 3rd Battalion, 124th Infantry Regiment. Well dug in and prepared to fight to the death to permit the escape of their comrades, the Japanese could not be dislodged on August 5th. Artillery and mortars made no dent in their positions. Colonel Starr, commanding Ted Force halted operations for the night. He brought up Major Lewis' 2nd Battalion, 169th Infantry. Major Lewis was ordered to pass around the Japanese flank at first light, and cut off their escape route. Meanwhile, Colonel Fowler's 2nd Battalion, 124th Infantry, was to support Colonel Williams.

Major Lewis moved his battalion off into the deep jungle and promptly became mired down in the thick jungle and difficult terrain. Although the 169th Infantry had fought in the jungles of the Northern Solomon islands, the New Guinea jungle completely disoriented them. The battalion lost its way so thoroughly that it could not even identify its night defensive position for supporting artillery to register for protection against a possible counterattack. Colonel Starr nevertheless ordered all three of his front line battalions to attack again at first light.

The Japanese moved first. Before dawn, the 3rd Battalion, 124th Infantry, was attacked by an estimated 400 Japanese. These soldiers, remnants of the *41st Infantry Division, 26th Field Artillery Regiment*, and *8th Independent Engineers* attacked with heavy supporting fire. The initial attack was stopped by the Americans, but the Japanese refused to withdraw and established themselves at the fringes of the Americans' perimeter, continuing a heavy suppressing fire. Colonel Williams' battalion was pinned down.

Colonel Fowler's 2nd Battalion, 124th Infantry, was not attacked and moved around the flank of the attacking enemy force. Colonel Starr ordered Colonel Fowler to try and turn the flank of the enemy attacking Colonel Williams. Colonel Fowler and his men tried, but soon found themselves under the same heavy fire that had pinned the 3rd Battalion. One of Colonel Fowler's companies did manage to slip around and locate a hill from which they could dominate the enemy's position. Advised of this Colonel Fowler moved the bulk of his battalion to this hill. Outflanked, the Japanese withdrew.

During this fierce action on August 6th, the 2nd Battalion, 169th Infantry remained lost in the jungle. Late in the day they encountered some Japanese fleeing from the battle with the

124th Infantry battalions, and engaged these soldiers. But at day's end the battalion was still out of contact with any other friendly force and still unable to pinpoint its position with certainty, again prohibiting artillery support. Care now had to be taken to ensure that the various American forces did not fire on one another. Colonel Starr estimated that some 350 Japanese had been killed during the day, with a loss to Ted Force of 11 killed and 2 wounded.

August 7th was a much more satisfying day for Ted Force. It advanced fairly quickly over difficult terrain, the Japanese having left only small rear guards to delay their advance. Some faulty American artillery ammunition caused more casualties than the enemy. The following morning, after more friendly fire killed and wounded some of Major Burns' soldiers, the objective was reached. Only Colonel Lewis' battalion remained unaccounted for, although not in any danger. This last unit of Ted Force came out of the jungle on August 10th, tired, but otherwise unharmed. Together with the rest of Ted Force, it was moved to the rear for rest and in the case of the 124th Infantry, to prepare for the journey to Morotai. Colonel Starr reported his force had killed some 1,800 Japanese for losses to itself of 50 men killed and 80 wounded.

While Ted Force was cleaning out the northern sector, the southern sector was also active. Here the 112th Cavalry and the 127th Infantry were left to finish the job that they had begun nearly a month before. Most of the cleaning up was done by patrols which remained as dangerous as ever. Opposition was disorganized and sporadic. Clearly, the Japanese had gone. Finally, on August 10th, relief for the hard-used cavalrymen and their infantry counterparts arrived in the form of the 103rd Infantry Regiment, 43rd Infantry Division. In quick succession the 112th Cavalry, the 127th and 128th Infantry Regiments were relieved by the now arriving 43rd Infantry Division and relieved from Persecution Task Force. In fact, Persecution Task Force ceased to exist, being replaced by the Tadji Defense Perimeter and Covering Force on August 15th. Commanded by Major General Leonard F. Wing, the commanding General of the 43rd Infantry Division, this new Task Force was charged with the final clean up of the Driniumor River line.

The 43rd Infantry Division was a New England National Guard division drawn from Maine, Connecticut, Rhode Island and Vermont. The division had been federalized and filled up with a group of draftees, most of whom coincidentally also came from New England. After training and occupation duty in New Caledonia, the division saw combat on Guadalcanal and New Georgia in the Solomon Islands. The division commander, Major General Leonard F. Wing, claimed to be a direct descendent of the American Revolution's "Green Mountain Boys," and was a native of Vermont. He had entered the service as a private and saw combat as an enlisted man in World War I. By the end of the war he was holding a commission as a first lieutenant. After the war he returned to civilian life, but also stayed active in the Vermont National Guard. Between the wars General Wing practiced law in Vermont, and was called to active duty with his division in February, 1941. The following February he was made the assistant division commander and during the bitter fighting on New Georgia he assumed command of the division which he now brought to Aitape after a brief rest occupying New Georgia. Still recovering from leg wounds received on New Georgia, and still new to division command, General Wing was another of those leaders who often could be found on the front lines determining the situation for themselves.

Fortunately for the injured General Wing and his tired division, the Japanese they had been sent to defeat had already accepted that fact. Mostly, the Japanese had gone. In the distance, near the Dandriwad River, the Japanese had set up strong delaying positions, but the Americans had no interest in that area, and so the Japanese were left in peace. The 43rd Infantry Division remained in the Aitape area, patrolling to ensure security for the Tadji Defense Perimeter, until relieved in October, 1944 by the 2/6th Cavalry (Commando) Regiment, Australian Army. Late in November the 6th Australian Infantry Division arrived and command of the area was passed from General Wing to Major General J. E. S. Stevens, Australian Imperial Force, the commander of the 6th Australian Division. Fighting continued in the area, as the Australians pushed eastward, until the war's end.

Allied losses until the end of major combat in the Hollandia-

Aitape campaign totaled 440 men killed, 2,550 wounded and 10 missing. Against this the Allies claimed some 8,821 enemy dead and 98 captured. To these figures must be added subsequent Australian casualties of 451 killed, 1,163 wounded and 3 missing. An additional 7,200 Japanese were reported killed and 269 captured by the Australians. The total casualties on both sides makes Aitape one of the most costly campaigns of the Pacific war.

The American advance up the north coast of Western New Guinea was extremely "painful" to the Japanese. Senior staff officers viewed the loss of Biak particularly as "the most critical crossroads of the war." Having been thoroughly defeated, the staff officers in Japan concerned themselves with defending the Philippines and the Central Pacific Bonin Islands. No such concerns affected the Japanese left behind in New Guinea. For them the only concern was survival.

Sergeant Masatsugu Ogawa had served with the *79th Infantry Regiment* of the *20th Infantry Division* in China before he had sailed with it to New Guinea in January of 1943. He had served throughout the campaign, a fighting retreat with his troops being pursued on land, sea and from the air by the ever stronger Allied military force. By 1944 he and those of his men who survived were refugees from the enemy and the jungle. Conditions were worse than could be imagined. The Japanese, moving ever west, towards an imagined safety at the western end of New Guinea, died of hunger, disease, and both enemy and friendly attacks.

"Soldiers who had struggled along before us littered the sides of the trail." Men fell by the wayside every yard of the route. Men who were no more than skeletons continued on until they could walk no more, then crawled on until they died by the trail. Once dead, the bodies were looted for the rags, especially boots, they wore by those still moving west. In many cases, as had already occurred on Noemfoor, cannibalism was practiced to ensure survival. Sergeant Ogawa was one of those struggling westward. "Many had gone mad. I couldn't get over the fact that delirious as they were, they still continued to march in the same direction. Nobody, no matter how insane, walked the wrong way." For the struggling Japanese, tens of thousands who undertook such miserable journeys in attempts to survive, the interior of New Guinea "was a desert of green."

Their weapons rusted from the constant rains. The leading soldiers usually cleaned out whatever natural food they found along the trail, leaving those following behind to starve. Those with wounds found that they would not heal under the miserable jungle conditions. If not cared for, infection, followed by death, soon appeared. "It went on without end, just trudging through the muddy water, following the legs of somebody in front of you." The Japanese survivors plodded on through the jungle, constantly pursued by some enemy force in addition to the jungle. "In New Guinea, we didn't know what was killing us." Sergeant Ogawa revised his earlier opinion of the Australian infantry pursuing him. From an earlier opinion, no doubt influenced by Japanese propaganda, he now "came to feel the Australian military was very strong indeed." Until the end of the war, Sergeant Ogawa and his men struggled to survive in the jungle. All told, some 148,000 Japanese troops perished in New Guinea.

In later years the campaign for Western New Guinea was often spoken of as a classic example of General MacArthur's skill in both strategy and tactics. The story told of the campaign usually relates how the Americans bypassed thousands of enemy troops and landed easily at Hollandia, Sansapor and Morotai. There is always mention of how little American blood was shed in these easy victories. And there the discussion usually ends, for little has been written about the campaign as a whole.

There is considerable truth in the stories of Hollandia, Sansapor and Morotai. In each case, as we have seen, the Americans landed unopposed and secured quickly the initial objectives with little or no loss. But that is not the whole story of the Western New Guinea Campaign. There is also the bloody struggle for Biak, the seizure of the Wakde Islands, and the long and deadly battles for Lone Tree Hill and the Driniumor River line. The men of the Sixth Army deserve more credit than being described as merely an occupation force. They fought some of the bloodiest battles of the Pacific war under unquestionably the most difficult conditions of that war.

One of the reasons that the New Guinea campaign has been glossed over is that it was soon used to compare General MacArthur's strategy with that of Admiral Nimitz's in the Central Pacific. In the debate, which began while the war was still going on, General MacArthur's supporters compared the favorable results of Hollandia and Sansapor with the bloody battles for Tarawa, Saipan and Iwo Jima. The argument was targeted to convince the American public that General Mac-Arthur was more competent than Admiral Nimitz and his Marine Corps generals, and that General MacArthur should be given overall command in the Pacific. Although General Mac-Arthur himself was too astute to come out publicly in support of this movement, he did his best to encourage it. That was one of his lesser reasons for declaring campaigns over while heavy fighting continued, as at Biak. The prime reason always remained his desire for an early return to the Philippines.

The conflict which occurred between the Army and the Marine Corps during the Mariana Campaign put all Army leaders, including those who held a lesser opinion of General MacArthur, on his side. During the battle for Saipan in the Marianas two Marine Corps divisions were aided by the 27th Infantry Division, a New York National Guard division parts of which had fought earlier in the Gilbert and Marshall Islands. Saipan was the first battle in which the 27th Infantry Division fought as a whole, and the first time its units fought under its own commander. During the battle, the overall Marine commander, Lieutenant General Holland M. Smith, recommended the relief of the commander of the 27th Infantry Division, so dissatisfied was he with its performance. The relief was approved and instituted by the Navy commander on the scene, which was appropriate under Navy-Marine Corps amphibious doctrine. The United States Army was enraged. A Marine Corps officer had relieved an Army commander, and that was unacceptable. Aside from being inaccurate, Admiral Raymond A. Spruance had relieved the division commander, it was no different than so many such reliefs occurring within Army units. There were several such during the campaign for Western New Guinea, most notably General Fuller at Biak, Colonel Herndon at Lone Tree Hill, and others.

So intense were the feelings about the relief at Saipan that it still surfaces to this day. Yet compared to the reliefs of General Fuller and Colonel Herndon, it was not at all unusual. By using the relatively easy victories at Hollandia and Sansapor, General MacArthur's skill as well as that of the U.S. Army, could be touted as better than the Navy-Marine Corps method. And so in a sense public relations denied the men of Sixth Army a just place in history.

Which was patently unfair. The Sixth Army, or Alamo Force, had defeated in detail the *18th Army*, had conquered some of the most difficult terrain in the world, and had advanced the Allied thrust against the enemy by thousands of miles. And it was not as easy as many histories make it seem. They had suffered equally with those who would fight in the Battle of the Bulge, at Normandy, Anzio, or on Okinawa. The only difference was they did their deeds under the cover of Sergeant Ogawa's "green desert" and General MacArthur's publicity blackout of anything viewed as less than successful. General MacArthur's need for quick victories to maintain his successful image as a great military leader, and to serve to support his possible Presidential bid, denied any prolonged discussion of his battles. As we have seen at Biak, within forty eight hours of the initial landings, he was declaring in his communiques that the battle was well advanced and would shortly be over. In reality the battle had barely begun. Most subsequent readers have taken the General at his communique, and questioned no further. This is unfair to the men, American and Australian, who served the General.

Nor were these battles as economical in lives as is often accepted, again from the official communiques. General Krueger often declared a battle over at a certain date, whether or not fighting was still going on. While this was not an uncommon practice, in the Southwest Pacific it is misleading. Aitape is a classic example. General Krueger declared the battle of Aitape over early in August. Yet after that date the entire 43rd Infantry Division was engaged in costly mopping up operations, and soon the entire 6th Australian Division moved against the remaining Japanese. This non-campaign resulted in additional casualties of 541 killed and 1,163 wounded for the Australians, who were under General MacArthur's overall command. This casualty total is actually more than occurred during the "official" battle for the Drinumor River line. By the simple expedient of combining the losses that the Americans suffered, 440 killed, 2,550 wounded and 10 missing with the losses of the Australians, the totals for the Aitape campaign become 981 dead, 3,713 wounded and 13 missing. These figures compare with those of the Navy-Marine assault on Tarawa, often touted as the worst example of the Navy-Marine Corps methods. When viewed in full disclosure, the two battles are roughly comparable in terms of casualties, although one battle lasted three days while the other went on for months.

What is clear is that each campaign, that in New Guinea and that in the Central Pacific, had its own demands, peculiarities and legends. Neither was directed less skillfully than the other. The bloody campaigns fought by the Navy and Marines in the Central Pacific were no less deadly or dangerous than that fought by the Army and Army Air Forces in New Guinea. In each the enemy was the same skillful, tenacious and deadly opponent. Physical conditions differed but took similar tolls on the troops. The jungle had its heat, disease and climate which encouraged illness while the Pacific islands often had no water, no place to hide and no shelter from the weather, also hot, or the enemy. Each campaign merited its success. Perhaps had General MacArthur controlled his press less and allowed the full story of his troops to be told their deeds would be recognized today.

General of the Army Douglas MacArthur

The central figure in the Western New Guinea Campaign was General of the Army Douglas MacArthur. He is also one of the most enigmatic figures in U.S. military history. Adored by some, despised by others, he nevertheless was a major figure in the Second World War. Born January 26th, 1880 into a military family, he never was interested in any other career. His father was a noted Civil War Union general and war hero, a winner of the Medal of Honor for conduct commanding Union troops at the battle of Lookout Mountain during the Chattanooga Campaign. His father, Captain Arthur MacArthur, was a career army officer and Douglas' early life was centered entirely on the military. Although his comments over the years varied in detail, they all concerned his vivid first impressions involving his childhood "in the Army."

One of the most important and lasting influences on Douglas MacArthur's life was his mother. Mary Pinkney MacArthur was a southern belle, and impressed on her son Douglas those old south virtues of a courtly manner and fastidiousness. She also had some less commendable traits which she passed on to her son as well. She has been described as a complex woman, meek and tough, petulant and sentimental, charming and emotional. Each of these traits would mark later descriptions of her son in his career. As was to be expected Douglas attended West Point as the son of a Medal of Honor winner. He was a top graduate in the class of 1903, and was commissioned into the Corp of Engineers, a position re-served for the top ten per cent of the graduating class each year.

He spent the next four years as a surveyor in the Philippines, a locale he had seen as a boy when his father served there. After duty there he served as an aide to President Theodore Roosevelt. He served as an aide to the General Staff and saw action during the American occupation of Vera Cruz in 1914. Now a major, he helped to organize and train the 42nd (Rainbow) Division and accompanied it overseas to the Western Front, where he distinguished himself by his personal bravery and competence. Here the first noticeable signs of his personal idiosyncracies appeared when he began to wear personal garments such as hats, scarfs and boots not part of the approved uniform.

Returning from the war, he was promoted brigadier general and appointed Commandant of West Point. After that assignment, he was again returned to the Philippines for another three years. At the conclusion of this assignment he was promoted again to major general. One of the major forces behind his relatively rapid advancement, other than his own competence, was Mrs. MacArthur. The General's mother wrote regularly to higher commanders and political leaders touting her son's virtues and complaining about his slow advancement within the Army. Her own husband had been denied an appointment as the army's Chief of Staff, a position he had wanted very badly, and it seemed as if his widow was now determined that if her husband couldn't have that premier position, her son would.

In her efforts to that end, she succeeded. Promoted to full general, Douglas MacArthur became Chief of Staff of the United States Army in November 1930. He held that position for an unusual five years. However, during his tenure he was called upon by the President, Herbert Hoover, to disperse a large group of World War I army veterans, gathered to protest their veteran's benefits. These men had brought their families with them and established a shanty town in the center of Washington, D.C. MacArthur gathered a force and forced the "Bonus Army" out of its tents and shacks. He ordered his troops to burn out the left behind "homes," leaving the families without shelter. Although his chief of staff, Major Dwight D. Eisenhower, protested, General MacArthur had the troops use force at the slightest evidence of protest. This "battle of Anacosta Flats" was one of the first times that General MacArthur was criticized for his actions, and he did not like it.

Retiring in 1938 from the United States Army, MacArthur went back to his home away from home, the Philippines, to assume the position of Field Marshall of the Philippine Army. His duties there were to prepare the Philippines for the promised independence from the United States. He was here when the Japanese attacked in December of 1941, thrusting MacArthur into World War II.

General MacArthur had been boasting that his preparation for the independence of the Philippines was progressing very well. He spoke of a force of 100,000 Philippine soldiers available to defend the Philippines. Yet he failed to mention that more than three quarters of these men were half-trained militia forces. Although he commanded the largest air force outside the United States, they too were unprepared for an attack from Japan. Most of his planes were destroyed in the first few days of the war, many lost on the ground without a chance to fight. His plans were to defend the entire group of Philippine islands, but after initial dispositions he changed his mind and pulled most of his troops into positions to defend Manila. American and Philippine weaknesses were quickly revealed when the Japanese landed on Luzon. Despite his best efforts MacArthur could not stop the oncoming Japanese, who despite his claims to the contrary, were outnumbered by his own forces. He ordered his troops to fall back into the Bataan Penninsula and to defend Corregidor, a fortified island in Manila Bay.

Here the General's reputation began to suffer severely. Visiting the Bataan front only once in three months, he acquired the nickname from his troops of "Dugout Doug," a reference to his deep underground shelter on Corregidor. This was the first time the General's personal courage had been questioned, in sharp contrast to his conduct at the front in World War I, and the nickname followed him for the duration of the war. Another, less well known, damage to his reputation was his acceptance of an award from Philippines President Manual Quezon of $500,000, supposedly as an affirmation of faith between the Philippines and its protector. What made it more damaging was the other gifts, one to General Sutherland of $75,000 and others, including Colonel Huff who received $25,000. Legally, at least a portion of these gifts were against U.S. Army regulations, since General MacArthur was now back on the U.S. Army payroll, as were his staff officers.

MacArthur's defeat in the Philippines made him a hero in the United States, but further tarnished his reputation in professional military circles. This dichotomy may explain why to this day there are two differing opinions of the General's service. His abandonment of his troops in the Philippines, although at Presidential order, was poorly received by many American officers. It did little to endear him to the enlisted men, either. His claim to have conducted a successful last ditch defense also did not bear scrutiny, as most of the success was due to the efforts of one of his subordinates left behind in the enemy's hands, General Jonathan Wainwright. Later, when President Roosevelt recommended that General Wainwright receive the Medal of Honor, General MacArthur tried to block the award. Whatever his reasons, it further damaged his reputation within military circles.

His relations with his allies in New Guinea were also less than should have been expected. His use of obvious deceit to keep the Australian command from overseeing American combat troops was insulting to the Australians, as where his derogatory comments about their troops. This, as we have seen, backfired when his own American troops performed no better their

first time in combat. It would leave a bad feeling among the Australians for the duration of the war.

The General's ego rose again when he laid claim to the creation of the island hopping campaigns, a proposal first suggested by Admiral William Halsey, a subordinate at the time. His mania for publicity was another factor which alienated many from the General. His comment to General Eichelberger when he sent him to Buna that if he succeeded, his name would be released to the press, was no small reward. Nearly all communiques from Southwest Pacific Headquarters referred only to troops "under the command of General Douglas MacArthur." Few commanders had their names in the press in the Southwest Pacific. Even General Krueger, who served General MacArthur the longest and most faithfully, was largely unknown even at the end of the war. Admiral Barbey, frustrated at this policy, finally had to invite correspondents to his ship regularly to get the Navy's story of its operations in the Southwest out to the American public. He probably only got away with this because of General MacArthur's reliance on him, and because he was not an Army officer.

One of the reasons for General MacArthur's press policies was his own aspirations to run for the presidency. This possibility was raised many times during the General's career, and despite protestations to the contrary, he was always interested. In each case, however, it failed to materialize until finally, during the General's command in Korea in 1952 it resulted in his relief from command and final retirement.

The military skills of General MacArthur were equally uneven. His disaster in the Philippines was not entirely of is own making, but he certainly contributed to it with his change of strategy, poor use of intelligence and overconfidence. In New Guinea he misused his Australian allies while overusing some of his American units. His use of intelligence improved, and resulted in some important victories, notably Hollandia, Sansapor and Morotai. Yet there were still problems. He continued to have faith in his "Bataan Gang" despite their repeated failures. The two most important of his subordinates, General Sutherland and General Willoughby, failed him repeatedly during the New Guinea campaign.

General Willoughby's nearly consistent misreading of some of the best intelligence sources any commander could hope for resulted in no change. Similarly, General MacArthur could not have been unaware of General Sutherland's general failure to maintain a working relationship with those under

his general's command, yet here again he took no action, not even discovering that his chief of staff had disobeyed his own direct order not to bring along to New Guinea his personal "secretary." Here loyalty was a failure in command.

The fact that General MacArthur was ultimately successful certainly helped his public image, and sustained his military reputation. Yet he claimed credit he did not deserve, protected subordinates beyond reason while approving the relief of field commanders whose relief may have been hasty, as in the case of General Fuller and Colonel Herndon. During the Philippine liberation, he ordered operations not in his strategic directives from Washington, taking unnecessary and unapproved casualties in both American and Australian units. His reasons for this were his own. Strange behavior for a general who prided himself on being economical with his soldiers' lives. All of which leads to the conclusion that while he may have been a good leader, he was not a great general.

Appendix

United States Military Casualties Western New Guinea Campaign—April to December 1944					
Operation	US Army KIA	US Navy KIA	US Army WIA	US Navy WIA	Totals
Hollandia	155	4	1,060	7	1,226
Aitape	450	0	2,550	0	3,000
Wakde-Sarmi	415	3	1,500	10	1,928
Biak	435	36	2,360	83	2,914
Noemfoor	70	0	345	3	418
Sansapor	15	0	45	0	60
Morotai	30	15	85	18	148
TOTALS	1,570	58	7,945	121	9,694

Imperial Japanese Army Casualties Western New Guinea Campaign—April to December 1944					
Operation	Killed in Action	Prisoner of War	Korean POW	Formosan POW	Totals
Hollandia	4,475	655	0	15	5,145
Aitape	8,825	100	6	25	8,956
Wakde-Sarmi	3,960	55	2	35	4,052
Biak	6,125	460	0	305	6,890
Noemfoor	1,960	245	2	625	2,832
Sansapor	695	95	7	160	957
Morotai	305	15	0	0	320
TOTALS	26,345	1,625	17	1,165	29,152

Inter-relation of Japan's Air and Ground Armies

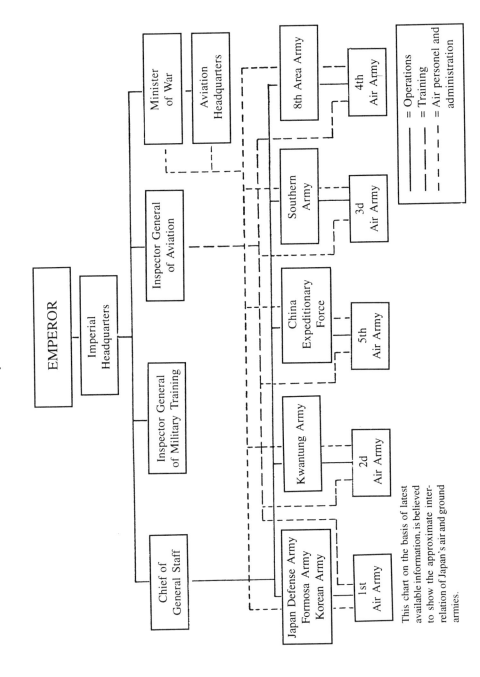

This chart on the basis of latest available information, is believed to show the approximate inter-relation of Japan's air and ground armies.

Abbreviated Army Chain of Command

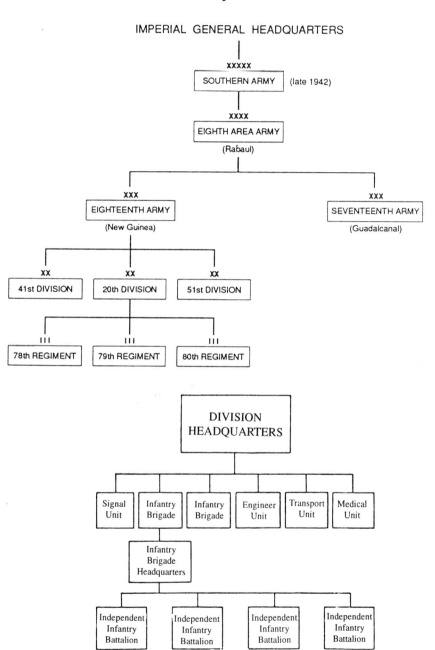

IMPERIAL GENERAL HEADQUARTERS

xxxxx
SOUTHERN ARMY   (late 1942)

xxxx
EIGHTH AREA ARMY
(Rabaul)

xxx
EIGHTEENTH ARMY
(New Guinea)

xxx
SEVENTEENTH ARMY
(Guadalcanal)

xx
41st DIVISION

xx
20th DIVISION

xx
51st DIVISION

III
78th REGIMENT

III
79th REGIMENT

III
80th REGIMENT

DIVISION
HEADQUARTERS

Signal Unit

Infantry Brigade

Infantry Brigade

Engineer Unit

Transport Unit

Medical Unit

Infantry Brigade Headquarters

Independent Infantry Battalion

Independent Infantry Battalion

Independent Infantry Battalion

Independent Infantry Battalion

Units	Standard Japanese Infantry Division												
	T/O	Operational	Horses	Rifles	Light machine gun	Grenade discharger	Heavy machine gun	Machine cannon or 20-mm antitank rifle	37-mm or 47-mm antitank rifle	70-mm battalion gun	75-mm regimental gun	75-mm field or mountain gun	Tankette or armored car
Division headquarters	300	300	(160)	(180)	(4)	( )							
Division signal unit	250	220	40	(100)	( )	( )							
Infantry group headquarters	71	70	18										
3 infantry regiments, each 3,843	11,529	9,000	2,130	6,393	(336)	324	108 (72)		18	18	12		
Division field artillery regiment	2,300	2,000	2,000	(450)	(1)							36	
Division reconnaissance regiment	730	650	(188)	(260)	28	16	4		4				7
Division engineer regiment	900	750	(150)	(700)	(9)								
Division medical unit	900	750	(110)	( )	( )	( )							
4 Field hospitals (Operational 3)	1,000	690	( )	( )	( )	( )							
Division ordnance unit	120	90	( )	( )	( )								
Division transport regiment	1,800	1,400	(1300)	( )	( )								
Divison ordnance unit	50	40	( )	( )									
Division veterinary unit	50	40											
Total	20,000	16,000	(7,500)	(9,000)	(382)	(340)	112 (76)		22	18	12	36	7

Lower Echelon Organization

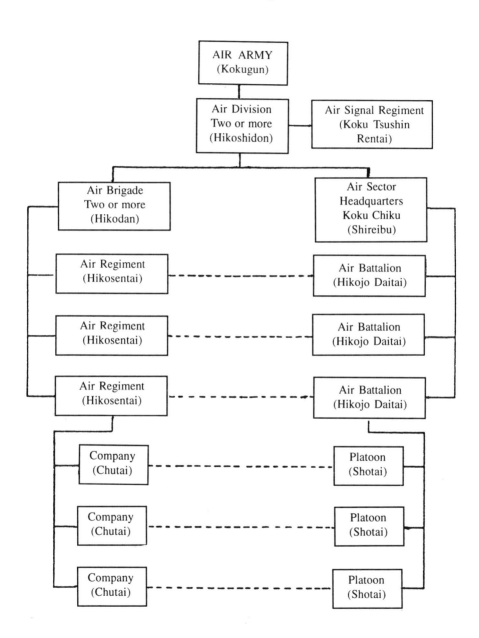

Characteristics of Operational Japanese Aircrafts			
	Type	Code name	Description
Mitsubishi A5M	96	Claude	Single-engine low-wing monoplane. Wings elliptical. Open cockpit. Fixed landing gear
Nakajima Ki-27	97	Nate	Single-engine low-wing monoplane. Tapered wings. Open or closed cockpit. Fixed landing gear
Mitsubishi A6M	0 (Mk.1)	Zeke	Single-engine low-wing monoplane. Tapered wings, rounded tips. High-set cockpit inclosure. Retractable landing gear.
	0 (Mk. 2)	Hamp	Single-engine low-wing monoplane. Tapered wings, square tips. High-set cockpit inclosure. Retractable landing gear.
Nakajima Ki-43	1 (Mk. 2)	Oscar, Mk. 2	Single-engine low-wing monoplane, Straight leading edges; tapered trailing edges. Full-length rudder. retractable landing gear; fixed tailwheel.
	2 (floatplane)	Rufe	Single-engine, single-float, low-wing monoplane. Similar to ZEKE, except for full-length rudder and floats.
Kawasaki Ki-45	2	Nick	Twin-engine, low wing, single -seat fighter. Wings stabilizer, and elevators tapered. Pointed nose. Long, slender fuselage. Tall fin and rudder.
Nakajima Ki-44	2	Tojo	Single-engine low-wing monoplane. Tapered leading, elliptical edges. retractable landing gear.
Kawasaki Ki-61	3	Tony	Single, inline engine, low-wing monoplane. Cockpit fairs into fuselage. Large aitscoop under fuselage. Resembles Hurricane.
Mitsubishi G3M	96 (Mk. 3)	Nell	Twin-engine, mid-wing monoplane. Sharply tapered wings, Junkers-type flaps and ailerons. twin fins and rudders.
Mitsubishi Ki-21	97 (Mk. 3)	Sally (Mk. 3)	Twin-engine, mid-wing monoplane. Tapered wings. Front cockpit rear dorsal turret. Single fin and rudder.
Nakajima Ki-49	100	Helen	Twin-engine, mid-wing monoplane. Fowler-type flaps and frise ailerons fitted. Has rear tail turret.
Mitsubishi G4M	1	Betty	Twin-engine, mid-wing monoplane. Cigar-shaped fuselage. Transparent nose and tail.

Nakajima B5N	97	Kate (Torpedo Bomber)	Single-engine low-wing monoplane. Long transparent cockpit inclosure.
Aichi D3A1	99 (Mk. 2)	Val Mk. 2. (Dive Bomber)	Single-engine low-wing monoplane. Elliptical wings. Dive-brakes. Long fin fairing on fuselage. Fixed landing gear.
Kawasaki Ki-48	99 (Mk. 1)	Lily Mk. 1. (Light Bomber)	Twin-engine, mid-wing monoplane. Resembles U.S. Martin "Baltimore" with abruptly-narrowing rear fuselage.

Japanese Ranks and Assignments

Grade	Name	Normal Command
General	Taisho	Army commander
Lieutenant general	Chujo	Division commander
Major general	Shosho	Infantry group or brigade comander
Colonel	Taisa	Regimental commander
Lieutenant colonel	Chusa	Second-in-command of regiment
Major	Shosa	Battalion commander
Captain	Tai-i	Company commander
First lieutenant	Chu-i	Platoon commander
Second lieutenant	Sho-i	Platoon commander
Warrant officer	Juni	Command and administrative duties
Sergeant major	Socho	First sergeant
Sergeant	Gunso	Squad (section) leader
Corporal	Gocho	Squad (section) leader
Lance corporal (leading private)	Heicho	
Superior private	Jotohei	
First-class private	Ittohei	
Second-class private	Nitohei	

Orders of Battle

Southwest Pacific Area
General of the Army Douglas MacArthur

Lieutenant General Richard K. Sutherland

Chief of Staff

ALLIED LAND FORCES
General Sir Thomas Blamey, A.I.F.

Major General F.H. Berryman, A.I.F.

Chief Of Staff

NEW GUINEA FORCE
General Sir Thomas Blamey, A.I.F.

7th Australian Division (Not Engaged In Campaign)

Major General George A. Vasey, A.I.F.

SIXTH U.S. ARMY (Alamo Force)
Lieutenant General Walter Krueger, U.S.A.

I U.S. Corps (Reckless Task Force)
Lieutenant General Robert L. Eichelberger, U.S.A.

24th Infantry Division

Major General Frederick A. Irving, U.S.A.

19th Infantry Regiment

21st Infantry Regiment

34th Infantry Regiment

3rd Engineer Combat Bn.

11th Field Artillery Bn.

13th Field Artillery Bn.

52nd Field Artillery Bn.

63rd Field Artillery Bn.

41st Infantry Division

Major General Horace H. Fuller, U.S.A. (To June 1944)

Major General Jens A. Doe, U.S.A. (From June 1944)

162nd Infantry Regiment

163rd Infantry Regiment

186th Infantry Regiment

116th Engineer Combat Bn

146th Field Artillery Bn.

167th Field Artillery Bn.

205th Field Artillery Bn.

218th Field Artillery Bn.

XI U.S. Corps (Persecution Task Force)
Major General Charles P. Hall, U.S.A

32nd Infantry Division

Major General William H. Gill, U.S.A.

126th Infantry Regiment

127th Infantry Regiment

128th Infantry Regiment

114th Engineer Combat Bn.

120th Field Artillery Bn.

121st Field Artillery Bn.

126th Field Artillery Bn.

129th Field Artillery Bn.

43rd Infantry Division

Major General Leonard F. Wing, U.S.A.

103rd Infantry Regiment

169th Infantry Regiment

172nd Infantry Regiment

118th Infantry Regiment

103rd Field Artillery Bn.

152nd Field Artillery Bn.

169th Field Artillery Bn.

192nd Field Artillery Bn.

112th Cavalry Regimental Combat Team

Brigadier General Julian W. Cunningham, U.S.A.

112th Cavalry Regiment

148th Field Artillery Bn.

Colonel Alexander M. Miller III, U.S.A.

Cyclone Task Force
Brigadier General Edwin D. Patrick, U.S.A.

158th Regimental Combat Team

Colonel J. Prugh Herndon, U.S.A. (To 30 May 1944)

Colonel Earle O. Sandlin, U.S.A. (From 30 May 1944)

158th Infantry Regiment
506th Medical Collecting Co.
147th Field Artillery Bn.
1st Platoon, 637th Medical
Collecting Company
503rd Parachute Regimental Combat Team
Colonel George M. Jones, U.S.A.
503rd Parachute Infantry
Regiment
462nd Parachute Field
Artillery Battalion
Company C, 161st Parachute
Engineer Battalion

Tornado Task Force
Major General Franklin C. Sibert, U.S.A.
(To 18 July 1944)
Major General John C. Persons, U.S.A.
(From 18 July 1944)
6th Infantry Division
Major General Franklin C. Sibert,
U.S.A. (To 24 August 1944).
Major General Charles E. Hurdis,
U.S.A. (From 24 August 1944).
1st Infantry Regiment
20th Infantry Regiment
63rd Infantry Regiment
6th Engineer Combat Bn.
1st Field Artillery Bn.
51st Field Artillery Bn.
53rd Field Artillery Bn.
80th Field Artillery Bn.
31st Infantry Division
Major General John C. Persons, U.S.A.
124th Infantry Regiment
155th Infantry Regiment
167th Infantry Regiment
106th Engineer Combat Bn.
114th Field Artillery Bn.
116th Field Artillery Bn.
117th Field Artillery Bn.
149th Field Artillery Bn.
33rd Infantry Division
Major General Percy W. Clarkson,
U.S.A.
123rd Infantry Regiment
130th Infantry Regiment
136th Infantry Regiment
108th Engineer Combat Bn.

122nd Field Artillery Bn.
123rd Field Artillery Bn.
124th Field Artillery Bn.
210th Field Artillery Bn.

Alamo Force Reserve
93rd Infantry Division
Major General Raymond G. Lehman
(To August 1944)
Major General Harry H. Johnson
(From August 1944)
25th Infantry Regiment
368th Infantry Regiment
369th Infantry Regiment
318th Engineer Combat Bn.
593rd Field Artillery Bn.
594th Field Artillery Bn.
595th Field Artillery Bn.
596th Field Artillery Bn.

SUPPORTING FORCES-SOUTHWEST PACIFIC AREA
3rd Engineer Special Brigade
533rd Engineer Shore
Regiment
543rd Engineer Amphibian
Regiment
593rd Engineer Boat Regiment
4th Engineer Special Brigade
534th Engineer Shore Regiment
544th Engineer Amphibian
Regiment
594th Engineer Boat Regiment
532nd Engineer Boat and
Shore Regiment
533rd Engineer Boat and
Shore Regiment
534th Engineer Boat and Shore
Regiment
542nd Engineer Boat and
Shore Regiment
543rd Engineer Boat and
Shore Regiment
544th Engineer Boat and Shore
Regiment
593rd Engineer Boat and
Shore Regiment
187th Engineer Aviation
Battalion

856th Engineer Aviation Battalion

860th Engineer Aviation Battalion

863rd Engineer Aviation Battalion

864th Engineer Aviation Battalion

872nd Engineer Aviation Battalion

875th Engineer Aviation Battalion

1881st Engineer Aviation Battalion

1884th Engineer Aviation Battalion

1887th Engineer Aviation Battalion

1896th Engineer Aviation Battalion

1897th Engineer Aviation Battalion

ALLIED AIR FORCES

Lieutenant General George C. Kenney, U.S.A.A.F.

Fifth U.S. Army Air Force
Lieutenant General George C. Kenney, U.S.A.A.F

ROYAL AUSTRALIAN AIR FORCE COMMAND, ALLIED AIR FORCES
Air Vice Marshall William D. Bostock, R.A.A.F.

Royal Netherlands East Indies Air Force

Thirteenth U.S. Army Air Force
Major General St. Clair Streett, U.S.A.A.F.

ALLIED NAVAL FORCES
Vice Admiral Thomas C. Kinkaid, U.S.N.

Seventh Fleet, United States Navy
Vice Admiral Thomas C. Kinkaid, U.S.N.

VII Amphibious Force
Rear Admiral Daniel E. Barbey, U.S.N.

ROYAL AUSTRALIAN NAVY (As Assigned)
Rear Admiral V.A.C. Crutchley, Royal Navy

ALLIED NAVAL FORCES
WESTERN NEW GUINEA CAMPAIGN

SEVENTH FLEET
VICE ADMIRAL THOMAS C. KINKAID

TASK FORCE 77
REAR ADMIRAL DANIEL E. BARBEY

TASK GROUP 77.1 WESTERN AT-TACK GROUP (Aitape Assault Force)
REAR ADMIRAL DANIEL E. BARBEY
SCREENING FORCE
COMMANDER W.S. VEEDER
DESTROYERS
SWANSON—Cdr. E.L. Robertson (Flagship)
Hobby—Cdr. G.W. Pressey
Grayson
Nicholson—Cdr. W.W. Vanous
Wilkes—Cdr. F. Wolseiffer
Grayson—LtCdr. W.V. Pratt
Gillespie—Cdr. J.S. Fahy

Kalk—Lt.Cdr. H.D. Fuller

TRANSPORT GROUP
CAPTAIN P.A. STEVENS
Henry T. Allen—Capt. John Meyer
H.M.A.S. Manoora—Cdr. A.P. Cousins, RANR
H.M.A.S. Kanimbla—Cdr. H.H. Shaw, RAN
L.S.D. Carter Hall—LtCdr. F.J. Harris
Triangulum—LtCdr. F.W. Parsons

TASK GROUP 77.2 CENTRAL AT-TACK GROUP
REAR ADMIRAL WILLIAM M. FECHTELER
SCREENING FORCE
CAPTAIN R.F. STOUT
DESTROYERS
REID—Cdr. S.A. McCornock (Flagship)
Stevenson—Cdr. F.E. Wilson
Stockton—LtCdr. W.W. Stark
Thorn—Cdr. E. Brumby
Roe—Cdr. F.S. Stich
Welles—Cdr. D.M. Coffee
Radford—Cdr. G.E. Griggs
Taylor—Cdr. N.J.F. Frank
DESTROYER TRANSPORTS
Humphreys—LtCdr. M.J. Carley
Brooks—LtCdr. C.V. Allen
Snads—LtCdr. L. C. Brogger
Gilmer—LtCdr. J.S. Horner
Herbert—LtCdr. J.N. Ferguson
TRANSPORT GROUP
Commander A.V. Knight, RANR
H.M.A.S. Westralia—Cdr. A.V. Knight, RANR
L.S.D. Gunston Hall—Cdr. D.E. Collins
Attack Transport (AK)—Ganymeade—LtCdr. G.H. Melichar

TASK GROUP 77.3 EASTERN AT-TACK GROUP
CAPTAIN A.G. NOBLE
SCREENING FORCE
CAPTAIN A.D. CHANDLER
DESTROYERS
Nicholas—Cdr. R.T.S. Keith
O'Bannon—Cdr. R.W. Smith
Howorth—LtCdr. E.S. Burns
Jenkins—Cdr. P.D. Gallery
Hopewell—Cdr. C.C. Shute

TRANSPORT GROUP
Commander D.L. Mattie
DESTROYER TRANSPORTS
Kilty—Lt. L.G. Benson

Ward—LtCdr. F.W. Lemly
Crosby—Lt. W.F. Sims
Dickerson—LtCdr. J.R. Cain
Talbot—LtCdr. C.C. Morgan
L.S.D. Belle Grove—LtCdr. M. Seavey
Schley—Lt.Cdr. E.T. Farley
Kane—Lt. F.M. Christiansen
Dent—Lt.Cdr. R.A. Wilhelm
Noa—Lt. H.W. Bond
AK Etamin—LtCdr. G.W. Stedman, U.S.C.G.

TASK FORCE 74 COVERING FORCE "A"
REAR ADMIRAL V.A.C. CRUTCHLEY, R.N.
CRUISER FORCE
H.M.A.S. Australia—Capt. E.F.V. Dechaineux, R.A.N.
H.M.A.S. Shropshire—Capt. J.A. Collins, R.A.N.
DESTROYER FORCE
H.M.A.S. Warramunga—Cdr. N.A. MacKinnon, R.A.N.
H.M.A.S. Arunta—Cdr. A.E. Buchanan, R.A.N.
Ammen—Cdr. H. Williams
Mullany—Cdr. B.J. Mullaney

TASK FORCE 75 COVERING FORCE "B"
REAR ADMIRAL RUSSELL S. BERKEY
CRUISER FORCE
Phoenix—Capt. J.H. Duncan
Nashville—Capt. C.E. Coney
Boise—Capt. J.S. Roberts
DESTROYER FORCE
Hutchins—Cdr. J.B. Cochran
Bache—LtCdr. R.C. Morton
Daly—Cdr. R.G. Visser
Abner Read—Cdr. T.B. Hutchins
Bush—Cdr. T.A. Smith

IMPERIAL JAPANESE ARMY

GENERAL HEADQUARTERS
General Hideki Tojo

Southern Army
General Count Hisaichi Terauchi, I.J.A.

2nd Area Army
General Korechika Anami, I.J.A.

18th Army
Lieutenant General Hatazo Adachi, I.J.A.
Lieutenant General Yoshihara Kane, I.J.A.
Chief of Staff

20th (Keijo) Division
Lieutenant General Katakiri Shigeru
  (K.I.A. 10 May 1944)
Major General Sadahiko Miyake
  (From 10 May 1944)
  78th Infantry Regiment
  79th Infantry Regiment
  80th Infantry Regiment
  26th Field Artillery Regt.
  20th Engineer Combat Bn.
  20th Transport Regiment

41st Division
Lieutenant General Mano Goro, I.J.A.
  237th Infantry Regiment
  238th Infantry Regiment
  239th Infantry Regiment
  41st Mountain Artillery Regt.
  41st Engineer Regiment
  41st Transport Regiment

51st (Utsunomiya) Division
Lieutenant General Nakano
  Hidemitsu, I.J.A.
  66th Infantry Regiment
  102nd Infantry Regiment
  115th Infantry Regiment
  14th Field Artillery Regt.
  51st Engineer Regiment
  51st Transport Regiment

2nd Army

Lieutenant General Fusataro Teshima,
  I.J.A.

32nd Division
(Not Engaged In This Campaign)

35th Division
Lieutenant General Shunkichi Ikeda,
  I.J.A.
  219th Infantry Regiment
  220th Infantry Regiment
  221st Infantry Regiment
  35th Field Artillery Regt.
  35th Engineer Regiment
  35th Transport Regiment
  35th Infantry Group Tankette
    Company

36th Division
Lieutenant General Hachiro Tagami,
  I.J.A.
  222nd Infantry Regiment
  223rd Infantry Regiment
  224th Infantry Regiment
  36th Mountain Artillery Regt.
  36th Engineer Regiment
  36th Transport Regiment
  36th Infantry Group Tankette
    Company

1st Independent Brigade
Major General Yuki Fukabori, I.J.A.

19th Army
(Not Engaged In This Campaign)

5th Division
(Not Engaged In This Campaign)

46th Division
(Not Engaged In This Campaign)

48th Division
(Not Engaged In This Campaign)

SERVICES OF SUPPLY AND SUPPORT
Major General Toyozo Kitazono, I.J.A. (M.I.A. April 1944)

4th Engineer Group
  16th Mobile Lumber Squad
  17th Mobile Lumber Squad
  16th Airfield Unit

103rd Airfield Unit
4th Field Searchlight Battalion
11th Debarkation Unit
24th Signal Regiment

42nd Machine Cannon
  Company
53rd Field Antiaircraft
  Battalion
54th Special Water Duty
  Company
91st Naval Garrison Unit
228th Independent Motor
  Transport Company
8th Independent Engineer Regiment
4th Field Transport Headquarters
2nd Field Base Unit

3rd Field Transportation Unit
16th Field Airdrome Construction Unit
17th Field Airdrome Construction Unit
51st Field Road Construction Unit
103rd Field Airdrome Construction Unit
107th Field Airdrome Construction Unit
108th Field Airdrome Construction Unit

FOURTH AIR ARMY

6th Air Division
Major General Masazumi Inada, I.J.A.
  10th Air Regiment
  14th Air Regiment
  45th Air Regiment

  13th Air Regiment
  24th Air Regiment
  208th Air Regiment
7th Air Division
(Not Engaged In This Campaign)

Bibliographic Essay

There is only one other work which covers in detail the Western New Guinea Campaign, and that is a volume in the U.S. Army's series United States Army In The Second World War by Robert Ross Smith entitled *Approach To The Philippines* (Washington. D.C., 1984). Yet even this excellent volume deals only with the ground operations and makes only passing reference to sea and air operations occurring at the same time. In order to get the complete story of naval operations there are at least three books available, each giving a different perspective on the offshore operations. First and most encompassing is Samuel Eliot Morison's *History of the United States Naval Operations in World War II. New Guinea and the Marianas* (Boston. 1960). This volume of his fifteen volume series deals with naval operations in both theaters during the summer of 1944, concentrating on fleet operations. For the specific details of the naval forces taking direct part in the conquest of Western New Guinea Rear Admiral Daniel E. Barbey's *MacArthur's Amphibious Navy, Seventh Amphibious Force Operations, 1943-1945* (Annapolis. 1969) is best, especially as it is written from the perspective of one of General MacArthur's trusted and most dependable subordinates. In addition Paul S. Dull's *A Battle History of The Imperial Japanese Navy 1941-1945* (Annapolis. 1978) gives the Japanese perspective on those operations. Air operations are covered in considerable detail by Wesley Frank Craven and James Lea Cate's *The Army Air Forces In World War II, The Pacific: Guadalcanal To Saipan* (Washington. 1950).

The principal commanders wrote their stories as well. General Douglas MacArthur's *Reminiscences* (New York. 1964) gives very little on his Western New Guinea Campaign, devoting only a few pages to it and speaking in generalities. What is interesting is that in these few pages the only personal reference is to the General himself. General Krueger wrote his own history, *From Down Under To Nippon, The Story of the Sixth Army In World War II* (Nashville, 1953) but while an interesting story gives little in the way of the General's personal decisions or feelings. General Eichelberger also wrote the narrative of his men, *Our Jungle Road To Tokyo* (New York. 1950) but more enlightening concerning the feelings of the General is the book by Jay Luvaas, *Dear Miss Em: General Eichelberger's War in the Pacific, 1942-1945* (Westport. 1972) which gives the General's personal perspective on the events in which he participated from his correspondence to his wife.

Biographies of the leaders are rare, with the exception of General MacArthur who had several written about him. Some of the more interesting are William Manchester's *American Caesar, Douglas MacArthur, 1880-1964* (Boston. 1978) and Michael Schaller's *Douglas MacArthur, The Far Eastern General* (New York. 1989) which detail the strengths as well as the foibles of this controversial general. For a strictly professional appraisal of the General, see Gavin Long's *MacArthur As Military Commander* (London. 1969). There is, of course, the work by the General's former staff officer, Major General Charles A. Willoughby and John Chamberlain entitled *MacArthur, 1941-1951*, but given the fact that the author was one of the "Bataan Gang" its objectivity is suspect. The most recent review of General Eichelberger's career is by John C. Shortal in his *Forged By Fire, General Robert L. Eichelberger and the Pacific War* (Columbia, S. C. 1987). For a view of the other theater of war in the Pacific, E. B. Potter's *Nimitz* (Annapolis. 1976) is the best overview. For one source covering all of General MacArthur's commanders, ground, sea and air, the best and perhaps only work is the collection of essays in William M. Leary's *We Shall Return, MacArthur's Commanders and the Defeat of Japan, 1942-1945* (Lexington. 1988). For an excellent work on the Buna-Gona campaign which preceded the move into Western New Guinea, see Lida Mayo's *Bloody Buna* (Garden City. 1984).

Books on the work of intelligence collection are still coming out, some with differing perspectives. Walter Lord's *Lonely Vigil, Coastwatchers of the Solomons* (New York. 1977) details the now nearly forgotten story of those brave men who lived for long periods behind enemy lines, with no hope of survival if caught. Edward J. Drea's excellent work on the use and misuse by Southwest Pacific Headquarters of the Ultra intelligence, *Mac-Arthur's Ultra, Codebreaking and the War Against Japan, 1942-1945* (Lawrence, Kansas. 1992), is essential reading to understand why many decisions were made during the campaign. David Kahn in his *The Codebreakers, The Story of Secret Writing* (New York. 1987) has some interesting opinions on the methods by which intercepted intelligence was handled at MacArthur's headquarters, as does Ronald Lewin in *The American Magic, Codes, Ciphers and the Defeat of Japan* (New York. 1982).

For the more personal perspective many of the participating combat units on the American side have had combat histories published about them, usually by one of their number. Arthur Anthony's *Bushmasters, America's Jungle Warriors of World War II* (New York. 1987) is a detailed history of the 158th Infantry Regiment. The division's own Public Relations Section produced *The Sixth Infantry Division In World War II, 1939-1945* (Washington. 1947). Although the 112th Cavalry has no known history, Edward J. Drea's *Defending The Driniumor, Covering Force Operations in New Guinea, 1944* (Kansas. 1984) is an excellent study of that regiment during the campaign. The story of the 503rd Parachute Infantry Regiment is told in Bennett M. Guthrie's *The Three Winds of Death, The Saga of the 503rd Parachute Regimental Combat Team in the South Pacific* (Chicago. 1985). An often neglected story is covered well by Brigadier General William F. Heavey in *Down Ramp!, The Story of the Army Amphibian Engineers* (Washington. 1947). The other major units of the campaign are covered by Walter T. Lauer's *The 32nd Infantry Division in World War II* (n.p. 1957) and William F. McCartney's *The Jungleers, A History of the 41st Infantry Division* (Washington. 1948). There is no single volume covering the contributions of the African-American troops in the Pacific, but a review of Mary Penick Motley's *The Invisible Soldier, The Experience of the Black Soldier, World War II* (Detroit. 1975) and Bernard C. Nalty's *Strength For The Fight, A History of Black*

Americans in the Military (New York. 1986) give a reasonable picture of their war. More books are appearing on this subject, but so far they have concerned themselves primarily with the African-American soldier in the Mediterranean Theater of Operations, where two major units saw action.

There is little available on the Japanese side, particularly on the ground forces, most probably because so few of them survived and due to the differences in language and culture. For some reason the Imperial Japanese Navy veterans have come up with several works in English. The most interesting of these are Captain Tameichi Hara's *Japanese Destroyer Captain* (New York. 1961), former submarine Captain Mochitsuro Hashimoto's *Sunk* (New York. 1954) and Zenji Orita and Joseph Harrington's *I-Boat Captain* (Canoga Park. 1976). Admiral Matome Ugaki's *Fading Victory, The Diary of Admiral Matome Ugaki* (Pittsburgh. 1991) details the confusion among the Japanese High Command as to the importance of the twin American thrusts towards Japan. A recent publication, Haruko Taya Cook and Theodore F. Cook's *Japan At War, An Oral History* (New York. 1992) gives a picture of the Japanese side of the war in all theaters, including one segment on New Guinea.

General histories usually relegate New Guinea to a footnote or a passing reference as a part of the larger war, an undeserved slight to the many thousands of Americans, Australians and Japanese who fought there.

Bibliography

Arthur, Anthony; *Bushmasters. America's Jungle Warriors of World War II.* St. Martins Press. New York. 1987.

Barbey, Vice Admiral Daniel D.; *MacArthur's Amphibious Navy. Seventh Amphibious Force Operations, 1943-1945.* U.S. Naval Institute Press. Annapolis, Maryland. 1969.

Blair, Clay; *MacArthur.* MCA Publishing. New York. 1977.

Blair, Clay; *Silent Victory. The U.S. Submarine War Against Japan.* Bantam Books. New York. 1975.

Committee On Veteran's Affairs, United States Senate; *Medal of Honor Recipients, 1863-1978.* U.S. Government Printing Office. Washington, D.C. 1979.

Cook, Haruko Taya and Theodore F. Cook; *Japan at War. An Oral History.* The New Press. New York. 1992.

Cortesi, Lawrence; *Pacific Strike.* Kensington Publishing Corp. New York. 1982.

Craven, Wesley Frank and James Lea Cate; *The Army Air Forces in World War II. Volume Four. The Pacific: Guadalcanal to Saipan, August 1942-July 1944.* U.S. Government Printing Office. Washington, D.C. 1950.

Division Public Relations Section, The; *The Sixth Infantry Division in World War II, 1939-1945.* Infantry Journal Press. Washington, D.C. 1947.

Devlin, Ferard M.; *Paratrooper! The Saga of U.S. Army and Marine Parachute and Glider Combat Troops During World War II.* St. Martins Press. New York. 1979.

Dod, Karl C.; *United States Army in World War II. The Technical Services. The Corps of Engineers; the War Against Japan.* Center Of Military History. U.S. Government Printing Office. Washington, D.C. 1987.

Drea, Edward J.; *Defending the Driniumor: Covering Force Operations in New Guinea, 1944.* Leavenworth Papers No. 9. Combat

Studies Institute, U.S. Army Command and General Staff College, Fort Leavenworth, Kansas. 1984.

Drea, Edward J.; *MacArthur's Ultra. Codebreaking and the War Against Japan, 1942-1945*. University Press of Kansas. Lawrence, Kansas. 1992.

Dull, Paul S.; *A Battle History of the Imperial Japanese Navy (1941-1945)*. Naval Institute Press. Annapolis, Maryland. 1978.

Dupuy, Colonel R. Ernest; *The National Guard. A Compact History*. Hawthorn Books, Inc. New York. 1971.

Eichelberger, Robert L. and Milton MacKaye; *Our Jungle Road to Tokyo*. Viking Press. New York. 1950.

Feldt, Commander Eric A.; *The Coastwatchers*. Oxford University Press. New York. 1959.

Gailey, Harry A.; *Howlin' Mad vs the Army. Conflict in Command, Saipan 1944*. Presidio Press. Novato, California. 1986.

Galvin, John R.; *Air Assault. The Development of Airmobile Warfare*. Hawthorn Book, Inc. New York. 1969.

Gill, Major General William H. and Edward Jaquelin Smith; *Always a Commander. The Reminiscences of Major General William H. Gill*. The Colorado College. Colorado Springs, Colo. 1974.

Greenfield, Kent Roberts; *American Strategy in World War II. A Reconsideration*. The John Hopkins Press. Baltimore. 1963.

Guthrie, Bennett M.; *The Three Winds of Death. The Saga of the 503rd Parachute Regimental Combat Team in the South Pacific*. Adams Press. Chicago. 1985.

Hara, Tameichi, Fred Saito and Roger Pineau; *Japanese Destroyer Captain*. Ballantine Books. New York. 1961.

Hashimoto, Mochitsuro; *Sunk*. Avon Publications, Inc. New York. 1954.

Heavey, Brigadier General William F.; *Down Ramp! The Story of the Army Amphibian Engineers*. Infantry Journal Press. Washington, D.C. 1947.

Ienaga, Saburo; *The Pacific War, 1931-1945. A Critical Perspective on Japan's Role in World War II*. Pantheon books. New York. 1968.

James, D. Clayton; *The Years of MacArthur, 1941-1945*. Houghton Mifflin Company. Boston. 1975.

Kahn, David; *The Codebreakers. The Story of Secret Writing*. Macmillan Company. New York. 1973.

Kennett, Lee; *G.I. The American Soldier in World War II*. Warner Books, Inc. New York. 1987.

Krueger, General Walter; *From Down Under to Nippon. The Story of the Sixth Army in World War II*. Battery Press. Nashville, Tennessee. 1989. (1953).

Lauer, Edward T.; *The 32nd Infantry Division in World War II*. 32nd Division Veterans Association. 1957.

Lee, Ulysses; *The Employment of Negro Troops. U.S. Army in World War II*. Office of the Chief of Military History. U.S. Government Printing Office. Wshington, D.C. 1966.

Leary, William M., (Ed.); *We Shall Return! MacArthur's Commanders and the Defeat of Japan, 1942-1945*. University Press Of Kentucky. Lexington, Kentucky. 1988.

Lewin, Ronald; *The American Magic. Codes, Ciphers and the Defeat of Japan*. Farrar, Straus, Giroux. New York. 1982.

Lockwood, Vice Admiral Charles A.; *Sink 'Em All! Submarine Warfare in the Pacific*. Bantam Books. New York. 1951.

Long, Gavin; *MacArthur as Military Commander*. B.T. Batsford, Ltd. London. 1969.

Lord, Walter; *Lonely Vigil. Coastwatchers of the Solomons*. Viking Press. New York. 1977.

Luvaas, Jay; *Dear Miss Em: General Eichelberger's War in the Pacific, 1942-1945*. Greenwood Press. Westport, Conn. 1972.

Mahon, John K. and Romana Danysh; *Army Lineage Series. Infantry, Part I. Regular Army*. Office of the Chief of Military History. Washington, D.C. 1972.

Manchester, William; *American Caesar. Douglas MacArthur, 1880-1964*. Little, Brown and Company. Boston. 1978.

Mayo, Lida; *Bloody Buna*. Doubleday and Company, Inc. Garden City, N. Y. 1974.

MacArthur, General of the Army Douglas; *Reminiscences*. McGraw Hill Book Company. New York. 1964.

McCartney, William F.; *The Jungleers. A History of the 41st Infantry Division*. Infantry Journal Press. Washington, D.C. 1948.

Morison, Samuel Eliot; *History of the United States Naval Operations in World War II. Volume VIII. New Guinea and the Marianas. March 1944-August 1944*. Little, Brown and Company. Boston. 1960.

Motley, Mary Penick (Ed.); *The Invisible Soldier. The Experience of the Black Soldier, World War II*. Wayne State University Press. Detroit. 1975.

Nalty, Bernard C.; *Strength for the Fight. A History of Black Americans in the Military*. Free Press. New York. 1986.

Orita, Zenji with Joseph D. Harrington; *I-Boat Captain*. Major Books. Canoga Park, California. 1976.

Potter, E. B., *Nimitz*. Naval Institute Press. Annapolis. 1976.

Rhoades, Weldon E. (Dusty); *Flying MacArthur to Victory*. Texas A & M University Press. College Station, Texas. 1985.

Riegelman, Colonel Harold; "Caves Of Biak" *Combat. The War with Japan.* Don Congdon, Editor. Del Publishing Company. New York. 1962.

Roscoe, Theodore; *United States Destroyer Operations in World War II.* Naval Institute Press. Annapolis, Maryland. 1953.

Sawicki, James A.; *Infantry Regiments of the U.S. Army.* Wyvern Publications. Dumfries, Virginia. 1981.

Schaller, Michael; *Douglas MacArthur. The Far Eastern General.* Oxford University Press. New York. 1989.

Sharpe, George, M.D.; *Brothers Beyond Blood. A Battalion Surgeon in the South Pacific.* Diamond Books. Austin, Texas. 1989.

Shortal, John F.; *Forged by Fire. General Robert L. Eichelberger and the Pacific War.* University of South Carolina Press. Columbia, S. C. 1987.

Smith, Robert Ross; *The Approach to the Philippines. U.S. Army in World War II.* Government Printing Office. Washington. D.C. 1984.

Stanton, Shelby L.; *Order of Battle. U.S. Army, World War II.* Presidio Press. Novato, California.

Stouffer, S. A., et. al.; *The American Soldier. Combat and its Aftermath. Volume II.* Princeton University Press. Princeton. 1949.

Toland, John; *The Rising Sun. The Decline and Fall of the Japanese Empire, 1936-1945.* Random House. New York. 1970.

Ugaki, Admiral Matome; *Fading Victory. The Diary of Admiral Matome Ugaki, 1941-1945.* University of Pittsburgh Press. Pittsburgh. 1991.

Weigley, Russell F.; *The American Way of War. A History of United States Military Strategy and Policy.* MacMillan Publishing Company, Inc. New York. 1973.

Weigley, Russell F.; *History of the United States Army.* Indiana University Press. Bloomington. 1984.

Williams, Mary H.; *Chronology 1941-1945. United States Army in World War II. Special Studies.* Office of the Chief of Military History. Washington, D.C. 1960.

Willoughby, Major General Charles A. and John Chamberlain; *MacArthur, 1941-1951.* MacGraw-Hill Book Company, Inc. New York. 1954.

Zimmer, Joseph E.; *The History of the 43rd Infantry Division 1941-1945.* Army Times Publishing Company. Baton Rouge, La. n.d.

Index